345 5 7 67

Connecting with
LAN Server 4.0

Connecting with LAN Server 4.0

Barry Nance

Ziff-Davis Press
Emeryville, California

Copy Editor	Margo R. Hill
Technical Reviewer	Tom Gordy
Project Coordinator	Ami Knox
Proofreader	Carol Burbo
Cover Illustration	Regan Honda
Cover Design	Regan Honda
Book Design	Paper Crane Graphics, Berkeley
Word Processing	Howard Blechman
Page Layout	M.D. Barrera and Tony Jonick
Indexer	Valerie Robbins

Ziff-Davis Press books are produced on a Macintosh computer system with the following applications: FrameMaker®, Microsoft® Word, QuarkXPress®, Adobe Illustrator®, Adobe Photoshop®, Adobe Streamline™, MacLink®*Plus*, Aldus® FreeHand™, Collage Plus™.

If you have comments or questions or would like to receive a free catalog, call or write:

Ziff-Davis Press
5903 Christie Avenue
Emeryville, CA 94608
1-800-688-0448

ISBN 1-56276-270-2

Manufactured in the United States of America
10 9 8 7 6 5 4 3 2 1

■ Contents at a Glance

■ Table of Contents

■ Introduction

LAN Server is a file, print, and application server that runs on OS/2. LAN
Server offers a high performance file system option, HPFS386, that leverages
Intel CPU Ring 0 architecture to achieve fast data transfers to and from the
server's hard disk. LAN Server's design assures excellent performance for sharing data files, application programs, and printers. For version 4.0, IBM added
TCP/IP support and an amazingly friendly graphical interface to LAN Server.
LAN Server is available in an "Entry" or an "Advanced" configuration. IBM
designed LAN Server Entry for use in small networks (2–100 users). LAN
Server Advanced supports up to 1,000 clients (workstations). Client workstations can run DOS, DOS-plus-Windows (either Windows 3.1 or Windows 95),
and, with a separately purchasable LAN Server add-on for Apple computers,
Macintosh System 7.

    Connecting with LAN Server 4.0 covers the latest version of IBM's client/
server-oriented network software. While NetWare has in the past held a commanding market lead in the networking industry, IBM's LAN Server product
provides all the features, functions, and performance of NetWare. LAN Server
additionally offers a rich environment for client/server computing—an environment difficult or impossible to achieve with NetWare. IBM's LAN Server product is poised to take networking beyond the simple file-and-printer-sharing
provided by NetWare. Over the next several years, people will create LAN
Server networks that share databases as well as files and printers, and these new
LANs will allow different parts of the software within an application to run on
different network computers. *Connecting with LAN Server 4.0* explains the differences between NetWare and LAN Server, shows how to plan for and install
LAN Server, covers administering, using, and troubleshooting LAN Server, and
even explores how to design computer programs that take advantage of the
LAN Server environment.

■ What's in This Book

Chapter 1 introduces you to both LAN Server and OS/2. LAN Server doesn't
contain its own operating system as Novell NetWare does. LAN Server is the
network operating system; OS/2 is the base operating system. Chapter 1 helps
you understand the LAN Server environment, including file sharing, printer
sharing, and client/server technology. Chapter 1 is a guided tour of LAN Server.

    In Chapter 2, you explore how local area networks (LANs) work. You
cover file servers, workstations, LAN cables, network adapters, and protocols.
Chapter 2 discusses accessing and administering the LAN, and it talks about
electronic mail and database servers.

Chapter 3 helps you plan for your LAN Server network. You learn the components of LAN Server, you discover LAN Server's hardware and software requirements, you analyze your organization's information sharing needs, and you develop a plan for your network.

Chapter 4 explains how to successfully install and begin using LAN Server. The chapter carefully describes how to install LAN hardware, the LAN Server software for the file server, and the client (workstation) software.

In Chapter 5 you begin administering LAN Server. You learn the role of a network administrator, come face to face with LAN Server's graphical and command line tools, and discover how to start and stop the file server. The chapter explores managing groups, logon accounts (users), and shared resources (disk drives, printers, directories, files, and modems). You cover LAN Server security as well as the contents of the PROTOCOL.INI and IBMLAN.INI configuration files.

Chapter 6 discusses LAN Server from a client (workstation) point of view. Chapter 6 gives you an understanding of the sharing of applications, files, modems, and printers. You learn the LAN Server commands you can use, and you cover connecting to a LAN Server file server from a DOS, Windows, or OS/2 workstation.

I hope you never need Chapter 7. However, problems sometimes arise on local area networks, and Chapter 7's troubleshooting advice should be your first line of defense when you encounter a problem. Chapter 7 explains the causes of network problems, describes network management tools (including the new Desktop Management Interface, or DMI), and helps you improve the performance of your network.

In Chapter 8, you turn to the running of application software on your LAN. Chapter 8 discusses the differences between single user and multiuser software products, reveals how to use Network Dynamic Data Exchange (NetDDE) to share data among workstations, explains which DOS disk diagnostic utilities you should avoid, and covers software products such as word processors, spreadsheets, communication programs, and database managers.

Chapter 9 is primarily for programmers who want to take advantage of LAN Server's client/server environment. Chapter 9 discusses information processing on a LAN, identifies computer languages you can use, covers batch file and REXX programming, introduces you to the LAN Server API, explores the use of NetBIOS to send data (in message form) from PC to PC, and provides helpful hints for testing and debugging your applications on a LAN.

Appendix A, the Command Reference, identifies the commands you can use to administer, configure, and view your LAN Server network.

Appendix B, the Programming Reference, augments the online programming documentation that comes with LAN Server. This reference section helps you find the right function to use in a particular programming situation, identifies the import libraries you need to use for each function, lists the operator rights (permissions) that each function requires, and provides an overall framework for your LAN Server programming efforts.

■ How to Use This Book

This book assumes you already know how to use DOS, Windows, and OS/2. While you'll find helpful information about these operating environments in this book, you should gain some familiarity with them before using this book (or before using LAN Server, for that matter). You won't find any assumptions in this book, however, regarding your level of expertise with local area networks. Because different network environments invariably use different terminology to describe themselves to you, this book helps you understand LANs by reducing the "acronym and buzzword glut" you face when you try to understand or use a local area network. This book also contains some important network planning strategies (Chapter 3) that you'll want to use to make your network a success.

Administrators will find the chapters on planning, installing, administering, and troubleshooting LAN Server invaluable. Everyone will find the chapters on using PCs as workstations and running applications on the LAN helpful, along with the Command Reference section. Finally, programmers will find the Programming Reference and chapter on programming LAN Server (Chapter 9) a practical roadmap for their exploration of client/server technology.

I've used a variety of network operating systems, from NetWare to LAN-tastic, and I've found LAN Server offers special advantages to both small and large organizations. Because I write for BYTE Magazine, the LANs I've created in my own office include several different types of file server software and network configurations. However, I've come to rely primarily on my two LAN Server PCs as my mainstay servers. I've included in this book the information you'll need to make your LAN Server network as useful, flexible, and reliable as mine. Turn the page and get started!

- *Exploring LAN Server*
- *Considering OS/2*
- *Defining the LAN Server Environment*
- *File and Printer Sharing*
- *The Benefits of Client/Server Technology*

1

Introducing LAN Server

WHEN YOU LINK COMPUTERS TOGETHER IN A LOCAL AREA NETWORK (LAN) and install network operating system software, the computers can share disk drives, printers, and sometimes other resources. The network operating system sends and receives information through the links between the computers.

You can use a LAN to make hard disks and printers attached to other computers seem like they are attached to your local PC. Because people whose computers are connected to the LAN can share one or more hard disks and the files on those disks, people can exchange files. With the appropriate multiuser software, several people can access the same files at the same time.

LAN Server, currently at version 4.0, is a software product from IBM that enables the sharing of files, printers, and modems on a LAN. This chapter explains LAN Server's basic features. Later chapters describe how to install LAN Server and discuss the administration, use, and troubleshooting of LAN Server.

■ Exploring LAN Server

IBM's LAN Server product allows DOS, OS/2, and even Macintosh computers to share files and printers on the LAN. The LAN Server product installs on a machine running OS/2 and turns that machine into a file server. Like many other network software products, LAN Server offers a NetBIOS communications interface and uses the well-documented, freely available Server Message Block (SMB) protocol to achieve file sharing and print redirection. A LAN administrator can configure LAN Server to use either the NetBEUI or TCP/IP transport layer protocols. LAN Server works with most popular Ethernet and Token Ring LAN adapters. The software also supports symmetrical multiprocessing, which is now available in OS/2 2.11. IBM also offers versions of LAN Server for its OS/400, AIX, MVS, and VM operating systems.

LAN Server Basics

In LAN Server and LAN Manager parlance, a *requester* is the software that lets a workstation log on to a domain and use network resources. Users have access to the network through the OS/2 LAN Requester program from OS/2 workstations and through the DOS LAN Requester program from DOS workstations. A server can share its files, printers, and even serial devices (such as modems) across the LAN. DOS requesters can't access a shared modem, but OS/2 requesters can.

During installation, the network administrator specifies a server to be a domain controller or an additional server. There is only one domain controller in a domain. A *domain* is a group of file servers and workstations with similar security needs. You can set up several domains on a large LAN Manager or LAN Server network. On a small LAN, a file server can also act as a domain controller. Domains provide a simple way for you to control user access to the network and the network's resources. A network user can have accounts in multiple domains, but he or she can log on in only one domain at a time. Users cannot start additional servers, nor can they log on if the domain controller is not running. Several domains can exist on the same LAN, each managed separately, but each file server belongs to only one domain. Domains are managed by network administrators who set up, maintain, and control the network, manage its resources, and support its users.

An *alias* is a nickname for a shared resource. On a server named ACCT-ING, an administrator might create an alias named OCTRCPTS to refer to the server's C:\RECEIPTS\OCTOBER directory. Workstations equate the OCTRCPTS alias to a drive letter, perhaps G, to gain access to the files in that directory. The alias specifies the server where the directory is located and the path to the directory, so people at workstations don't have to remember server names and directory structures. An alias remains defined after the domain controller is stopped and restarted, but a netname does not.

An administrator assigns a *netname* to a resource (disk directory, printer, or serial device) to define the resource temporarily. Like an alias, a netname identifies a shared resource on a server. However, to use a resource through its netname, you specify the server name in addition to the netname. Unlike an alias, a netname does not remain defined if the domain controller is stopped.

A UNC (Universal Naming Convention) name consists of a server name and a netname, which together identify a resource in the domain. A UNC name has the following format:

```
\\servername\netname\path
```

Note the use of the double backslash characters preceding the server's name.

If you assign LPT1 to a shared print queue, you override your local printer port and your print jobs go to the network printer. On the other hand, you can't override local drive letter assignments. If you have a C drive on your computer, you must use other drive letters besides C to refer to file server disk resources.

Security

User-level security on a LAN Manager or LAN Server network consists of logon security and permissions. Each user account has a password; the user specifies a user ID and the password to gain access to the network through a domain. A network administrator can limit a particular user's access to certain times of the day or the workstation(s) from which the user can log in. Permissions limit the extent to which a user can use shared resources. The network administrator, for example, can create a COMMON directory that everyone can use, and the administrator can create an UPDATE directory with files only certain people can modify but everyone can read.

The network administrator grants, restricts, or denies access to a shared resource by creating an access control profile. Each shared resource can have just one access control profile. An administrator can put individual logon accounts in an access control profile, or the administrator can set up named groups of accounts and insert group names in the access control profile. Group names are more convenient and they help keep the profile to a manageable size. Each individual or group name has a list of permissions and security restrictions the administrator can use. The access permissions allow or disallow these operations:

- Run programs
- Read and write data files
- Create and delete subdirectories and files
- Change file attributes
- Create, change, and delete access control profiles

Version 4 Features

IBM's OS/2 LAN Server 4.0 provides resource sharing for files, printers, and serial devices among LAN Server, DOS LAN Requester (with and without Windows), and OS/2 LAN Requester systems on a Token Ring or Ethernet LAN (LAN Server also supports the broadband-based PC Network adapters). With the LAN Server for Macintosh option, Apple Macintosh computers on an AppleTalk network can access server machines on an IBM OS/2 LAN Server network and exchange System 7.0 files with DOS and OS/2 files.

IBM has made some major changes and additions to OS/2 LAN Server in version 4.0. The LAN Server administrative tools now use the object technology in the OS/2 Workplace Shell by representing all network resources as OS/2 icons. A user can be added to a group by simply picking up the icon with the mouse and dropping it on the group. Administrators can manage multiple domains from any workstation, regardless of where the domain servers are located. To share server resources, the administrator just has to open a menu for the given object's icon to have the option of sharing, denying, and managing access rights, including printers, CD-ROM drives, and asynchronous resources. Public applications stored on the server can be allocated to a user or a group by dropping the application on that icon. The command-line interface is still supported for all version 4.0 functions, however. The following are other key enhancements that IBM made to LAN Server 4.0:

LAN adapter detection: To address third-party adapter support issues, LAN Server includes a detection facility to identify a machine's installed network adapter and the jumper and switch settings on the card.

Multiple domain browse: LAN Server clients have always had the option of a single log-on into multiple domains, but version 4.0 allows for global resource availability (regardless of a user's native domain). These cross-domain links allow users to access the tools they need, regardless of where they log on. In addition, LAN Server's aliasing feature lets users reference network resources without knowing where they're located on the network.

Enforced disk-space limits: Network administrators can now enforce disk-space limitations on network users through the GUI or command-line interface.

Performance improvements: OS/2 symmetric multiprocessing is supported in LAN Server 4.0; OS/2 and LAN Server support up to four processors. To exploit Pentium processors, version 4.0 supports native-mode operation in caching. Peer-to-peer support is now available for DOS, DOS/Windows, and OS/2 clients, and Microsoft's Windows for Workgroups and Windows NT clients can connect directly to LAN Server machines.

DOS enhancements: LAN Server takes advantage of client-server caching to reduce the number of DOS clients' cross-network requests for data, resulting in reduced network traffic. The DOS client now ships with an optional GUI that enables point-and-click connection, peer messaging, application launching, and resource sharing.

Transport improvements: LAN Server is implemented with OS/2's MPTS (Multi-Protocol Transport Services), which allows for integration into a number of networking environments. On the protocol side, it includes full TCP/IP support and a new version of the NetBIOS API for TCP/IP that is faster than earlier versions. Also, NetBIOS caching has been added to the OS/2 NetBIOS over the TCP/IP component.

As in version 3.0, the latest IBM NOS offering comes in two packaged versions: OS/2 LAN Server Entry and OS/2 LAN Server Advanced. LAN Server Advanced differs from LAN Server Entry on three key capabilities and functions that are available only on the high-end product: 386 HPFS (High-Performance File-System) support, fault tolerance for fixed disks (to support disk mirroring and disk duplexing), and local security support for the 386 HPFS partitions.

However, LAN Server does not support global naming of all network objects, and may in some instances require that a person use multiple logon accounts to access resources located in multiple domains.

LANQuest LABS, which conducted head-to-head tests of LAN Server 4.0 against NetWare 4 and NT Server 3.5, made the following observation: "For a server with a single CPU and 800 equivalent users, LAN Server Advanced was 38 percent faster than Windows NT Server and 11 percent faster than NetWare. Surprisingly, LAN Server Advanced with a single CPU was 10 percent faster than Windows NT Server on a server with dual-CPUs

for the same equivalent 800 users." LANQuest went on to say, "LAN Server
has best performance at every load point from 200 to 800 equivalent users."
And in comparing LAN Server Entry to LAN Server Advanced, "LAN
Server Entry provides very good performance for the small to medium network (20 to 80 users)."

File Servers—Past and Present

File servers let other computers share their disk space, files, and printers. The
Corvus company was one of the pioneers in desktop computer resource sharing. Late in the 1970s, Apple Computer's very popular Apple II computer
was expensive. Large-capacity disk drives for the Apple II were likewise expensive. Local school systems wanted to purchase Apple II computers to
help schoolchildren learn, but the cost of the disk drives—even small
ones—was prohibitive. And the computers were not nearly as useful without
disk drives. Corvus saw a need and began selling one of the first local area
networks to local boards of education. The school system could purchase a
single large-capacity disk drive, purchase Apple II computers without disk
drives, connect the computers and the disk drive through a local area network, and give access to the single, shared disk drive to each Apple II user.
The idea caught on rapidly, although the Corvus software wasn't able to let
multiple people concurrently access a shared disk file. Corvus is no longer a
major vendor of local area networking products.

In 1983, Novell began selling a network operating system product that
greatly improved on what Corvus had done. NetWare for the first time allowed multiple workstations to concurrently access shared files. The multiuser sharing of files, along with NetWare's evolution toward hardware
independence, made NetWare popular. NetWare's ability to let workstations
treat the hard drive on a LAN-attached PC as a shared device, via a phan-
tom drive letter, was a turning point in local area networking, one that gave
rise to the term *file server*. Novell uses its secret, proprietary NetWare Core
Protocol (NCP) to achieve file and print redirection.

By properly programming an application with shared file awareness, including record locking and workstation identification, developers of LAN-
aware programs could enable multiple people to use multiple instances of
the application, running on LAN-attached PCs, at the same time. However,
developers found it difficult and costly to write programs that ran inside the
file server (alongside NetWare) or that tried to make use of the NetWare
Core Protocol.

Toward the latter part of the 1980s, IBM's LAN Server product grew
in features to encompass virtually all the functions available in NetWare.
Version 3.0 of LAN Server, which embodies 32-bit code, several optimiza-
tions, and the same level of hardware independence exhibited by NetWare, is

actually faster than NetWare 3.11 (as measured by NSTL, the National Systems Testing Laboratory). LAN Server provides shared files and shared printers to workstation applications. In addition, LAN Server 3.0 excelled at providing shared LAN access to CD-ROM drives and even modems. LAN Server 4.0 extends the capabilities of version 3.0 with a graphical user interface, support for TCP/IP, and several other significant features.

■ Considering OS/2

While the network software components of NetWare use a proprietary operating system (built into NetWare), LAN Server runs on the general purpose operating system OS/2.

OS/2 Features

IBM released Version 2.0 of OS/2 in March, 1992. In late spring of 1993, Version 2.1 of OS/2 became available. OS/2 Warp, released in November of 1994, has the following key features:

- Simple graphical-user-interface installation
- System integrity protection
- Virtual memory
- Preemptive multitasking and task scheduling
- Fast 32-bit architecture
- Overlapped, fast disk file access
- DOS compatibility
- More available memory for DOS applications (typically about 620K of conventional memory)
- Capability to run concurrently OS/2, DOS, and Windows 2.1, 3.0, and 3.1 software
- Multiple concurrent DOS sessions
- High Performance File System (HPFS)
- Presentation Manager (PM) graphical user interface
- Object-oriented Work Place Shell (WPS)
- National Language Support (NLS)
- Interactive online documentation and help screens

- Capability to run OS/2 on IBM and IBM-compatible hardware
- Support for popular Super Video Graphics adapter (SVGA)
- Support for additional printers
- Support for popular SCSI CD-ROM drives
- Advanced Power Management (APM) support
- Personal Computer Memory Card International Association (PCMCIA) support

Almost all the items in this list help OS/2 to be a good file server platform.

LAN Server and OS/2

On an OS/2 computer, LAN Server runs in an OS/2 session. You can have multiple OS/2 sessions running on the file server, if you want. The LAN Server network operating system software does most of its work (the sharing of files, disk space, and perhaps a LAN printer across the network) in the background. The network operating system also performs administrative tasks, such as recognizing workstations as LAN users log in and forgetting about workstations when those users log out.

OS/2 offers a High Performance File System (HPFS) option especially designed for hard disks. OS/2 can access files in an HPFS partition much more rapidly than files in a FAT partition. The difference in performance is most dramatic for large files. HPFS gives you the ability to use long file names (up to 254 characters) and to include spaces and several periods in such a name. OS/2-based computers—either the file server or OS/2 workstations—can see and use these files.

Programmability is the biggest reason that people talk about client/server in connection with the OS/2-based network operating system, LAN Server. OS/2 is easily programmed, perhaps even more so than DOS. LAN Server can share the network adapter with other OS/2 application software running on the file server computer. OS/2 *multitasks*, which means that it runs several computer programs concurrently. One such computer program is the network operating system. Another may be a database server application. The workstations can see and use the extra drive letters provided by the network operating system. Your programming staff also may program the workstations to send and receive special requests and responses to and from the file server (or a separate computer, for that matter). These custom-programmed requests and responses may, for example, carry SQL statements and relational database records.

■ Defining the LAN Server Environment

A LAN is a combination of computers, LAN cables, network adapter cards, network operating system software, and LAN application software. On a LAN, each personal computer is called a workstation, except for one or more computers designated as file servers. Each workstation and file server contains a network adapter card. LAN cables connect all the workstations and file servers. In addition to DOS, each workstation runs network software that enables it to communicate with the file servers. In turn, the file servers run network software that communicates with the workstations and serves up files to those workstations. LAN-aware application software runs at each workstation, communicating with the file server when it needs to read and write files.

LAN Hardware

A LAN is made up of computers. You will find two kinds of computers on a LAN: the workstations, usually manned by people, and the file servers, which are usually located in a separate room or closet. The workstation works only for the person sitting in front of it, while a file server enables many people to share its resources.

In contrast to the workstations, a *file server* is a computer that serves all the workstations—primarily storing and retrieving data from files shared on its disks. File servers are usually fast 486- or Pentium-based computers, running at 25 MHz or faster and with 16MB or more of RAM. File servers usually have only monochrome monitors and inexpensive keyboards, because people do not interactively use file servers: They normally operate unattended. However, a file server almost always has one or more large, fast, expensive hard disks.

LAN cable comes in different varieties. You can use thin coaxial wire (referred to as *Thinnet* or *Cheapernet*) or thick coaxial wire (*Thicknet*). You can use shielded twisted pair (*STP*), which looks like the wire that carries electricity inside the walls of your house; or unshielded twisted pair (*UTP*), which looks like telephone wire. You can even use fiber optic cable. The kind of wire you use will depend mostly on the kind of network adapter cards you choose.

A network adapter card, like a video display adapter card, fits in a slot in each workstation and file server. Your workstation sends requests through the network adapter to the file server. Your workstation receives responses through the network adapter when the file server wants to deliver a portion of a file to you.

Only two network adapters may communicate with each other at the same time on a LAN. This means that other workstations have to wait their turn if the network is in use. Fortunately, such delays are usually not noticeable. The LAN gives the appearance of many workstations accessing the file server simultaneously.

Two of the most popular kinds of network adapters are Ethernet and Token Ring. Ethernet-based LANs enable you to interconnect a wide variety of equipment, including UNIX computers, Apple computers, IBM PCs, and IBM clones. You can buy Ethernet cards from dozens of competing manufacturers. Ethernet comes in three varieties (Thinnet, UTP, and Thicknet) depending on the thickness of the cabling you use. Thicknet cables can span a greater distance, but they are much more expensive. Ethernet operates at a rate of 10 million bits per second (10 Mbps).

Except for fiber optic cables and adapters, Token Ring is the most expensive type of LAN. Token Ring uses shielded or unshielded twisted pair cable. Token Ring's cost is justified when you have a great deal of traffic from many workstations. You will find Token Ring in large corporations with large LANs, especially if the LANs are attached to mainframe computers. Token Ring operates at a rate of 4 or 16 Mbps.

LAN Software

In addition to LAN hardware, you must have a network operating system. (You sometimes will see *network operating system* abbreviated as *NOS*.) DOS by itself cannot use a network adapter to talk to a file server. Just as you need DOS to manage applications in a stand-alone computer, you need a network operating system to control the flow of messages between stations. In the simplest case, this network software makes the disk drive on the server appear to be an extra drive (perhaps F) on each workstation. The network operating system also may make a LAN printer in another room appear to be locally attached to your workstation. Most ordinary computer programs are thus totally unaware of the LAN even though they use files on the remote drive F or print to the LAN printer through the LPT1 port.

On some networks, a separate, unattended computer acts as a file server. This is a *server-based* LAN. On other, smaller LANs, a workstation may be both a file server and a workstation at the same time. This is a *peer-to-peer* LAN (sometimes called a peer LAN).

The network operating system components on each workstation and on the file server communicate with each other using a computer language called a protocol. One common protocol is IBM's NetBIOS, short for Network Basic Input Output System. Several vendors besides IBM use NetBIOS.

■ File and Printer Sharing

People on a LAN Server network can share files, printers, and serial devices (such as modems). These people can also use the LAN to exchange e-mail correspondence and share multiuser application software.

Shared Resources

LAN Server can help a team of people share information. This means the members of the team can store files in one or more common, public directories that everyone can access. A common directory might be on a team member's PC (peer access), or the directory might be located on a separate, unattended PC that you use just for file storage (server access). With most applications, however, only one team member at a time can access a given file. You need to purchase multiuser software to have concurrent access to files. (This is true for all networks.)

Team members who use LAN Server can share printers as well as disk files. Using LAN Server's administrative functions, you designate the PCs that should share disk directories and those that should share printers. When you share a disk directory or printer from a PC, you give the shared resource a name by which other team members can refer to that resource. Other members establish connections to shared resources by also using LAN Server functions. Establishing the connection assigns a new drive letter (perhaps D) to a shared directory and, for a shared printer, redirects the parallel printer port (LPT1) across the LAN to the shared printer.

You can tell LAN Server to remember the connections you've established. LAN Server will automatically recreate each connection each time you log on.

With your new drive letter(s) and printer(s), you can work with files on other PCs as if the files existed on your PC's hard disk. When you print, the pages appear on the shared printer. You have access to shared directories and printers from within Windows, from within OS/2, and from within DOS.

How Resource Sharing Works

Network adapter cards send packets of information from one computer to another, under the direction of the network operating system. Adapters don't understand file and printer sharing; the adapter merely sends or receives packets. The network operating system accomplishes the file and printer sharing by doing the same job for the extra drive letter or the remote printer that DOS or OS/2 does for your local hard drive or local printer. Making another computer's hard disk or printer seem to be attached to your PC is called *redirection*.

The network software embedded in LAN Server exists in three basic layers. The lowest layer is the software driver for the network adapter. The middle layer is IBM's popular LAN protocol NetBIOS, which stands for Network Basic Operating System. IBM calls the current version of the NetBIOS protocol NetBEUI (for NetBIOS Extended User Interface). The top layer of software, the redirector, is the component that redirects disk and printer information from PC to PC.

The results of the interaction of these layers of software are the extra disk drives and printers you can access from your PC even though these resources exist on a separate computer.

The first use you'll find for your new network is the sharing of files without first having to copy them to disk. You can simply make files available to others by putting the files in a common, public directory on your hard disk (or perhaps by making your entire hard disk available to other people).

NOTE. *You'll need to be careful about file collisions on the LAN; you wouldn't want your recent changes to a file overlaid by another person who happens to type slower than you do. Two people who want to edit the same file at the same time need to coordinate with one another.*

You can designate certain printers in the office for certain kinds of print jobs. By organizing and designing your team's approach to sharing printers, you can make your printouts look their best while you keep paper handling (such as changing forms) to a minimum.

Multiuser Software

With the appropriate multiuser software, you and other people can concurrently access the same files at the same time. Examples of such software include Borland's Paradox for Windows and Microsoft's Access products. You'll notice that both these examples are database managers, for which multiuser access is a natural environment. It doesn't make sense (at least with today's software technology) to concurrently access word processing documents on a Windows-based LAN.

In the area of spreadsheets, Lotus Development, Microsoft, and Novell are working on ways to allow several people to simultaneously update portions of the same worksheet.

LAN Server, besides enabling the sharing of files and printers, implements *Network Dynamic Data Exchange* (Network DDE). The basic concept behind DDE is that of a conversation. There are two applications interacting: a client and a server. The client initiates and controls the conversation flow, and the server responds to requests from the client. Applications often act as both client and server, carrying on multiple conversations simultaneously. As long as you understand the basic conversation verbs, you can establish communications between applications at will.

DDE is an open-ended, language-independent, message-based protocol that lets applications exchange data or commands in any mutually agreed-on format. In a conversation between client and server, the client is the initiator.

■ The Benefits of Client/Server Technology

IBM and Microsoft developed OS/2 to be the successor to DOS. These companies wrote an operating system that can run multiple programs simultaneously, has more than 640K of RAM available to applications, and performs well in difficult situations. These characteristics make OS/2 a powerful operating system for a file-server environment.

While they developed OS/2, IBM and Microsoft also worked together to create file server software suitable for OS/2. IBM developed IBM LAN Server and Microsoft developed LAN Manager, but you will find few differences between the products. The IBM programmers in Austin, Texas, and the Microsoft programmers in Redmond, Washington, shared their work constantly as they created their almost-twin network operating systems. Both companies want LAN Server and LAN Manager to outsell Novell NetWare, but as yet this has not happened. Novell maintains a commanding lead in the LAN industry, but the IBM and Microsoft products do have an important attribute that makes the OS/2-based file server software attractive.

Because an OS/2 file server is highly programmable, it can do more than just manage files for workstations. An OS/2 computer, even while it acts as a file server, can run software that aids the workstations in special ways.

In a conventional workstation/server relationship, when a workstation needs to look through a large file for some data, the file—in message-sized pieces—must travel through the LAN cable to the workstation to be inspected. This process can cause quite a bit of LAN traffic and can slow down other workstations. A better approach has the workstation telling the file server what it is looking for. The search for the data can occur directly in the server. When the server finds the data, it can return just that data to the workstation in only a few LAN messages. This is called *client/server technology*. Unfortunately, in most cases, client/server requires the efforts of a programmer to implement the special processing that occurs inside the server.

■ Summary

This first chapter introduced you to local area networks (LANs), OS/2, and LAN Server itself. The next chapter explains networking in more detail. Later chapters discuss the installation, administration, and use of LAN Server.

- *Examining the LAN*
- *Working with File Servers*
- *Sharing a Printer*
- *Using Workstations*
- *Using Macintosh Computers on a LAN*
- *Connecting through LAN Cables, Adapters, and Protocols*

- *NDIS and ODI*
- *NetBIOS*
- *Using the OSI Model*
- *Accessing the LAN*
- *Administering the LAN*
- *Communicating with Electronic Mail*
- *Client/Server Architecture*

2

Looking at Local Area Networks

LOCAL AREA NETWORKS (LANS) ARE POPULAR ENOUGH THAT
you're probably already familiar with many of the characteristics
of a LAN. This chapter will refresh your familiarity and expand
your understanding of local area network technology: You'll gain a
good grasp of the context in which LAN Server operates.

■ Examining the LAN

You can share files, applications, databases, disk space, printers, fax machines, modems, and interoffice mail on a local area network (LAN). A typical LAN consists of one or more file servers, one or more database servers, shared printers, and several workstations. You'll get a broad look at these LAN features and components in the next few sections of this chapter; later sections of this chapter will provide a more detailed picture of LAN technology.

A LAN Overview

Through a combination of hardware and software, a LAN lets people share information. Just as a leader or manager can turn a group of people into an organized, functioning team, a LAN turns a group of computers into an organized, functioning team, which in turn supports the work of a team of people.

People can share computer resources as well as information on a LAN. A shared resource might be a disk drive, a printer, or another computer component. The shared information might be a list of customers, an inventory of parts, a schedule of events, a list of products and prices, a collection of documents, a schedule of classes, a list of students, a tabulation of accounting entries, the result of observations or inspections, or other data.

Local area networks connect computers located in a relatively small, or local, geographic area and allow those computers to share information. The small geographic area can be a department of people, a small office, or perhaps a small building. A single LAN cannot connect computers more than about 300 feet away from each other. You can, however, connect two or more LANs in a wide area network (WAN). Special telephone lines let the WAN-connected LANs transfer information among themselves.

The hardware components of a LAN typically consist of network adapter cards, cables, central hubs to which the cables connect, and the computers that make up the LAN. The software components of a LAN typically consist of driver programs that provide access to the network adapters, communications programs that make it possible for the computers to send and receive messages, and network operating system (network operating system) programs that extend the computer environment of a PC to also include the shared resources (disk drives, printers, and so on) that are part of the LAN.

Sharing Files, Disk Space, and Printers

A *file server* is usually a fast PC with lots of RAM and large, fast hard disks. The quality and appearance of the file server's keyboard and monitor usually don't matter on a *server-based LAN*, because the file server operates in unattended mode much of the time. However, the quality and reliability of the file server's computer circuits and the file server's hard disks are important, because the file server does the work of many computers as the server responds to the file and print service requests of the workstations on the LAN.

In contrast, a *workstation* is an attended PC on the LAN that people interact with and that typically has a good-quality monitor and keyboard. The workstation often obtains information from a file server, processes the information under your direction, and stores the result on the file server. When you print a document or report, a shared network printer located somewhere in the office may produce the printout.

Some computers on the network may act as both file server and workstation at the same time. In contrast to a server-based LAN, a network on which computers are both workstations and file servers is a *peer LAN*. On some small networks, using a PC as both server and workstation saves the cost of a separate file server computer. However, such a configuration runs the risk of occasionally losing data when a workstation application crashes the computer. When this happens, the file server software also halts, causing LAN down time until you reboot the computer.

On some LANs, unattended computers may run computer programs that perform work in a background mode. These programs might, for example, perform lengthy calculations in response to requests from workstations for database access or update or they might process communication requests from workstations, thus acting as a communications gateway machine. These unattended computers are neither file servers nor workstations. They are called database servers, calculation engines, or gateway servers. Sometimes a separate PC performs each of these background tasks. In other situations, a multitasking operating system like OS/2 lets a single unattended computer perform several background tasks concurrently.

Each time the workstation application you're running loads or saves a file on the file server, the network operating system sends the operation to the file server as a series of LAN messages, usually called *frames* or *packets*. The file server responds to each LAN message by performing the requested operation and returning the result to the workstation. The network operating system makes the file server's shared resources seem like local resources to the workstation. From DOS-based workstations, you see the file server as one or more additional drive letters that didn't exist before you logged in. From UNIX-based workstations, you see the file server as one or more extra file systems that you can mount. From Macintosh workstations, you see the file server as extra folders that you can open and manipulate.

Connecting the Computers

The network adapters, cables, and hubs that connect the computers in a local area network form an organized web of communications links between the computers. Computers connected by network hardware are called *nodes*. Most of the nodes are workstations, while others are file servers, print servers, database servers, or perhaps gateway servers. The communications links provide the pathway through which the network software sends redirected file-load and file-save I/O requests. The network adapter sends messages to and receives messages from among the LAN computers, and the cable carries the messages.

Understanding LAN Cables

LAN cable comes in many varieties. The kind of wire you use depends mostly on the kind of network adapter cards you choose. You'll find more detail on cable types later in the chapter. Your LAN may use thin coaxial wire (referred to as *Thinnet* or *Cheapernet*) or thick coaxial wire (*Thicknet*). *Shielded twisted pair* (*STP*) wire, which looks like the wire that carries electricity inside the walls of your house, and *unshielded twisted pair* (*UTP*) wire, which looks like telephone wire, are also popular LAN cables. Another option is *fiber-optic cable*, which works over longer distances and at faster speeds than other types of cable. But fiber-optic cable installation and fiber-optic–based network adapters can be expensive.

Each workstation is connected with cable to the other workstations and to the file server. Sometimes a single piece of cable wends from station to station, connecting all the servers and workstations along the way. This cabling arrangement is called a *bus* or *daisy-chain* topology. (*Topology* is simply a description of the way the workstations and servers are physically connected.)

In a *star* topology, a separate cable runs from a central place, such as a file server, to each workstation. Sometimes the cables branch out repeatedly from a root location, forming a *star-wired tree*. Daisy-chained cabling schemes use the least cable but are the hardest to diagnose or bypass when problems occur.

Sending and Receiving LAN Messages

At the lowest level, networked PCs communicate with one another and with the file server using frames (message packets). These frames are the foundation on which all LAN activity is based. The network adapter, along with its support software, sends and receives these frames. Each computer's network adapter has a unique address on the LAN: Other computers target a particular node as the recipient of a frame by inserting this unique address in the destination portion of the frame. A particular frame might open a communications session between two computers, send part of a file from a file server to a workstation, acknowledge the receipt of a frame, broadcast a message, or close a communications session.

Only one frame at a time travels through the LAN cables. On a busy network, one network adapter sends a frame to its destination (another adapter), and then a different adapter sends a frame back. The rapid rate at which each pair of computers exchanges LAN messages makes it seem like all the PCs on the LAN are communicating at the same time. Frames travel quickly enough from adapter to adapter (workstation to file server, for example) to make it appear that the LAN gives concurrent access to all the workstations. In reality, only one adapter may send a frame at any given moment.

The layering of protocols in each computer is what turns the group of computers into a local area network. A *protocol* defines the format, or layout, of the information in the messages. One protocol might contain a LAN message whose format is that of another protocol, in the same way that an envelope can contain a smaller envelope. This layering of protocols is a powerful concept. The lowest layer knows how to tell the network adapter to send a message, but that layer is ignorant of file servers and file redirection. The highest layer understands file servers and redirection, but knows nothing about Ethernet or Token Ring. Together, though, these layers give you a local area network.

Summarizing Network Adapters

Ethernet is the most popular type of network adapter, followed by Token Ring, ARCNet, and Fiber Distributed Data Interface (FDDI). ARCNet adapters, connected by coaxial cables, pass tokens as in Token Ring, but in a different format. ARCNet is an older LAN technology that is becoming obsolete. FDDI, however, is a new LAN technology that uses pulses of light, through fiber-optic cables usually made of plastic, to send LAN messages.

The type of network adapter and cable in your LAN depends on your organization's budget, the need to connect to a mainframe computer, the distances between the nodes, and other considerations.

Ethernet Adapters

Ethernet is a LAN standard based on the Experimental Ethernet network designed and built in 1975 by Xerox at the Palo Alto Research Center (PARC). IEEE 802.3 is a LAN standard similar to Ethernet. The first edition of IEEE 802.3 was published in 1985. The differences between the two Ethernet standards are in the areas of network architecture and frame formats.

Ethernet-based LANs enable you to interconnect a wide variety of equipment, including UNIX, Apple, IBM, and IBM clone computers. You can buy Ethernet network adapter cards from dozens of competing manufacturers. Ethernet adapters can use one of several varieties of cabling—Thinnet, unshielded twisted pair (UTP), shielded twisted pair (STP), or Thicknet—depending on the number of nodes on your LAN and the distances between the nodes. Thicknet cables can span a greater distance than Thinnet, but Thicknet is more expensive. Many Ethernet installations use less expensive UTP wire, with hubs and repeaters, to save money and create LANs with hundreds of nodes. Ethernet operates at a rate of 10 million bits per second (10 mbps).

Between *data transfers* (requests from and responses to the file server), Ethernet LANs remain quiet. After a workstation sends a request across the LAN cable, the cable falls silent again. What happens when two or more workstations (and/or file servers) attempt to use the LAN at the same time? The messages collide in the LAN cable. Suppose that one of the workstations wants to request something from the file server, just as the file server is sending a response to another workstation. (Remember that only one computer may communicate through the cable at a given moment.) A collision occurs, and both computers—the file server and the workstation—back off and try again. Ethernet network adapters use *Carrier Sense, Multiple Access/ Collision Detection* (CSMA/CD) to detect the collision, causing each to back off for a random amount of time. This method effectively prevents another collision by enabling one computer to go first. With higher amounts of traffic, the frequency of collisions rises, and response times become worse and worse. When this happens, an Ethernet network may actually spend more time recovering from collisions than sending data. IBM and Texas Instruments, recognizing Ethernet's traffic limitations, designed Token Ring to solve the problem.

Token Ring Adapters

Except for fiber optic cables and adapters (discussed later in this chapter), Token Ring is the most expensive type of LAN. Token Ring uses shielded or unshielded twisted-pair cable. The Token Ring's cost is justified in situations where there is a great deal of traffic from many workstations. You will find Token Rings in large corporations with large LANs, especially if the LANs are attached to mainframe computers. Token Ring operates at a rate of either 4 or 16 million bits per second (4 mbps or 16 mbps).

On a Token Ring network, even when there is no traffic, all the workstations continuously play a game of "hot potato," passing around an electronic *token*, a short 3-byte message indicating that the network is idle. If a workstation has nothing to send, as soon as it receives the token, it passes the token on to the next workstation. Only when a workstation receives the token can it send a message on the LAN. If the LAN is busy and you want your workstation to send a message to another workstation or server, your workstation must wait patiently for the token to come around. Only then can your workstation send its message. The message circulates through the workstations and file servers on the LAN, all the way back to you, the sender. During the circulation of the message, one of the workstations or file servers recognizes that the message is addressed to it and begins processing that message. The sender then sends a token to indicate that the network is idle again.

Token Ring is not as wasteful of LAN resources as this description makes it sound. The token takes almost no time at all to circulate through a LAN, even with 100 or 200 workstations. It is possible to assign priorities to certain workstations and file servers so that they get more frequent access to the LAN. And, of course, the token-passing scheme is much more tolerant of high traffic levels on the LAN than is the collision-sensing Ethernet.

Sometimes a station fumbles and "drops" the token. LAN stations watch each other and use a complex procedure to regenerate a lost token. Token Ring is quite a bit more complicated than Ethernet, and the LAN adapter cards are correspondingly more expensive.

Using Network Software

Just as you need an operating system to manage applications in a stand-alone computer, you need a *network operating system* to make a file server's hard disk appear to your workstation as a shared resource. The network operating system gives you access to shared resources by extending the functions of your computer's operating system. The file and print operations you do at your workstation turn into LAN messages that flow to a file server, and the file server sends responses back to your workstation. The network operating system uses a network protocol to send and receive LAN messages.

Surveying Popular Protocols

The network operating system components on each workstation and on the file server communicate with each other through a protocol. *Protocols* make sure that messages arrive at their destination undamaged (by electrical interference, for instance). Protocols also help workstations identify each other on the LAN. Primarily, protocols give applications and network software the means to send and receive LAN messages.

One common protocol is IBM's *NetBIOS*, short for *Network Basic Input Output System*. Several vendors besides IBM use NetBIOS. Another protocol is Novell's *IPX*, which stands for *Internetwork Packet Exchange. TCP/IP, Transmission Control Protocol/Internet Protocol*, is a popular protocol for connecting LAN components from different vendors.

The network software running at a workstation sends file-load and file-save (file-read and file-write) requests to file servers using one of these protocols. When you log on, your workstation uses a protocol to send your account name and password to a server for verification. Workstations also use a protocol to convey database update or access requests, processing requests, and communications requests to and from database servers, calculation engines, and gateway servers.

Accessing a File Server

In the simplest case, network software makes the disk drive on the server appear as an extra drive letter (perhaps *F*) on each DOS-based workstation. On a UNIX workstation, the network software makes the server's disk drive appear as an extra file system. Network software on a Macintosh computer makes the server's disk appear as an extra folder. The network operating system also may make a LAN printer in another room appear to be locally attached to your workstation. Most ordinary computer programs are thus totally unaware of the LAN even though they use files on the remote drive F or print to the LAN printer through the LPT1 port.

A network operating system intercepts each file-load and file-save operation at your workstation and determines if the I/O operation refers to a file on a file server. The network operating system lets the local operating system on your workstation perform the I/O operation if you're accessing a file located on your local hard disk. For I/O operations that access files on a file server, the network operating system software running on your workstation converts the I/O request into a LAN message and sends the message to the file server. Upon receiving a response from the server, the workstation network operating system software converts the response into the completed I/O operation that your application software is expecting.

Using Databases, Gateways, and Other Resources

The network operating system isn't the only software that can use the protocols available on your LAN. A database server accepts insert, update, and query requests from workstations in the form of LAN messages. The database server responds by returning to the workstation one or more LAN messages containing the results of the database operation.

Similarly, establishing a communications session with a host computer attached to your LAN causes LAN messages to flow through the LAN cables. A gateway server forwards your communications data (screens of data, keyboard input, or transferred files) to and from the host computer.

A client/server application often takes advantage of how a LAN works to separate the collection of input data from the calculation of results and the printing of reports. Some attended workstations run software that accepts and edits input. Other unattended workstations run software that performs calculations or does other application-oriented work. The client/server application components running on the different computers often coordinate their efforts by sending and receiving LAN messages.

■ Working with File Servers

A file server is often the hardest working computer on the LAN. The server, usually unattended, receives file I/O requests from workstations, performs the requested operation, and sends the result back to the workstations. You can think of the file server as Grand Central Station for the LAN messages that flow through the LAN cables. The file server imposes rules for sharing files and usually participates in the printing of reports or documents on a shared LAN printer.

Distinguishing Peer LANs and Server-Based LANs

The network operating system you install on your server may be just one or a few TSR (terminate and stay resident) programs that enable the computer to be shared across the network. Such simple network software usually leaves the computer running DOS and able to act as a workstation and a server at the same time. This is called a *peer-to-peer* network operating system. On the other hand, the network operating system may not be DOS-based at all. The network operating system may replace DOS completely once it has been loaded into memory, or the network operating system may use a high-power operating system such as OS/2 or UNIX in place of DOS. Such a network operating system is a *server-based* network operating system. The NetWare product consists of a combination operating system and server-based network operating system.

Of course, you may install a peer-to-peer network operating system but choose not to use the server computer as a workstation, enabling the computer instead to concentrate on its role as a file server. This configuration is a *dedicated server*. The file server still runs DOS, but you do not have to worry about the possibility that an application running on the server/workstation will crash and thus stop the entire network. A server-based network operating system is, by definition, a dedicated server environment.

Looking at File Server Activity

On a busy LAN, the following example dialog between the workstation and file server happens tens to hundreds of times each minute.

Workstation	File Server
Open file "EXPENSES.WK1".	Okay; file is open.
Send me the contents of the file.	Okay; here is the data.
Close the file.	Okay; file is closed.

This dialog is typical of about 99 percent of the activity that occurs between workstations and a server on an average LAN. The LAN cable carries the exchange of messages back and forth between the workstations and file server. The network operating system, running in both the workstation and the file server carries on the dialog. The network operating system gives the applications running at the workstation the illusion that the file-server hard disk is just another drive. To enable the workstation to treat the file server hard disk as just another drive, the network operating system does all the tasks DOS would do. These tasks occur through the LAN cable, rather than just locally inside the workstation.

File-Sharing Collisions

If two workstations both want the file EXPENSES.WK1 at *approximately* the same time, and if the people at both workstations have rights to modify the file, trouble can erupt. Suppose that one user loads the file into his spreadsheet program, types some new data onto the worksheet, and saves the file. You do the same thing, but you type different data and type faster than the other user. You save your changes to the file quickly, but the slower typist saves his changes a minute or two later. Clearly, the other user's changes will take effect while yours are ignored. This is probably not what you intended to happen. You and the other user should coordinate the use of the file in order to avoid these problems.

If two workstations access EXPENSES.WK1 at *exactly* the same time, the file server opens the file for one workstation but denies access to the other workstation. You may update the file without noticing a problem, but the other user may see the dreaded message

```
Sharing Violation; Abort, Retry, or Ignore?
```

You can avoid file-sharing problems in a number of ways. The simplest method is to coordinate the updating of the files with other workstations (electronic mail can help you accomplish this). Another procedure involves giving people copies of files from one central source and having only one person responsible for updating the central file. One person may be in charge of files in a manner similar to that of a librarian in a public library. The network operating system can also help you enforce good file-sharing techniques.

Knowing What Makes a Good File Server

You need a place to store the files that you want the workstations to share. You can turn one of the office's personal computers into a file server, or you may choose to use a different kind of computer—a minicomputer, perhaps, or what is called a *superserver*, a PC designed especially to be a file server—as the file server. Either way, you have four criteria to apply to your server:

- You need fast access to the files on the server.
- You need the file server to have the capacity to hold files and records for many users.
- You need some measure of security for the files.
- You need the file server to be reliable.

If you choose something other than a PC to be a file server, you also need to verify that the computer is compatible with the LAN and that it can behave as a file server. You will most likely need to discuss LAN options with your minicomputer vendor.

On the other hand, if you use a PC as a file server, choose a PC that is faster and has larger, faster disks than do the other machines. Why should the file server be a faster computer if the software applications run on each individual PC on the LAN and not on a central machine? During busy periods, the server receives many requests for disk files and records; it takes a certain amount of CPU effort as well as disk rotation and access time to respond to each request. Requests should be serviced quickly so that each user gets the feeling of being the only one using the file server at any given moment.

The CPU

The file server's CPU (central processing unit), hard disk, RAM, and network adapter play significant roles in how fast your LAN shares files. The file server's CPU tells the hard disk what to store and retrieve. The CPU is the next most important file server component after the hard disk. The CPU in a computer executes the instructions given to it by the software you run. Applications will run more quickly if the CPU is fast. Similarly, a network operating system will run more quickly if the CPU is fast. Some network operating systems absolutely require certain types of CPU chips. Novell NetWare version 2, for example, requires at least an 80286 CPU. NetWare version 3 requires at least an 80386. IBM LAN Server version 3 and version 4 require that OS/2 2.x be running on the server computer; OS/2 2.x itself requires an 80386 or better CPU.

The Hard Disk

The hard disk is the most important component of a file server. The hard disk stores the files of the people using the LAN. To a large extent, the reliability, access speed, and capacity of a server's hard disk determine whether or not people will be happy with the LAN and will use the LAN productively. The most common complaint about the average LAN is that the file server runs out of disk space. For this reason, most manufacturers of file server computers put gigabyte-sized hard disks in their computers.

A common bottleneck in the average LAN is the time it takes to access the hard disk in the file server. In general, disk access speed is measured by two things: data transfer rate and average seek time. *Data transfer rate* refers to the number of bytes of data that the hard disk and its controller card can deliver to the computer in one second. *Average seek time* represents the time taken by the disk to move the read/write head a small distance and then wait about a half-revolution of the disk platter for a given sector to appear under the head. File servers generally have disk subsystems with 10-millisecond average access times and 10-megabyte-per-second data transfer rates.

RAM

The network operating system loads into the computer's RAM just like any other application does. You need to have at least enough RAM in the computer for the network operating system to load and run. You can realize significant performance gains with a faster CPU and extra RAM because of something called *caching*. If the file server has sufficient memory installed, it can "remember," or cache, those portions of the hard disk that it previously accessed. When the next user asks for the same file represented by those portions of the hard disk, the server can hand them to the user without having to actually access the hard disk. Because the file server is able to avoid waiting for the hard disk to rotate into position, the server can do its job more quickly.

The Network Adapter

The server's network adapter card is the server's link to all the workstations on the LAN. All the requests for files enter the server through the network adapter, and all the response messages containing the requested files leave the server through the network adapter. As you can imagine, the network adapter in the server is a busy component. Within any one of the protocols used by network adapters, you will find that some network adapters perform better than others. One network adapter may be faster than another at processing messages because it has a large amount of on-board memory (RAM), because it contains its own microprocessor, or perhaps because the adapter uses a 16-bit or 32-bit computer slot and thus can transfer more data between itself and the CPU at one time. A faster, more capable network adapter is an ideal candidate for installation in the file server.

■ Sharing a Printer

When you send your documents to the LAN printer, the network operating system stores each one in a temporary spool file on the file server. When the printer is finished with its current print job, the network operating system sends the next spool file in line to the printer as a print job and deletes that temporary spool file. Typically, the network operating system prints a *banner page* or *job separator page* between printouts to identify each one. The banner page shows the account ID of the person printing the document, along with some other information about the print job.

In other words, the file server acts as a buffer for all the printouts. The server sends each file to the printer, one by one. On a busy LAN, you may have to wait for other documents to print before the server prints yours.

■ Using Workstations

Most workstations on local area networks use DOS as their operating system. Most of the LAN designers' efforts have gone into making DOS-based access of file servers as transparent as possible. However, if you use Microsoft Windows on your DOS-based computer, for example, your view of the LAN will be different. If you use OS/2's capability to give you both multiple DOS and multiple OS/2 sessions, your view also will be different, as will your view if you use a Macintosh. The UNIX operating system shows the LAN in yet a different way.

Accessing the LAN From DOS

A DOS user will notice certain changes in his or her computer's behavior when it's connected to the LAN. Your DOS-based computer can access extra drive letters and print to the LAN printer (if one exists, of course). In addition, there are new commands and utilities you can run. Some DOS commands behave differently on a LAN. Your applications may have less memory in which to run. The DOS PATH statement for your computer almost certainly will change as a result of your connection to the LAN. You may find it necessary to change entries in your CONFIG.SYS file because your computer is attached to the LAN. And, unless you have a diskless workstation, you will have new network-related files stored on your computer.

At boot time, DOS assigns drive letters whose values depend on the number of floppy-disk drives, number of hard-disk drives, and number of DOS-formatted partitions on those hard-disk drives. DOS always reserves drives A and B for floppies, even if you do not have a drive B. DOS assigns drive C to your first hard disk. DOS uses drive D, E, and other drive letters to refer to your second hard disk, your additional DOS partitions, and your additional floppy-disk drives. The network operating system also assigns drive letters, but not until you perform the login sequence. With many network operating systems, you can choose which drive letters you want the network operating system to assign. However, in practice, most network administrators preassign your drive letter assignments for you. The preassignment lets you consistently have access to the same shared disk drives that other people in your organization have.

The DOS TSR program SHARE.EXE is especially important on a LAN. The SHARE command enables file sharing. You should run SHARE immediately after logging in. You probably will want to make SHARE part of the batch file program (BAT file) that loads the network software.

The following DOS commands do not work on a file server hard disk across the LAN:

ASSIGN

CHKDSK

DISKCOMP

DISKCOPY

FDISK

FORMAT

LABEL

RECOVER

SYS

UNDELETE

UNFORMAT

In addition, you should note that most third-party disk diagnostic and maintenance utilities do not work on a file server hard disk. These utilities include such products as Norton Utilities and PC Tools. The following DOS commands, however, operate on a file server disk just as well as they do on your local hard disk:

ATTRIB

BACKUP

COMP

COPY

FC

RESTORE

SORT

TREE

XCOPY

Using Windows on a LAN

If you install it on each individual computer, Microsoft Windows occupies from 5MB to 7MB of disk space on each computer's hard disk. On a large LAN with many Windows users, the total disk space consumed by Windows files is considerable. You can share certain Windows files from one or more file servers if you configure things properly, using Windows's built-in menuing facilities to create application menus for individuals and groups. The object-oriented Windows menus can, of course, use file server search paths.

Sharing Windows files from a file server has several advantages. The most important advantages to people on the LAN are the access and management of LAN resources through the Windows interface. You can connect and disconnect remote printers with the Control Panel, view and manage remote files with the File Manager, and view or change the status of print jobs on LAN printers with the Print Manager. Probably the next most important advantage is the savings in disk space you realize. The savings become even more significant if the LAN workstations consist of personal computers with relatively small hard disks.

You should look closely at the mix of software applications, users, and hardware configurations that make up your LAN as you contemplate storing Windows files on your LAN. If only a few people use Windows in your office, you may find that putting Windows on the file server is not cost effective. Installing Windows on a network is usually difficult and tedious: The effort is worthwhile only if Windows is a popular operating environment in your office. You also need to choose whether to have Windows run automatically on the workstations, or whether to make it an option for people on the LAN. You should study how people in the office use Windows and find out whether the majority of applications people use are DOS or Windows applications.

If you have used Windows, you know that it requires computers and adapter cards that are compatible with the IBM PC standard. You also know that Windows requires a computer with a certain amount of speed and internal memory. These requirements become key issues if you want to integrate Windows with your network.

Keep in mind that Windows executes in the workstation, not in the server. You cannot improve the performance of Windows on a slower personal computer by installing Windows on a high-performance file server. The server only acts as a place to store the files that make up the Windows environment.

A special version of Windows called Windows for Workgroups has networking software built into it. Windows for Workgroups is a network operating system and Microsoft Windows combined.

Using OS/2 on a LAN

IBM's newest edition of OS/2, Version 2.x, has a number of features not found in DOS, earlier versions of OS/2, or Windows. Because IBM designed and developed OS/2 2.x after networks became popular, this latest version of OS/2 understands networks and does not need as much tweaking and fine-tuning as other environments do.

When you log onto the LAN from your OS/2 computer, you will notice the extra drive letters, the capability to print to the LAN printer, and many of the other differences noted earlier for DOS-based workstations. The network software, however, does not use conventional memory under OS/2. You do not have the same memory issues to deal with, and you do not need a memory manager product to reclaim usable memory.

OS/2 2.x gives you several operating environments: multiple OS/2 sessions (full screen or windowed), multiple DOS sessions (full screen or windowed), Windows sessions, and Presentation Manager sessions. You manage these operating environments from your OS/2 desktop, which is called the Workplace Shell. The Workplace Shell is LAN-aware, and you can manipulate remote objects (those that are LAN-attached rather than local to the workstation) in the same manner as you manipulate local objects.

Once you log into the network and map your file server drives as drive letters, each new DOS session or OS/2 session you create has equal access to the file server drives. A CAPTURE command issued in one DOS or OS/2 session affects all the other sessions. You can print from any environment in OS/2 after issuing the printer redirection command.

You normally will want your workstation to automatically attach itself to the LAN each time you boot your computer. Under OS/2, you do this with batch file statements you place in the file STARTUP.CMD. You may, for example, create a STARTUP.CMD file containing statements similar to the following:

```
@echo off
c:
cd \muglib
logon barry
```

OS/2 is a multitasking operating system. You may start a long-running print job in one session under OS/2, and then switch your attention to another session to get other work done. The print job continues in the background while you work. If you start another print job in a different session, the OS/2 spooler and the network spooler work together to keep the printouts separate.

OS/2 and the LAN also work together to protect the integrity of your data files. If, for example, you edit a document with a word processor in one session and try to edit that same document from another session, you receive a *Sharing Violation* error message from OS/2. The same mechanism that protects multiple users on the LAN from editing the same file at the same time also protects your multiple OS/2 and DOS sessions from colliding.

■ Using Macintosh Computers on a LAN

If you use a Macintosh as a workstation, you probably will notice very few changes in your Mac's behavior when it is on the LAN. The current version of the Mac operating system, System 7, contains some significant networking enhancements. System 7's new LAN-related capabilities include peer-to-peer file sharing, Ethernet and Token Ring drivers, Interapplication Communication (IAC), and Apple events messaging.

Three Macintosh Control Panels (CDEVs—Mac configuration utilities) enable you to start or stop file sharing, arrange access rights to your Mac and to shared objects, and monitor user access. The Sharing Setup CDEV switches file sharing on or off. It also sets a network name and password for your Mac, and it determines whether or not other users can use the IAC function to link applications. The Users & Groups CDEV enables you to configure access privileges for your Mac and the shared objects. Finally, a File Sharing Monitor CDEV shows the shared objects and a list of users who are currently accessing your Mac.

Interapplication Communication (IAC) is a System 7 feature that enables applications to exchange information by forwarding document updates across the network or by exchanging commands and information with other LAN-aware applications. IAC links applications running on different AppleTalk workstations.

The simplest form of IAC is the Publish/Subscribe mechanism. One Mac user (the person who "owns" the information and who has responsibility for updating it) tells an application to *publish*, or make available to other users, all or part of the information. IAC automatically makes this data available to another Mac user on the LAN, who "subscribes" to that data through the Standard File dialog box that appears when he or she chooses Subscribe from the Edit menu. Each time the information changes, System 7 passes the revised information to the subscribers through an edition file created by the application that publishes the data.

In System 7, applications can share information using special messages called *Apple events*. With this feature, one Mac application can request the services of another Mac application on the LAN (or within the same computer, for that matter). Apple events are a form of client/server architecture.

System 7 comes with both Ethernet drivers and Token Ring drivers. AppleTalk itself operates at the relatively slow rate of 230K per second, and supports a recommended maximum of 32 networked computers. The Ethernet and Token Ring drivers enable you to connect your Mac to larger, faster Ethernet and Token Ring networks.

Using UNIX on a LAN

If you use a UNIX-based computer as a workstation on a LAN, you will be able to share files with DOS and Mac users. A DOS user sees the file server as a drive letter with directories and files; the Mac user sees objects and folders. On a UNIX workstation, you'll see additional file systems, directories, and files. If you use an environment like X-Windows on your UNIX machine, you'll see icons and folders as well. Your new commands and utilities include such tools as RLOGIN, RCOPY, and RWHO, which are network versions of their UNIX counterparts. You also get telnet (for executing programs on remote computers), ftp (for transferring files), and smtp (for sending electronic mail).

Most UNIX networks are based on the TCP/IP protocol. TCP/IP is not a network operating system; you must get additional software to be able to access a file server. Sun Microsystems's Network File System (NFS) product is a popular way to connect UNIX-based computers. Several other computer manufacturers have licensed NFS, including IBM.

■ Connecting through LAN Cables, Adapters, and Protocols

Next we'll look closely at the Ethernet and Token Ring standards, the NDIS and ODI standards, and the NetBIOS and TCP/IP protocols; you'll also learn about the OSI Reference Model.

Communicating with Ethernet

In the collision-sensing environment often referred to as *CSMA/CD* (*carrier sense, multiple access, with collision detection*), when the network adapter card has a frame to send, it listens to the network. If the adapter hears that another card is sending a frame at that moment, the card waits a moment and tries again. Even with this approach, collisions (two workstations attempting to transmit at exactly the same moment) can and do happen. It is the nature of CSMA/CD networks to expect collisions and to handle them by retransmitting frames as necessary. These retransmissions are handled by the adapter card and are not seen or managed by you or your applications. Collisions generally happen and are handled in less than a microsecond.

On an Ethernet network, data is broadcast throughout the network in all directions at the rate of 10 megabits per second. All machines receive every frame, but only those meant to receive a frame (by virtue of the frame's destination network address) respond with an acknowledgment.

Passing Data with Token Ring

Token Ring networks can operate at either 4 or 16 megabits per second (but not both on the same LAN). You can think of a token-passing network as a ring; even though the network may be wired electrically as a star, data frames move around the network from workstation to workstation in a circular fashion. A workstation sends a frame to the MSAU (multistation access unit), which routes the frame to the next workstation.

Each network adapter card receives a frame from its upstream neighbor, regenerates the electrical signals making up the frame, and passes the result along to the next (downstream) workstation. The frame may consist of some data that one computer is sending to another, or the frame may be a token.

When a workstation wants to send a frame, the network adapter waits for the token. The adapter then turns the token into a data frame containing a protocol-layered message.

The frame travels along from adapter to adapter until it reaches its destination, which acknowledges reception of the frame by setting certain bits in the frame. The data frame continues its journey around the ring. When the sending station receives its own frame back, and if the frame was properly received by the destination adapter, the sender relinquishes use of the LAN by putting a new token into circulation. This design ensures that collisions never occur.

Although most people think of a Token Ring as a single piece of cable that all the workstations tap into, a Token Ring actually consists of individual point-to-point linkages. One workstation sends the token (or a data frame) to your workstation, your workstation sends the token or frame downstream to the next workstation, and so forth. From a communications standpoint, the messages go directly from one PC to another.

Not all workstations on the ring are peers, although the differences are invisible to the outside world. One of the workstations is designated as the *active monitor*, which means that it assumes additional responsibilities for controlling the ring. The active monitor maintains timing control over the ring, issues new tokens (if necessary) to keep things going, and generates diagnostic frames under certain circumstances. The active monitor is chosen at the time the ring is initialized and can be any one of the workstations on the network. If the active monitor fails for some reason, there is a mechanism by which the other workstations (standby monitors) can decide who becomes the new active monitor.

Using FDDI

The Fiber Distributed Data Interface (FDDI) is a much newer protocol than Ethernet or Token Ring. Designed by the X3T9.5 Task Group of ANSI (the American National Standards Institute), FDDI passes tokens and data frames around a ring of optical fiber at a rate of 100 megabits per second. FDDI was designed to be as much like the IEEE 802.5 Token Ring standard as possible. Differences occur only where necessary to support the faster speeds and longer transmission distances of FDDI.

If FDDI were to use the same bit-encoding scheme as that employed by Token Ring, every bit would require two optical signals: a pulse of light and then a pause of darkness. This means that FDDI would need to send 200 million signals per second to have a 100-megabit-per-second transmission rate. Instead, the scheme used by FDDI—called 4B/5B—encodes 4 bits of data into 5 bits for transmission so that fewer signals are needed to send a byte of information. The 5-bit codes (symbols) were chosen carefully to ensure that network timing requirements are met. The 4B/5B scheme, at a 100-megabit-per-second transmission rate, actually produces 125 million signals per second (125 megabaud). And because each carefully-selected light pattern symbol represents 4 bits (a half-byte, or *nibble*), FDDI hardware can operate at the nibble-and-byte level rather than at the bit level, making it easier to achieve the 100-megabit-per-second data rate.

■ NDIS and ODI

Network Driver Interface Specification (NDIS) and Open Datalink Interface (ODI) are two competing standards for how the network operating system controls the network adapter.

NDIS, developed jointly by 3Com Corporation and Microsoft, is a cornerstone of the LAN Server network operating system. A network adapter manufacturer makes its network adapters compatible with LAN Server by supplying NDIS-compliant software drivers with the network adapters.

ODI, developed jointly by Novell and Apple Computer, performs many of the same functions as NDIS does, but NDIS and ODI are incompatible with each other. A network adapter manufacturer makes its adapters compatible with NetWare, the most popular network operating system, by supplying ODI-compliant software drivers with the boards.

As you would expect, network adapter manufacturers supply both NDIS and ODI drivers with their products.

■ NetBIOS

NetBIOS accepts communications requests from the file-redirection portion of the network operating system or from an application program (such as a database server or an electronic mail product). NetBIOS requests fall into four categories:

Name support	Each workstation on the network is identified by one or more names. These names are maintained by NetBIOS in a table; the first item in the table is automatically the unique, permanently assigned name of the network adapter. Optional user names (such as BARRY) can be added to the table for the sake of convenient identification of each workstation. The user-assigned names can be unique or, in a special case, can refer to a group of users.
Session support	A point-to-point connection between two names (workstations) on the network can be opened, managed, and closed under NetBIOS control. One workstation begins by listening for a call; the other workstation calls the first. The computers are peers; both can send and receive messages concurrently during the session. At the end, both workstations hang up on each other.
Datagram support	Message data can be sent to a name, to a group of names, or to all names on the network. A point-to-point connection is not established and there is no guarantee that the message will be received.
Adapter/ session status	Information about the local network adapter card, other network adapter cards, and any currently active sessions is available to application software that uses NetBIOS.

Many network operating system products, including LAN Server, use NetBIOS to send and receive LAN messages.

Using TCP/IP

TCP/IP, which stands for *Transmission Control Protocol/Internet Protocol*, was designed by the Department of Defense for ARPANET, a geographically large network (not a LAN) that connects the various sites of the DoD Advanced Research Projects Agency. TCP/IP is a layer of protocols, not a LAN operating system.

TCP, like the session-oriented functions of NetBIOS, provides point-to-point, guaranteed delivery communications between nodes. IP provides datagram communications between nodes on a network. TCP/IP is like NetBIOS in several ways. A set of fairly standard utilities exist for transferring files (ftp), doing simple remote program execution (telnet), and sending electronic mail (smtp) over TCP/IP networks. These utilities do not perform file redirection.

Because TCP/IP is a public, not proprietary, protocol, it has become extremely popular as the basis for interconnecting LANs from different vendors.

Using Named Pipes

A *pipe* is a stream of data between two programs. One program opens the pipe and writes data into it; the other program opens the pipe and reads the data from the first program. If this sounds easy and simple to program, that's because it is. A named pipe is a file whose name has a particular format, as follows:

```
\PIPE\path\name.ext
```

OS/2 provides a set of functions for opening, using, and closing named pipes. The application that wants to create the pipe (called the server—but don't confuse this with a file server) starts the communication session, and another application (called the client) joins in. An application can treat named pipes as simple data streams or, if the programmer desires, as message pipes. In the latter case, each read operation fetches one message at a time from the pipe.

Because named pipes do so much work yet require only a programmer to code a few simple program statements, named pipes are popular on OS/2-based LANs.

■ Using the OSI Model

ISO, the International Standards Organization, has published a standard called the Open System Interconnection (OSI) Model. Most vendors of LAN products endorse the OSI standard but have not yet implemented OSI fully. The OSI Model describes how communications between two computers should happen. Sometime in this decade, this theoretical standard will become a practical one as more and more vendors switch to OSI.

The OSI Model divides LAN communications into seven layers; most network operating system vendors use three or four layers of protocols. The OSI Model specifies that each of these seven layers be insulated from the others by a well-defined interface. The following list identifies the seven layers of the OSI Model.

One of the factors that makes the network operating system of each vendor proprietary (as opposed to having an open architecture, or nonproprietary), is the vendor's noncompliance with the OSI Model.

Physical
This part of the OSI Model specifies the physical and electrical characteristics of the connections that make up the network (twisted pair cables, fiber optic cables, coaxial cables, connectors, repeaters, and so forth). You can think of it as the hardware layer. Although the remainder of the layers may be implemented as chip-level functions rather than as actual software, the other layers are software in relation to this first layer.

Data Link
At this stage of processing, the electrical impulses enter or leave the network cable. The network's electrical representation of the data (bit patterns, encoding methods, and tokens) is known only to this layer. It is at this point that errors are detected and corrected (by requesting retransmissions of corrupted packets). Because of its complexity, the Data Link layer often is subdivided into a Media Access Control (MAC) layer and a Logical Link Control (LLC) layer. The MAC layer deals with network access (either token passing or collision sensing) and network control. The LLC layer, operating at a higher level than the MAC layer, is concerned with sending and receiving the user data messages.

Network
This layer switches and routes the packets as necessary to get them to their destination. This layer is responsible for addressing and delivering message packets.

Transport
When more than one packet is in process at any one time, the Transport layer controls the sequencing of the message components and regulates inbound traffic flow. If a duplicate packet arrives, this layer recognizes it as a duplicate and discards it.

Session   The functions in this layer enable applications running at two workstations to coordinate their communications into a single session (which you can think of in terms of a highly structured dialog). The Session layer supports the creation of the session, the management of the packets sent back and forth during the session, and the termination of the session.

Presentation   When IBM, Apple, DEC, NeXT, and Burroughs computers want to talk to one another, obviously a certain amount of translation and byte reordering needs to be done. The Presentation layer converts data from one machine's native internal numeric format to another's.

Application   This is the layer of the OSI Model seen by an application program. A message to be sent across the network enters the OSI Model at this point, travels downward toward layer 1 (the Physical layer), zips across to the other workstation, and then travels back up the layers until the message reaches the application on the other computer through its own Application layer.

Measuring Distance Limitations

Local area networks are local because the network adapters and other hardware components cannot send LAN messages more than about a few hundred feet. Table 2.1 reveals the distance limitations of different kinds of LAN cable. In addition to the limitations shown in Table 2.1, keep in mind that you can't connect more than 30 computers on a Thinnet Ethernet segment, more than 100 computers on a Thicknet Ethernet segment, more than 72 computers on an unshielded twisted pair Token Ring cable, or more than 260 computers on a shielded twisted pair Token Ring cable. An FDDI-based LAN, however, can connect up to 1,000 nodes.

■ Accessing the LAN

Most LAN messages from workstations are file-oriented. Some are administrative in nature, having to do with logging in, logging out, and identifying who's who on the LAN. Others carry material to be printed on a shared LAN printer.

Table 2.1

Network Distance
Limitations

Network Adapter	Cable Type	Maximum	Minimum
Ethernet	Thin	607 ft.	20 in.
	Thick (drop cable)	164 ft.	8 ft.
	Thick (backbone)	1,640 ft.	8 ft.
	UTP	328 ft.	8 ft.
Token Ring	STP	328 ft.	8 ft.
	UTP	148 ft.	8 ft.
FDDI	Fiber optic	6,547 ft.	8 ft.
ARCnet (passive hub)	393 ft.		Depends on cable
ARCnet (active hub)	1,988 ft.		Depends on cable

Logging In

When you start up your computer, the network software loads into memory but you cannot yet access the file server's hard disk. You need to log in by typing your account ID and password. On a NetWare LAN, for example, if you can change to the file server drive letter (typically F) after loading the network software, you'll find yourself in the \LOGIN directory. You cannot access any other directory until you log in. One of the few computer programs in the \LOGIN directory is LOGIN.EXE. When you run the LOGIN program, the software asks you for your account ID and password. The password does not appear on screen as you type it. With IBM LAN Server, on the other hand, the LOGIN computer program resides on your workstation, and the server is not even minimally available to you until you log in.

Even before you type your account ID and password, the workstation sends messages through the LAN cable. The very first of these messages is a broadcast message directed to any and all computers on the LAN. This particular broadcast message asks file servers to identify themselves. When a file server responds, the workstation knows it can then ask you for your account ID. If your workstation cannot find a file server, an error notification will appear on your computer screen.

During the login process, the file server looks up the account ID in one of its internal tables. Your password, rights and permissions, workgroup ID (the name of your team), default directory, disk space restrictions, and other network restrictions reside in these internal tables. Naturally, the password and other information exists in encrypted form to prevent tampering.

Other network-specific administrative tasks may take place during the login process. On a simple peer LAN, these tasks may be called out in the BAT file that turns the computer into a workstation. On a NetWare LAN, a login script tells the LOGIN.EXE program how to configure your workstation.

Mapping Drives

Different personal computers contain different drive letter assignments, even before the network software loads. DOS assigns these initial drive letters based on the number of disk drives (both floppy and hard) in the computer and the number of partitions on the computer's hard disk(s). One computer may have a drive A (floppy) and a drive C (one hard-disk partition). On another computer, DOS may assign drives A, B, C, D, and other drive letters. To complicate matters, the file server may contain multiple disk drives. The network also may have multiple file servers. How should the network software assign drive letters in such cases?

The process of assigning network drive letters is called mapping drives. On a NetWare LAN, you run the MAP.EXE utility program to assign drives. By default, NetWare begins assigning drive letters starting with F or, if you already have several DOS-assigned drive letters on your computer, the next available drive letter. You can map additional nondefault network drives by using MAP.EXE. Typically, a network administrator invokes MAP in the system login script so that everyone gets the same drive letter assignments when he or she logs in. On a LAN Server network, you use a NET USE command to assign drives. Many peer LANs also use a NET USE command to assign drive letters. One peer LAN, WEB (from WebCorp), assigns a single drive W and establishes each different server computer as a directory on this networked drive W. The name of a server's directory is based on the machine name that you gave the server at installation time.

Macintosh computers do not map drive letters. If you have a Mac, you will see additional folders you can access once you have logged in. The Chooser enables you to see these additional network resources. A UNIX-based computer, on the other hand, sees the network drives as additional file systems. With Network File System (NFS), for example, the UNIX workstation mounts a network drive over an empty directory (thus making the UNIX mount command work almost the same for network drives as for local file systems).

After you have logged in and mapped the network drives as drive letters (or folders or file systems), you can access applications and data files on the network. You can also print to the shared LAN printer (as discussed later in this chapter). As you run applications, you should notice little or no difference between using your local hard disk and using the file server's hard disk.

The File Server

Depending on how the network operating system implements its security features, you may observe that network files and directories behave differently from what you are accustomed to. On a NetWare LAN, for example, you may not have any rights at all in a particular directory, when you use the DOS DIR command, you may see no files listed, or when you try to copy a file into that directory, you may see an error message on your screen. You can run the NetWare utility RIGHTS.EXE to find out what rights, if any, you have in a given directory.

Some DOS-based utilities and commands do not work on network drives. In particular, CHKDSK and disk diagnostic software such as Norton Utilities and PC Tools, when run at a workstation, cannot operate on network drives.

The file server itself can help you administer good file-sharing techniques. You can use the network operating system's rights and permissions capabilities to divide people into teams. Each team may be given its own public directory on the server. Coordination among members of the team, perhaps in the form of a published procedure and personal assignments of responsibility for certain files, will go a long way toward preventing file-sharing problems.

A server-based network operating system typically uses something other than DOS to access the hard disk. For example, you cannot boot a NetWare file server with a DOS disk and run the DOS CHKDSK utility on the hard disk; the hard disk does not use a formatting scheme that DOS recognizes. A DOS-based workstation, however, can use NetWare files as if they were DOS files because the workstation and file server conspire to make the server's files look like DOS files. The workstation component transforms the responses from the server into operating system responses to the application.

Sharing a Printer

The print spooler module in the network operating system constantly switches its attention between two functions. One function consists of receiving print material in the form of LAN messages and storing that material as temporary disk files. The other function consists of knowing which disk file should be printed next and sending that next print job to the printer. After the spooler prints a file, it deletes that disk file. Each disk file is a separate print job. If you and another person both happen to send reports to the printer at the same time, the spooler places each print job in a separate file in a queue. After detecting that the data for both has been received, the spooler first prints one report and then the other. Unless confused by too-short time-out periods, the spooler will keep the pages of each printout from mixing with one another.

The spooler puts the most recently received printout at the end of a queue. Associated with each printout is information you have specified at the workstation, such as whether you want a banner page printed, whether you want the network operating system to eject the last printed page (you may have already embedded a page-eject command at the end of your printout), and what type of paper the network operating system should use to print your output. Each printout, as it is received from a workstation, goes to the end of the queue and waits there for its turn to print. Most network operating systems provide utility commands you can issue to find out how far down in the queue your print job is. Many of these utilities also enable you to cancel a waiting print job or hold the job for later printing.

Different people use different fonts (typefaces) in their memos and letters. Most laser printers and some dot-matrix printers support a variety of fonts. Most laser printers can even print reports sideways, in Landscape mode, so that the long edge of the paper is the bottom rather than the side of the page.

Almost all printers stay in the most recently selected mode (Portrait or Landscape) and use the most recently selected font until told otherwise. On a shared LAN printer, if one person tells the printer to use a Letter Gothic font in Landscape mode, the next person's printout may appear in that same mode and font. This may not be what that person intended.

■ Administering the LAN

There are four reasons to implement security on your LAN: to limit inadvertent damage, protect confidentiality, prevent fraud, and reduce the chance of malicious damage by a disgruntled employee. The network operating system helps you protect the information stored on the LAN by requiring people to have account IDs and passwords and by allowing each person to have different access rights to different directories and files.

Administering Account IDs and Passwords

On the file server, the network operating system keeps track of each LAN user's login name (account ID), password (in encrypted form), directory rights, and other attributes. The network operating system protects the files containing these attributes: You cannot edit these files with a text editor, for example.

When a network operating system's login process detects an invalid account ID and password, the network operating system of course denies LAN access to the intruder. Some networks even enable the system administrator to specify that a given account ID can log in only once (rather than at several workstations concurrently), can log in only during certain hours of the day or only from certain workstations.

Granting Rights and Permissions

Even if every person on the LAN has the best of intentions, mistakes happen. A DIR *.* command may turn into a DEL *.* command. Or a well-intentioned person may overzealously try to do LAN-management tasks (such as copying a new application's executable files to a public area of the LAN) that can disrupt the day-to-day operation of the office. To prevent these and other similar situations from happening, most network operating systems enable the system administrator to restrict the access rights of each account ID on a directory-by- directory basis. Typically, these rights allow (or disallow) a person's ability to open, read, write, create, or delete files. Additionally, these rights permit (or prohibit) a person's ability to create directories, change directories, or modify a file's attributes.

Identifying the Network Administrator

The utility program the system administrator runs to add new account IDs to the LAN or to modify people's access rights requires, as you may expect, that the person running the program have special rights. Such rights by default only exist for a certain account ID. On NetWare LANs, this special user ID is *supervisor*. On LAN Server networks, the special account ID is *admin*. The person in the office who knows the password for this special ID can perform network administration tasks on the LAN.

Creating New Account IDs

One of the first tasks that should be performed on a new LAN, and one that should be performed each time your office hires new employees, is the adding of account IDs to the network. The utility program that the system administrator runs to create new account IDs is usually menu-driven and simple to use. (Vendors of network operating systems know that system administrators are busy people who do not have time to look up complex commands and parameters.)

For all network operating systems, the basic process of adding an account ID involves establishing the ID, its initial password, its directory rights, and other security attributes, and perhaps creating a home directory for the new user. The home directory usually has the same name as the account ID and is the default initial directory the user sees after logging in.

The process of removing a user from the LAN when someone leaves the office is simply the opposite of adding a new user. The system administrator removes the ID and deletes the user's home directory.

■ Communicating with Electronic Mail

Electronic mail is a simple yet potent facility. When used officewide, e-mail becomes more valuable and useful than the telephone for helping people communicate information. You can use e-mail to convey information that is difficult or impossible to read over the telephone, including reports, tables, statistics, charts, and images.

How E-mail Works

In its simplest form, e-mail consists of a mechanism for transferring a file of text from one person to one or more people. On a LAN, this may take the form of merely copying a text file into a personal post-office directory on the file server so the recipient can open and read his or her mail. This simplest of approaches does nothing for privacy and security, however. Most products elaborate greatly on this approach, using file encryption or directory and file permissions to enforce security.

E-mail systems that use file servers are fairly straightforward. A central database contains the names and locations of all mail users. A second database holds individual mail messages and attached files. You will find that LANs are the most frequently used medium for routing e-mail from place to place. The more sophisticated packages also can send messages across longer distances—by way of a modem (over dial-up lines), through dedicated (leased) telephone lines, or through LAN bridges.

E-mail software packages include a post-office component and a user-interface component. The software post-office component, like the real U. S. Postal Service, takes a completed mail message, decodes the address, and sends the message to its destination. Depending on the address, your message may be routed across the office through the LAN, through other computer systems in your office to another LAN, or across the country via gateways and bridges. Software post offices should be invisible, reliable, and prompt. And if you expect people in your office to use e-mail instead of inter-office paper memos (or instead of Federal Express), the product must have a good interface.

E-mail Standards

E-mail systems do not adhere to a universal standard for addressing and sending messages. Such a standard exists, in the form of the CCITT X.400 specification, but X.400 is difficult and cumbersome to administer and use. Most e-mail products instead use a de facto standard created by Action Technologies—Message Handling Service (MHS).

Using X.400

The international e-mail interexchange standard, X.400, is so complex and costly to implement that currently only large enterprisewide networks and commercial e-mail service providers use X.400 gateways.

X.400 is a CCITT standard; it defines how an intersystem mail message is addressed. "X.400" usually refers not only to the addressing standard but also a number of other CCITT e-mail standards. Among these are X.401, which describes the basic intersystem service elements, and X.411, which defines message-transfer protocols.

The most important member of the X.400 family of standards is X.410, which defines mail-handling protocols. X.410 deals with how Open Systems Interconnection (OSI) protocols work for e-mail applications. True e-mail interoperability is possible through these standards. Not all X.400 systems implement the standards properly, however. Some systems, for example, cannot reliably send binary files or Group 3 faxes (the most popular high-speed fax standard) from one network to another, even though such file transfer is part of the X.400 standard.

X.400 is becoming popular for international e-mail. U.S. Sprint, with its Telemail software, is a leader in providing overseas e-mail links. Administrators of Telemail networks, however, sometimes do not activate every connection with every possible e-mail domain, so you may not have access to overseas e-mail even if you use Telemail. On the other hand, some IBM proprietary e-mail systems do have X.400 gateways to Telemail.

To send an X.400 mail message, the sender formats the text file with address elements that are defined in the standard. The e-mail system administrator assigns a unique originator/recipient name to every user. The format for an originator/recipient identifier follows:

```
keyword:value, keyword:value
```

Each keyword is an address element. Most e-mail systems use only a few address elements, but X.400 enables a system to use a dozen or more.

Every address contains certain common elements. For example, all X.400 addresses include an ADMD—Administrative Management Domain. An ADMD is a public-mail system (such as MCI Mail) that serves as a message-transfer system. A private mail domain (PRMD) such as a LAN e-mail system can be attached to public networks like Telemail or MCI Mail.

A user name, user number, or a combination of first name and surname uniquely identifies an individual in his or her home mail system. For example, a WidgetMail user who worked at the Widget Company might be identified like this:

```
ADMD:MCIMail, PRMD:WidgetMail, FN:Barry, SN:Nance
```

The exact order in which the keywords and values appear does not matter.

Using MHS

Before the Message Handling Service (MHS) was created, each electronic mail product stored its messages in files formatted in such a way that other products could not use the files. The addressing schemes used to identify recipients were proprietary. Action Technologies published the MHS standard to overcome these limitations. Action Technologies also wrote software that implements MHS on NetWare LANs, and Novell bundles MHS with each copy of NetWare it sells.

An MHS gateway requires its own dedicated server, but MHS is a convenient way of moving information between e-mail systems. Because many vendors of e-mail products support MHS, it has become the lowest common denominator for interconnecting workgroup e-mail systems.

MHS provides a standard directory-and-file structure on the file server, into which any mail application can drop messages. MHS puts the incoming messages in specific locations and manages the physical flow of messages between mail centers. When MHS is installed, a publicly accessible server directory structure is created. Anyone on the network can create a message and give it to MHS for delivery. After the user creates the message, the MHS utility software sees the message and processes it.

A standard MHS packet is an ASCII text file containing several information items, each in a special format. A version number appears first and tells MHS that this is an MHS mail packet. The next line has the To field, and the following line has the From field. The sender's e-mail software has the responsibility of handling the addressing and providing complete MHS addresses.

If the user addresses the message to a user on the same MHS server, the server simply copies the file to the recipient's MHS mailbox. Periodically, an MHS e-mail software module polls the mailbox looking for new messages. When the module finds a new message, the MHS module copies it from the MHS mailbox to the e-mail mailbox. If the address is for another mail center, MHS moves the message to an out-basket directory for further processing. At a time determined by the MHS scheduler, the MHS server picks up the out-basket mail and sorts it by destination. The server uses the modem to establish a connection to the other mail center and then transfers the mail to the remote MHS site.

In turn, the remote MHS server collects the messages and sorts them by address. After a mail message is sorted, it is handled like all other messages on that LAN. As far as a user at the remote site is concerned, the only difference is that delivery of mail is not instantaneous. The e-mail software does not have to know about gateways and bridges. It just puts an address (in an MHS-recognizable format) on the mail message and hands the message to MHS.

■ Client/Server Architecture

If you operate your LAN in the simplest of ways, you share disk space on the file server and you share files by making those files available to other people in publicly accessible directories. You can make your LAN work harder, however. With *client/server architecture*, the LAN is integrated with one or more applications. Database servers are a good example of client/server architecture. You may designate one of the workstations on the LAN as a database server, for example, and use a product such as IBM's DB2 for OS/2, Microsoft's SQL Server, or perhaps Oracle to store your records. Client/server technology goes beyond mere file and printer sharing as offered by file servers and network operating systems. This new area of computing enables different computers on the LAN to perform the different tasks that make up an overall application system.

Database Servers

Beyond treating a file server as just another drive letter lies a whole area of software technology—that of database servers. A *database server* is an unattended computer on the LAN that serves up records to the application(s) running on other workstations. One of the goals of a database server is to take some of the workload away from the file server and from the workstations.

Looking at Database Server Advantages

Accessing one or more large files located on a file server can be a slow process if each workstation has to read most or all the files through the services of the network operating system. Each time the workstation reads a portion of the file, the network software turns the read operation into a LAN message and sends the message to the file server. The file server performs the actual read operation and sends the resulting file material back to the workstation. Large files cause thousands (or more) of read requests and corresponding LAN messages. For a large file accessed by several workstations, the file server repeatedly sends the file, in great numbers of small portions, to each of the workstations. If the file has a separate index, the burden of managing the index falls on the application software running on the workstation. The index management processing workload, the volume of LAN I/O messages, and the repetitious nature of the file server's responses to the workstation's requests usually form a rather inefficient, unproductive, and poorly performing environment.

In a database server environment, the application's file access logic (not the network operating system) controls the message passing. The application retrieves a record by sending the desired key to the database server as a

LAN message. The database server sends back the desired record (or a "record-doesn't-exist" indication). This process greatly reduces LAN message traffic. More importantly, it puts the indexed file I/O burden on a separate machine. The workstation only has to inform the database server of the kinds of data the workstation desires from the large, shared file that is the database.

On a busy LAN, a database server helps distribute the processing evenly and fairly. You can select a computer and operating system for the database server based on criteria that may be different from the criteria you used to pick the file server machine. You may even go so far as to use Macintoshes for user workstations and a high-powered superserver as the database server computer. Because the workstation no longer has to contain the actual file I/O logic, the application can be smaller by saving whatever memory those file I/O routines consume.

Identifying Database Server Disadvantages

When you need to ensure good performance and control the LAN environment more closely than a particular network operating system allows, you can build a database server into your LAN architecture. Unfortunately, you almost certainly will need the services of a programmer (or a staff of programmers) to implement a database server. You will incur the cost of programming (or reprogramming) the primary application on the LAN to use the database server. Simply installing a database server product on your LAN is not enough. You must somehow connect the application to your new database server. However, database front-end software such as Microsoft's Access and Borland's Paradox eases the burden of needing a programmer by allowing skillful people within your organization to use easy-to-understand scriptlike computer languages.

■ Summary

We've covered the basics of local area networking technology in this chapter. You learned how file servers and workstations use network hardware and run network software to create a LAN. You know how LANs work and how they behave. We've identified the essential components of a local area network.

The next chapter extends your understanding of local area networks by comparing LAN Server with other network operating systems.

- *The Components of LAN Server*
- *LAN Server Terms and Concepts*
- *Hardware and Software Requirements for LAN Server*
- *Analyzing Your Information-Sharing Needs*
- *Developing a Network Plan*
- *Designing the Basic Network*

- *Documenting Your Network*
- *Upgrading from NetWare*

3

Planning for LAN Server

Planning for a LAN server network takes careful thought and consideration. You need to understand the components that make up LAN Server, familiarize yourself with LAN Server terminology, know LAN Server's hardware and software requirements, think about your information sharing needs, and then develop your plan. This chapter explains these issues and provides you with the guidance you'll need as you develop a network plan.

■ The Components of LAN Server

In LAN Server terminology, a *requester* is software that lets a workstation log on to a domain and use network resources. People have access to the network through the OS/2 LAN Requester program from OS/2 workstations and through the DOS LAN Requester program from DOS workstations and DOS and Windows workstations. A server can share its files, printers, and even serial devices (such as modems) across the LAN. DOS requesters can't access a shared modem, but OS/2 requesters can.

A network operating system (NOS), LAN Server is the software that enables a group of PCs whose network adapters are connected by cables to become a functioning local area network (LAN). The following list shows the LAN Server components:

- OS/2 LAN Server (file server component, Entry Level or Advanced version)

- OS/2 LAN Requester (turns OS/2 PCs into workstations)

- DOS LAN Services (DOS Requester for DOS PCs and Windows PCs)

- Multi-Protocol Transport Services (MPTSs): (drivers for network adapters)

- LAN Support Program (more drivers for network adapters)

- LAN utility programs (miscellaneous software)

Most PCs on a LAN Server network are workstations; the remainder (perhaps just one PC) are file servers. You install requester software on the workstations and you install LAN Server itself on the file server(s). Technically, the LAN Server software on the file server consists of both requester and server components. The combination of requester and server components running on the file server allows you to log on to the file server to perform administrative tasks. The server component of LAN Server version 3.*x* and version 4.*x* runs only on machines that have an 80386, 80486, or Pentium CPU, because the server operates the CPU in 32-bit mode. A workstation might run in 16-bit mode (DOS or DOS and Windows) or in 32-bit mode (OS/2 2.*x* or higher). The component DOS LAN Services provides requester services on a DOS-based machine. OS/2 LAN Requester provides requester services on an OS/2-based machine and on the file server itself. Requester services typically consist of sharing files, disk space, and printers.

After you log on to the network, the requester at each workstation makes the file server's shared resources seem like local resources. Your workstation can access extra drive letters, as well as a shared printer, after you log on. When you run application or utility software at a workstation, the requester at that workstation redirects that software's file operations (loading or saving a file, for example) across the LAN to a file server. The file server does the actual file operation and returns a response to the workstation. The requester performs the work of transforming the file operation into a LAN message that the requester sends to the file server, and the requester also receives the response from the server. The LAN Support Program component and the LAN Adapter and Protocol Support (LAPS) component are driver modules that can send and receive LAN messages through the network adapters installed in your PCs. To send or receive the LAN messages they've created, the requester and server use either the LAN Support Program or the LAN Adapter and Protocol Support components to do the actual message handling.

You can buy either the Entry or Advanced version of LAN Server. The Advanced version offers features that help a large LAN perform better, give you extra security, and provide fault tolerance; but, in general, the Entry and Advanced versions are similar and they both supply the same ability for workstations to share files and printers. You can buy both versions in either CD-ROM or disk form. The CD-ROM or disk media contain LAN Server, the two requesters (OS/2 LAN Requester and DOS LAN Services), migration utilities you'll use if you're upgrading from an earlier version of LAN Server, the LAN Support Program and Multi-Protocol Transport Services (including LAPS), Productivity Aids, and online documentation. Both versions come with printed documentation as well.

In contrast to the licensing arrangements for some other network operating system products, such as Novell NetWare, you purchase a license (one at a time or in bundles) from IBM for workstations you add to your network. You need to purchase a license for each requester (OS/2 or DOS) that you run at each workstation. Each license allows you to make an extra copy of the requester software in your LAN Server package. The DOS and OS/2 requesters are the same for both the Advanced and Entry versions of LAN Server.

NOTE. *You may find that Windows for Workgroups version 3.11 PC can connect to a LAN Server file server without using (or needing) to run DOS LAN Services.*

LAN Server-Entry

On a small network (perhaps 25 workstations or less), the less expensive LAN Server-Entry product might very well be the appropriate choice. On a larger LAN, you might use LAN Server-Entry machines as print servers or domain controllers while other PCs run LAN Server-Advanced. LAN Server-Entry includes server and requester functions, First Failure Support Technology/2 (FFST/2, an error monitor and error logging feature), a graphical user interface, LAN Server Applications Development Toolkit (if you have programmers who wish to write LAN-aware computer programs), a Migration Import Utility (for upgrading from the PC LAN Program network operating system software), Network DDE and network-shareable Clipboard, network messaging, online documentation, a server configuration/installation utility, and support for uninterruptible power supplies (UPSs).

LAN Server-Advanced

LAN Server-Advanced includes all the components and features of the Entry version and adds features that enhance performance, reliability, and security. For better performance, the Advanced version includes a special 32-bit version of OS/2's High Performance File System (HPFS) called 386HPFS. This special version is optimized to perform well in a file server environment. You can increase the reliability of your file server by configuring LAN Server-Advanced to mirror multiple disk drives in your file server. With mirroring, LAN Server-Advanced keeps duplicate copies of files on multiple disks and keeps running if one hard disk crashes. The mirroring feature is useful if even short periods of idle time would cost your organization to lose significant productivity. However, you pay for the mirroring not only in the extra price of the Advanced version but also in the price of the extra disk drive(s) on which you mirror the data.

The 386HPFS feature enhances security as well as performance. You can password-protect a file server that's running 386HPFS and thus keep prying eyes and fingers away from confidential files stored on the file server. You can also impose directory size limits with 386HPFS to prevent any one person from using too much disk space on the file server.

Note that if you choose to not install the 386HPFS or disk-mirroring features of LAN Server-Advanced (they're options you select at install time), you are essentially running the LAN Server-Entry version. Many offices spread the LAN workload across multiple LAN Server-Entry file servers, make frequent backup copies of important data files, and keep the file server in a secure location.

Using the DOS Requester

For both the Advanced and Entry versions of LAN Server, the requester running on DOS (or DOS and Windows) workstations is the same. Called DOS LAN Services, this requester enables workstations to access the file server(s) as one or more DOS drive letters and enables the workstations to print to a shared printer. DOS LAN Services includes its own graphical user interface for those who don't use Windows, and also includes Windows software for those who do. Both interfaces let you log on to the network, change your password, show who's logged on, send and receive messages, log and later view your messages, connect or disconnect to and from shared file server resources, and manage print jobs.

During the installation of DOS LAN Services, you choose whether DOS LAN Services will offer its own interface or the Windows interface. You must also install Windows if you'd like to access network resources through the Windows interface. If you have more than 640K of memory in your workstation, you'll probably be able to load part of the DOS LAN Services modules into upper memory and thus conserve the 640K of conventional memory in which you run DOS application software.

When you load DOS LAN Services, you should also load the program SHARE.EXE, which comes with DOS. SHARE enables file sharing in a LAN environment. You're then ready to log on to the LAN and begin running your application software. When you log on, DOS LAN Services connects to the shared resources assigned to you by the LAN administrator.

Using the OS/2 Requester

In general, the requester you install on OS/2-based PCs provides OS/2 users with the same functions that the requester for DOS (or DOS and Windows) supplies. Besides letting an OS/2 PC share a file server's disk drives, directories, and printers, the OS/2 Requester also lets OS/2-based communications software share a file server's modems. Each DOS, Windows, and OS/2 program you run on an OS/2-based PC can concurrently access any of the disk drives, directories, and printers that you've set up as shared resources on your LAN. The Requester itself, along with the network adapter driver software, doesn't consume conventional memory, which means that each DOS session and each Win-OS/2 session has more of the 640K of DOS memory at its disposal. Because OS/2 is a multitasking operating system, file sharing is always in effect. You don't need to separately load the DOS utility SHARE.EXE on OS/2-based workstations. By the same token, OS/2 protects the individual DOS, Windows-OS/2, and OS/2 sessions from accessing the same file at the same time. This file-sharing protection operates between concurrent sessions running on an OS/2 PC the same way it operates across the LAN, between individual workstations.

■ LAN Server Terms and Concepts

LAN Server introduces new concepts and terminology into your organization. The following sections explain these concepts and terms.

Domains

During installation, the network administrator specifies a server to be a domain controller or an additional server. There is only one domain controller in a domain. A *domain* is a group of file servers and workstations with similar security needs. You can set up several domains on a large LAN Server network. On a small LAN, a file server can also act as a domain controller. Domains provide a simple way to control access to the network and the network's resources. A network user can have accounts in multiple domains, but can log on in only one domain at a time. Users cannot start additional servers or log on if the domain controller is not running. Several domains can exist on the same LAN, each managed separately, but each file server belongs to only one domain. Domains are managed by network administrators who set up, maintain, and control the network, manage its resources, and support its users.

Using Aliases to Identify Shared Resources

A UNC (Universal Naming Convention) name consists of a server name and a netname, which together identify a shared resource in the domain. A UNC name has the following format:

```
\\servername\netname\path
```

Note the use of the double backslash characters preceding the server's name.

If you assign LPT1 to a shared print queue, you override your local printer port and your print jobs go to the network printer. On the other hand, you can't override local drive letter assignments. If you have a C drive on your computer, you must use other drive letters besides C to refer to file server disk resources.

An *alias* is a nickname for a shared resource. On a server named ACCTING, an administrator might create an alias named OCTRCPTS to refer to the server's C:\RECEIPTS\OCTOBER directory. Workstations equate the OCTRCPTS alias to a drive letter, perhaps G, to gain access to the files in that directory. The alias specifies the server where the directory is located and the path to the directory, so people at workstations don't have to remember server names and directory structures. An alias remains defined after the domain controller is stopped and restarted, but a netname does not.

LAN Server encourages you to use aliases to refer to shared resources. Suppose that you have a LAN Server machine named PRODUCTION that shares a printer with an alias of REPORTS. The full name of the shared printer is \\PRODUCTION\PRINTER1. LAN Server workstations can share the alias REPORTS or the full name \\PRODUCTION\PRINTER1 to access that printer.

LAN Server Security

Account-level security on a LAN Server network consists of logon security and permissions. Each logon account has a password; the user specifies a logon account ID and the password to gain access to the network through a domain. A network administrator can limit a particular user's access to certain times of the day or limit the workstations from which the user can log in. *Permissions* limit the extent to which a user can use shared resources. The network administrator, for example, can create a COMMON directory that everyone can use, and the administrator can create an UPDATE directory with files only certain people can modify but everyone can read.

The network administrator grants, restricts, or denies access to a shared resource by creating an *access control profile*. Each shared resource (usually a disk directory) can have just one access control profile. The administrator can put individual logon accounts in an access control profile, or the administrator can set up named groups of accounts and insert group names in the access control profile. Group names are more convenient and they help keep the profile to a manageable size. Each individual or group name has a list of permissions and security restrictions the administrator can use. The access permissions allow or disallow these operations:

- Run programs

- Read and write data files

- Create and delete subdirectories and files

- Change file attributes

- Create, change, and delete access control profiles

■ Hardware and Software Requirements for LAN Server

Before installing LAN Server on a PC, you first must install OS/2. I recommend you use version 2.1 or higher. The following sections will look at the hardware requirements for OS/2, LAN Server, and the requester software that runs at the workstations.

Running LAN Server

OS/2 version 2.1 takes advantage of the Intel-designed 80386 or 80486 CPU chip to run 32-bit computer programs (such as LAN Server). OS/2 can also concurrently run multiple DOS and Windows programs. OS/2 has system integrity protection, which means that a failure in one computer program won't crash the computer, and OS/2 has virtual memory management, which means OS/2 can transfer infrequently used portions of software to disk. OS/2 cannot offer these capabilities on the older 80286 or 8088 CPU chips used in the IBM AT and the original IBM PC. Intel created two distinct types of 80386 CPU chips; OS/2 works with both the sx and dx designations.

OS/2 needs at least 6 megabytes (MB) of internal memory (RAM); the operating system performs better with even more memory. You should consider putting at least 16MB of RAM in your computer before you install LAN Server. LAN Server and the 386HPFS module can use the extra memory for caching (storing frequently accessed portions of files in memory for fast retrieval), and the extra memory will come in handy when you want to run client/server applications inside your file server alongside LAN Server.

OS/2 supports several types of hard disks and hard-disk controllers, including MFM, ESDI, IDE, and SCSI. OS/2 doesn't need special software drivers for MFM, ESDI, or IDE disks. For SCSI disk controllers and disks, OS/2 includes drivers for popular SCSI interfaces (Future Domain, Adaptec, Trantor, DPT, and of course, IBM).

You need a high-capacity floppy-disk drive to install and use OS/2. If you use 5¼-inch disks, the disk drive must be a 1.2MB drive. If you use 3½-inch disks, the disk drive must be a 1.44MB or 2.88MB drive. You can use the lower capacity 360K (5¼ inch) or 720K (3½ inch) drives to store files you create, but you can't use these drives to install OS/2.

You can use a variety of video displays (adapters and monitors) with OS/2, but VGA (Video Graphics Array) and XGA (Extended Graphics Array) work best.

You might be able to use any network adapter that comes with a Network Driver Interface Specification (NDIS) module for OS/2 (the LAN Server documentation refers to such driver modules as "non-shipped NDIS drivers"). However, LAN Server directly supports certain network adapters. You should consider getting a supported network adapter to use in your file server.

The following list summarizes the recommended hardware for OS/2 2.x and LAN Server 4.x:

- 80386 (sx or dx), 80486, or Pentium CPU

- 16MB or more of internal memory (RAM)

- MFM, ESDI, SCSI (possibly with a software driver), or IDE hard disk, with about 70MB of free disk space

- 1.2MB drive (5¼-inch disk) or 1.44MB drive (3½-inch disk) floppy disk drive

- Mouse

- Supported network adapter
- Printer (optional)

You can use one of the following types of video systems with OS/2 and LAN Server:

- VGA (Video Graphics Array), color or monochrome
- Some SVGA (Super VGA) displays
- IBM 8514/a or equivalent
- XGA (Extended Graphics Array)

The following list identifies the network adapters that LAN Server directly supports for use in the file server:

- IBM Token-Ring Adapter II (non-Micro Channel)
- IBM Token-Ring 16/4 Adapter (non-Micro Channel)
- IBM PC Network Broadband Adapter II (non-Micro Channel)
- IBM PC Network Adapter II-Frequency 2 (non-Micro Channel)
- IBM PC Network Adapter II-Frequency 3 (non-Micro Channel)
- IBM PC Network Baseband Adapter (non-Micro Channel)
- 3Com 3C503 EtherLink** II Adapter (non-Micro Channel)
- Ungermann-Bass** NIU**pc Adapter (non-Micro Channel)
- SMC EtherCard PLUS** Adapter (non-Micro Channel)
- 3278/79 Emulation Adapter (non-Micro Channel)
- IBM Token-Ring Adapter/A (Micro Channel)
- IBM Token-Ring 16/4 Adapter II (Micro Channel)
- IBM Token-Ring 16/4 Adapter/A (Micro Channel)
- IBM Token-Ring 16/4 BusMaster Adapter/A (Micro Channel)
- IBM PC Network Broadband Adapter II/A (Micro Channel)
- IBM PC Network Adapter II/A-Frequency 2 (Micro Channel)
- IBM PC Network Adapter II/A-Frequency 3 (Micro Channel)
- IBM PC Network Baseband Adapter/A (Micro Channel)
- Ethernet LAN Adapter (Micro Channel)
- Ethernet LAN Adapter/A (Micro Channel)

- Adapter/A for Ethernet Networks (Micro Channel)

- 3Com 3C523 EtherLink/MC Adapter (Micro Channel)

- Ungermann-Bass NIUps Network Adapter (Micro Channel)

- SMC EtherCard PLUS/A Network Adapter (Micro Channel)

- 3270 Connection Adapter for 3174 (Micro Channel)

Running the Requesters

An OS/2-based workstation on a LAN Server network requires at least the minimum hardware to install and run OS/2, but a DOS LAN Services workstation has fewer requirements.

An OS/2-based PC can run the OS/2 requester software that comes with LAN Server 4.*x* if that workstation uses OS/2 version 2.1, has 9MB or more of RAM and 12MB of free disk space, and contains a supported network adapter. A DOS (or DOS and Windows) PC can run the DOS LAN Services requester software if that workstation has 640K of RAM, at least 5MB of free disk space, IBM DOS or MS-DOS 3.3 (or higher), and a supported network adapter. DOS LAN Services will work with version 3.1 of Microsoft Windows or versions 3.1 or 3.11 of Microsoft Windows for Workgroups. A Windows for Workgroups 3.11 PC might not need DOS LAN Services in order to connect to a LAN Server file server; the next chapter explains how to find out whether this is true in your situation.

Table 3.1 identifies the network adapters directly supported by DOS LAN Services. If your preferred network adapter is not in the list, note that DOS LAN Services uses the NDIS interface to communicate with a network adapter. You can usually install and use any network adapter that comes with a DOS-mode NDIS driver.

Table 3.1 ▬▬▬▬▬▬▬▬▬▬▬▬▬▬▬▬▬▬▬▬▬▬▬▬▬▬▬▬▬▬▬

DOS LAN Service
Supported Network
Adapters

3Com EtherLink

3Com EtherLink 16

3Com EtherLink II or IITP (8- or 16-bit)

3Com EtherLink III

3Com EtherLink/MC

3Com EtherLink Plus

3Com TokenLink

Table 3.1 (Continued)	
DOS LAN Service Supported Network Adapters	Advanced Micro Devices AM2100/PCnet
	Amplicard AC 210/XT
	Amplicard AC 210/AT
	ArcNet Compatible
	Artisoft AE-1
	Artisoft AE-2 or AE-3
	Artisoft A E-2 (MCA) or AE-3 (MCA)
	Artisoft AE-3
	Cabletron E2000 Series DNI
	Cabletron E2100 Series DNI
	Data Systems Z-Note
	DEC Ethernet (All Types)
	DEC DEPCA
	DEC EE101 (Built-In)
	DEC EtherWorks LC
	DEC EtherWorks LC/TP
	DEC EtherWorks LC/TP_BNC
	DEC EtherWorks MC
	DEC EtherWorks MC/TP
	DEC EtherWorks MC/TP_BNC
	DEC EtherWorks Turbo
	DEC EtherWorks Turbo/TP
	DEC EtherWorks Turbo/TP_BNC
	DECpc 433 WS (built-in)
	IBM Token Ring
	IBM Token Ring (MCA)

**Table 3.1
(Continued)**

DOS LAN Service
Supported Network
Adapters

IBM Token Ring II

IBM Token Ring II/Short

IBM Token Ring 4/16Mbps (megabits per second)

IBM Token Ring 4/16Mbps (MCA)

Intel EtherExpress 16 or 16TP

Intel TokenExpress EISA 16/4

Intel TokenExpress 16/4

Intel TokenExpress MCA 16/4

National Semiconductor Ethernode *16AT

National Semiconductor AT/LANTIC EtherNODE 16-AT3

NCR Token Ring 4 Mbps ISA

NCR Token Ring 16/4 Mbps ISA

NCR Token Ring 16/4 Mbps MCA

NE1000 Compatible

NE2000 Compatible

Novell/Anthem NE1000

Novell/Anthem NE2000

Novell/Anthem NE1500T

Novell/Anthem NE2100

Novell/Anthem NE/2

Olicom 16/4 Token-Ring Adapter

Proteon ISA Token Ring (1340)

Proteon ISA Token Ring (1342)

Proteon ISA Token Ring (1346)

Proteon ISA Token Ring (1347)

Proteon MCA Token Ring (1840)

**Table 3.1
(Continued)**

DOS LAN Service
Supported Network
Adapters

Proteon Token Ring (P1390)

Proteon Token Ring (P1392)

Pure Data PDI508+ (ArcNet)

Pure Data PDI516+ (ArcNet)

Pure Data PDI9025-32 (Token Ring)

Pure Data PDuC9025 (Token Ring)

Racal NI6510

RadiSys EXM-10

SMC ArcNet PC

SMC ArcNet PC100, PC200

SMC ArcNet PC110, PC210, PS110, PS210, PC250

SMC ArcNet PC130/E

SMC ArcNet PC120, PC220, PC260

SMC ArcNet PC270/E

SMC ArcNet PC600W, PC650W

SMC (WD) EtherCard (All types except 8013/A)

SMC (WD) EtherCard PLUS (WD/8003E)

SMC (WD) EtherCard PLUS 10T/A (MCA) (WD 8003W/A)

SMC (WD) EtherCard PLUS 16 with Boot ROM Socket (WD/8013EBT)

SMC (WD) EtherCard PLUS/A (MCA) (WD 8003E/A or 8003ET/A)

SMC (WD) EtherCard PLUS TP (WD/8003WT)

SMC (WD) EtherCard PLUS with Boot ROM Socket (WD/8003EB)

SMC (WD) EtherCard PLUS with Boot ROM Socket (WD/8003EBT)

SMC (WD) EtherCard PLUS Elite (WD/8003EP)

SMC (WD) EtherCard PLUS 10T (WD/8003W)

SMC (WD) EtherCard PLUS Elite 16 (WD/8013EP)

Table 3.1 (Continued)

DOS LAN Service
Supported Network
Adapters

SMC (WD) EtherCard PLUS Elite 16T (WD/8013W)

SMC (WD) EtherCard PLUS Elite 16 Combo (WD/8013EW or 8013EWC)

SMC (WD) StarCard PLUS (WD/8003S)

SMC (WD) StarCard PLUS/A (MCA) (WD 8003ST/A)

SMC (WD) StarCard PLUS with On-Board Hub (WD/8003SH)

■ Analyzing Your Information-Sharing Needs

The types of applications you use will play a part in determining your need to share information. The other factors you need to weigh as you evaluate a network include the following:

- How quickly the network performs

- The capacity of the network to handle your organization's workload

- The ability of the network to grow with your organization

- The network's compatibility with the hardware and software you already own

- The levels of security the network offers

- The data integrity and reliability the network provides

Making the Network Perform Quickly

In each workstation, the biggest performance factors are the speed of the CPU, the software you run, and the type and quality of the network adapter. These factors determine how quickly your workstation can request files from a server and process the response messages. Your applications seem to run faster because the network supplies files to those computer programs faster.

A faster CPU means the application and network software will process requests and responses faster. Regardless of whether or not a network is present, Windows runs better on computers with fast CPUs (80486 or Pentium), lots of memory (8MB or more of RAM), and fast video adapters (because Windows operates in graphics mode).

The application software you run may or may not be well written; if the application software doesn't use the computer (CPU, video adapter, and so on) efficiently, longer periods of time will pass between the sending of each network message to a server. In this case, the application software is the bottleneck.

Finally, some network adapters are faster than others. All Ethernet adapters send and receive data at the rate of 10 Mbps (megabits per second); Token Ring adapters, either 4 or 16 Mbps; and ArcNet adapters, 2.5 Mbps. Better-quality adapters are faster because they prepare messages for sending faster, or they process incoming messages faster. The message travels at the published speed of the network once that message gets into the LAN cable. Processing the message before or after it travels through the cable can take significant effort. A 16-bit network adapter is generally faster than an 8-bit adapter. Some adapters have on-board processors or extra memory to help process messages more quickly.

In a server computer, you have the same considerations as you would for a workstation, plus a few others. It's important to install your faster, higher-quality network adapters in your file server computers. File servers receive and send more messages than do other computers and so need a better network adapter.

A file server can usually respond to file request messages more quickly if the server has more RAM installed. The server can use the extra RAM to remember the contents of frequently accessed files. When a request arrives at the server for a file partly or wholly in server memory, the server can honor the request directly from memory. The server doesn't have to go through the laborious steps involved in accessing the hard drive. For those file requests that do require hard drive access, it's important that the hard drive controller and the hard drive itself be fast, high-quality units.

If you haven't yet decided on the type of network adapter you should get, and you're wondering whether it's worthwhile to get 16 Mbps Token Ring adapters instead of 10 Mbps Ethernet adapters, the answer is "perhaps." Sixteen Mbps Token Ring adapters, if they're of high quality (16-bit boards with extra on-board memory and possibly an on-board processor), will outperform equal-quality Ethernet adapters on heavily used networks. Other considerations, as explained in subsequent sections of this chapter, also enter the picture.

LAN Server-based networks use OS/2 to access files. File servers based on OS/2 access files more quickly because the underlying operating system is faster than DOS. If performance is a key concern, and if any of the following conditions apply:

- The files you'll share are large

- The files are numerous and exist in extensive directory structures

- More than about 25 people will access files concurrently on the LAN

then you may want to consider using OS/2's High Performance File System (HPFS) on your file server instead of the old-fashioned DOS "FAT" file system. Additionally, with LAN Server-Advanced, you can achieve extra performance with the 386HPFS driver. But even the HPFS driver that comes with OS/2 gives a performance boost to LAN Server-Entry file servers.

The network operating system is part of the performance puzzle. The processing of messages inside the network adapter, as you've learned, can happen quickly or slowly. Similarly, the translation of file requests into messages by the workstation's network software, and the processing of those messages by the file server's network software, also take a certain amount of time. LAN Server networks generally perform better at processing file request messages than do other LANs. This is especially true on heavily loaded LANs.

Considering Network Capacity

You'll need to make sure your network can handle the volume of work you will ask it to do. This means the hard drive in the file server needs to be large enough to hold all the data files and programs that people will use. It also means having network software that supports enough network connections for all the workstations. The networking hardware should be capable of supporting both the number of computers and the distances between the computers.

There are other capacity-related issues to address. You have to choose between having one very fast file server with one or two very large hard drives and having perhaps two, three, or four file servers on the network. In general, it's best to distribute the workload among multiple servers. You can put some files on one server and other files on other servers. As people access files, multiple servers will respond more quickly than would a single server doing all the work.

The network software, the number of servers, and the organization of data on those servers should help you manage your network—the number and sizes of the files you want to share and use, the number of people who will use the network, the security your organization requires, and the number and kind of printers you want to use.

Your network hardware and network operating system software will need to grow with your organization. If you are near the upper limit of the usefulness of the hardware or software at the time you make your purchase, your investment will not last very long. For example, if you purchase a single, small file server computer with no hard disk expansion potential, you might very well find yourself throwing out the old system and buying a new one. You might as well start with one or several servers with plenty of capacity for the work your group does. In terms of growth, you'll want to consider the disk capacity, speed, and physical size (distance between computers) of the network. Estimate your needs for the next year or two to account for the people who will use the LAN now and in the foreseeable future. If, for example, you suspect that you'll use nearly all the available disk space in the first month or two of the network's existence, you'd be wise to invest in more disk space at the time you install the network.

Compatibility

As you choose network hardware and software, one of your biggest questions should be: "What network products can safely intermix on the same LAN?" In other words, which combinations of hardware and software will work together and which will not?

There are enough competing standards and overstated vendor marketing claims of "openness" and "interoperability" that it's often difficult to find networking products that actually do work together. You learned in Chapter 2 about the distinct and separate NDIS, ODI, and OSI Model standards for how network software should work with the different brands of network adapters. One of the benefits of NDIS is that many vendors offer NDIS-compatible software for their hardware.

In addition, LAN Server itself (and the operating system it runs on, OS/2) is compatible with virtually all LAN-aware software products. The cc:Mail and Notes products from Lotus Development, for example, run well in a LAN Server environment.

Security

One of the functions of the network operating system is security. Even in the friendliest of office environments, it's often appropriate to restrict access to certain files. Not all people in the organization should have full access to all information. Certain files contain confidential data and should be available only to certain people (payroll files are a good example). In addition to enabling redirected access to files and printers on other computers, the NOS keeps track of which people are authorized to use the network. Some network operating systems can restrict a person's access to certain times of the day, limit the number of concurrent logins from multiple workstations by one person, and permit logins only from certain workstations.

All network operating systems allow the network administrator to place restrictions on the types of file access a person can perform. Some networks implement security at a higher level. Some networks can, for example, prevent a person from creating new directories on the file server but allow other types of access in a given directory. LAN Server gives network administrators several ways to restrict network access, including (with the LAN Server-Advanced 386HPFS feature) the ability to limit the amount of disk space one person can use on a file server.

Data Integrity and Reliability

Data integrity is one of the goals of the network's security system, in addition to privacy. Because of the close relationships between network functions, this book could have just as easily discussed many of the aspects of data integrity in the earlier section of this chapter on reliability. However, as one of the criteria for evaluating network operating systems, data integrity is worth treating separately.

With OS/2 and LAN Server, you can use read-only access to prevent a butterfingered person from erasing everyone's files in that directory by typing DEL *.* instead of DIR *.* in a directory. However, read-only access also prevents that person (and the applications that person runs) from writing (updating) those files. Other more sophisticated network operating systems allow read/write access to files while they prevent inadvertent file erasures.

Fault tolerance describes a file server's ability to continue processing in the face of hardware or software failures. If you and your applications demand a higher level of fault tolerance, you may want to take a close look at PCs designed especially to be file servers. If your organization depends heavily on the LAN, the server becomes a critical resource. You can think of the file server as the most important link in the chain of components that enable file and printer sharing. The productivity of every person on the LAN depends on the server. If that server gets bogged down with heavy traffic or crashes at a time when people absolutely must get work done, productivity suffers. A hard drive failure on a person's single-user PC may cause that one person to go into a frenzy. A crashed drive on a file server can put an entire team or department out of business until it's fixed.

A dedicated file server computer combines high performance components (CPU, hard drive, and network adapter) with a fault-tolerant design. The dedicated server may offer some or all of the following features:

- Error-correcting memory, to prevent memory chip failures from halting the file server

- RAID (Redundant Array of Inexpensive Disks) technology, to enhance data integrity

- The ability to replace hard drives and other components even while the server is still operating

- Special diagnostic and monitoring software to help detect and repair problems early

- Detection of network operating system problems and graceful recovery from those problems

Dedicated file server computers include the SystemPro/XL from Compaq, the Advanced Logic Research (ALR) PowerPro Array, the Dell 433SE, the Tangent Multi-Server, and the Tricord PowerFrame.

RAID and Data Integrity

Using arrays of three or more disks to form a RAID (Redundant Array of Inexpensive Disks) offers two benefits. The first is performance. In a RAID implementation, data is scattered evenly across every disk in the array using a technique called striping. Overall throughput improves because each disk in the array can more or less evenly divide the load of system disk reads and writes.

The second benefit is data redundancy. Every RAID level but one specifies a method whereby data is stored redundantly on the array so that the failure of one disk does not result in data loss. There are six RAID levels: These levels differ in how they implement striping and redundancy.

- *RAID level 0* consists of a series of disks where striping is the only RAID feature implemented. No provision is made for data redundancy. Because a RAID 0 array provides all the performance benefits of striping and none of the overhead entailed by writing redundant failure recovery data, it is the configuration to choose when performance is important and failure protection is not.

- *RAID level 1* implements disk mirroring along with data striping. Each disk in the array is mirrored by another; the second disk in the mirrored pair stores an exact copy of the first disk's information. A four-disk RAID 1 array consists of two mirrored pairs and the equivalent capacity of two disks to use for data storage. If all disks can perform reads and writes simultaneously, disk mirroring will probably subtly improve disk-read performance, since a read request will be satisfied by the first drive in the pair to seek the information. Write requests slow down because they have to be completed for both disks in the pair.

- *RAID level 2* is the first to set aside the capacity of one disk to perform data recovery for the remaining ones. Striping is implemented at the bit level. The first bit for a unit of information is written to the first disk, the second to the second disk, and so on.

(continued)

- *RAID level 3* typically implements striping at the byte level, and one disk (often called the parity drive) is set aside to store error-correcting information. The error-correcting code stored by the parity drive is calculated by performing bitwise arithmetic on the bytes on the data drives. In a process not unlike finding the value of a variable in a simple algebraic equation, the missing byte on a failed disk is calculated by using a bitwise operation to combine the byte values on the remaining disks and comparing that value with the value on the parity drive. Commercial RAID 3 implementations often optimize disk-read performance by synchronizing the spindle rotation of each drive so that parallel reads of a range of bytes can be readily performed. For this reason, RAID 3 units should be particularly fast when doing sequential reads of large files. RAID 3 performance suffers when doing heavy disk writes because the parity drive must be written to in every write operation.

- *RAID level 4* sets aside a single disk in the array as the parity drive. RAID 4 stripes in units of disk blocks rather than bytes, a disk block being the amount of data transferred to or from the disk in one write or read operation.

- *RAID level 5* spreads the error-correction data evenly across the drives in the array. The data is striped in units of blocks. RAID 5 arrays should handle multiple simultaneous disk writes more quickly than RAID 3 or 4 arrays, because no single disk must be written to during every write operation. Because they stripe in block increments, RAID 5 arrays should handle multiple simultaneous random reads well, because each disk can independently retrieve an entire disk block.

LAN Server provides *disk mirroring* and *disk duplexing* capabilities. These features write data to the hard drive multiple times to make sure you always have at least one good copy of your files, even if one hard drive fails. LAN Server performs disk mirroring by causing the hard disk controller card to write the same data on a second disk. In the event of a disk drive failure, the network operating system falls back to using the mirrored second disk as the primary disk drive, with minimal loss of service as the network software switches to the backup drive. In this kind of system, the twin disk is often called a *hot backup*. The benefit of disk mirroring is excellent data integrity. The disadvantage is that the redundant storage of file data uses up half the disk capacity in the file server. Performance can also suffer somewhat, because the network operating system must do twice as many disk write operations to make the second copy of the data.

Disk mirroring provides no protection against the failure of a hard disk controller card. In single-controller systems, if the controller card fails the file server fails (whether or not mirroring is in effect). Disk duplexing uses both duplicate hard disk controller cards and duplicate disks to guard against failure. With duplexing, even a complete controller failure won't bring down a system. However, disk mirroring and disk duplexing can be expensive—you have to buy the extra hardware to make the redundant storage possible.

LAN Server and several other network operating systems can detect and handle power failures through the use of an uninterruptible power supply (UPS). If commercial (electric company) power fails, the UPS not only steps in to run the server with electricity from a battery but also notifies the network operating system that battery power is being used. If the electric company doesn't restore power before the batteries run down, the network operating system gracefully closes files and shuts down. A power failure that happens in the middle of a file server operation won't corrupt files if you use a UPS and a network operating system (such as LAN Server) that recognizes the UPS.

With the LAN Server-Entry version, the reliability of your LAN depends on the health of each and every component in your file server computer. If the hard disk fails, your LAN will be idle (at least with respect to that one server) until you replace the disk and use your backup copies of files to restore the server to a previous state. LAN Server-Advanced, as you learned earlier in this chapter, implements disk mirroring, disk duplexing, and extra file server security.

Note that other LAN components can affect the reliability of your LAN. A bad LAN cable, failed network adapter in a workstation, or nonfunctioning hub (or access unit) can cause workstations to drop their connections to your file server(s).

■ Developing a Network Plan

The first item in the general plan is a basic map of the network. The map expresses the essential relationships between the computers. You'll find it useful to post this map on a bulletin board in your office after installation is complete. This chapter includes several sample maps that show how to chart your new network.

The next part of the general plan shows your determination of which computers on the network will share what data. You'll use a photocopy of the network map to make notes regarding the file-sharing and file-using roles each computer will play on the LAN.

The general plan also includes a shopping list for the network hardware and software you selected in the previous chapter. Don't write a check yet, though; some parts of the detail plan (discussed later in this chapter) will affect your shopping list. The general plan merely helps you identify the categories of hardware and software you'll need.

Once you have a general plan consisting of a network map, a rough idea of who will share what resources, and a shopping list, you can create a detailed plan. The detailed plan contains a more specific map of the network, a list of computers categorized by their file server, print server, and pure workstation roles, and a shopping list accurate enough to take to the computer store (or give to your purchasing department). The detailed plan can optionally also identify the specific network configurations you've chosen for each computer. The configuration information will come in handy as you maintain and troubleshoot the network. The final section of the detailed plan is a list of the user accounts you'll create. This list identifies each person using the network and shows that person's rights, privileges, and resource-sharing needs.

■ Designing the Basic Network

The first step in creating the general network design is mapping the LAN. You draw a rough layout of the office space your LAN will encompass and add networking features to that layout. In essence, you network your office on paper before you actually connect computers together. Trying different configurations with pencil, paper, and an eraser is certainly easier than with computers, network adapters, and cables.

Your network map should reveal the name of the person who uses the computer, the basic type of each computer, and the distance between the computers. The distances on the map are not point-to-point; each distance value includes

- The distance to the wall

- The distance up through the wall, across the ceiling, and back down again

- The distance from the second wall to the second PC

If you are going to cable the computers directly without going through the walls and ceiling, your distance measurements will be smaller. However, be careful about running cables directly between the computers in your office. The loose cables can be unsightly, they can cause injuries if people trip over them, and they can become damaged if people handle or pull on the cables. In general, the only situation in which it's appropriate to run cables directly from computer to computer is if the PCs' desks are arranged in a back-to-back fashion.

The cable distance values tell you approximately how much cable and what lengths you'll need to buy. The distances also tell you if you are close to exceeding any cable-length limitations for the type of network you've chosen. Table 2.1 in Chapter 2 explained the distance limitations for the different kinds of cable and network adapter you want to use in your LAN.

■ Documenting Your Network

You've selected the type of LAN cabling and the network adapters, and you've categorized the computers according to the functions they'll perform on the LAN. You can now create a detailed network map. The detailed map of your network will contain the following information:

- Brand name of each computer on the LAN

- CPU type, CPU speed, installed RAM, and free disk space of each computer

- Name of the person who uses the computer

- Brand of each printer connected to computers on the LAN

- Identification of the domain controller, file server, and print server computers

- Major categories of the applications people use

- Exact lengths of the LAN cables

- Brand, slot size, and connector type of each network adapter card

This is valuable information for you to use in the future. Keep the detailed map up-to-date; you'll be glad you did.

The detailed network map doesn't show certain configuration options for the computers that will soon connect to the LAN. You should make a separate list of these options. Your list should include the following information for each computer:

- Operating system (DOS, OS/2, Macintosh System 7, and so on) and version

- Memory manager (if any)

- Windows version (if any)

- Number and type of floppy-disk drives

- Number of DOS drive letter partitions on the hard drive

- Number and type (ISA, MCA, EISA) of available slots

- Device drivers loaded in the CONFIG.SYS file

- TSRs loaded by the AUTOEXEC.BAT file

- Number of parallel (LPTx) ports

- Number of serial (COMx) ports

- Video adapter brand and type (VGA, SuperVGA, 8514, etc.)

Then, for each adapter in each computer, you should document the items in the following list:

- Adapter type and brand

- IRQs used

- Memory addresses

- I/O addresses

You'll find the detailed network configuration list valuable as you install requester software on each computer. You'll quickly be able to see which computers need special treatment as you install and configure LAN Server requesters. The list will be important in the future, too; you'll have a picture of the computers on your LAN that will help you manage changes and upgrades when they occur.

■ Upgrading from NetWare

Replacing NetWare with LAN Server on your file server, as opposed to simply adding a LAN Server file server to an existing NetWare LAN, can be somewhat disruptive. You'll want to plan the installation work for a time when the network isn't being used by anyone (a weekend, perhaps), and you'll want to provide training to the people who will have to become familiar with LAN Server commands and utilities. If you decide to replace Net-Ware with LAN Server on the same file server, you'll want to make sure you have reliable backup copies of all your files.

PCs are fairly inexpensive, especially in relation to the cost of the data they hold. I recommend that, instead of replacing NetWare with LAN Server on the same PC, you install OS/2 and LAN Server on a separate PC. You can then log on to the NetWare file server from the OS/2 machine, copy files from the NetWare server to the OS/2 PC, and save yourself a great deal of time. After installing OS/2 on the LAN-attached PC you've chosen to be your new LAN Server file server, install the NetWare Requester for OS/2. You can then log on to NetWare file servers and copy files from one server to the other over the wire.

IBM offers a free migration kit for LAN Server customers who are upgrading from NetWare. The kit is available electronically through Compuserve, the OS/2 BBS, and the Internet (you can ftp to software.watson.ibm.com, ftp.cdrom.com, or networking.raleigh.ibm.com to obtain the kit via modem). For a small shipping and handling fee, you can order the kit on floppy disk from IBM by calling your local IBM sales office.

■ Summary

This chapter gave you considerations to think about and perhaps some ideas for how you can best use a LAN Server network. In the next chapter, you'll install and begin using LAN Server.

- *The Installation Roadmap*
- *Installing the LAN Hardware*
- *Installing the Server Component*
- *Installing Network Adapter Support*
- *DOS LAN Services on Workstations*

Installing LAN Server

T HIS CHAPTER PROVIDES AN OVERVIEW OF THE INSTALLATION PROCESS
(a road map) so you don't get confused or lost during the installation. The chapter follows the road map to lead you, step by step,
through the process of installing network adapters and network
adapter software, installing LAN Server on the file server, and
using DOS LAN Services to turn PCs into workstations.

In a book about a simple software product, you often find that the installation instructions are relegated to an appendix. For a sophisticated networking product like LAN Server, however, installation deserves a chapter of its own. Installing LAN Server may very well be your first experience with the product, and the configuration options you select during the installation process will affect the performance and behavior of the product in later day-to-day use.

■ The Installation Road Map

The starting point for your road map is a collection of PCs, at least one of which is already running OS/2 version 2.11 or later. If you have more than one OS/2-based computer, you'll probably choose the most powerful one as your file server. Of the other computers, some may run DOS, some DOS and Windows, and some OS/2. These other computers will become workstations on the LAN.

The first step toward installing your network consists of inserting the network adapter cards in the PCs and configuring the cards. Next, you connect the LAN cable to each PC's network adapters. These two steps comprise the hardware-oriented portion of the installation. To install the software, you begin with the Server/Install disk. You'll next insert the AnyNet disks, then the Requester disks, and finally the Server disks (this means you'll insert the Server/Install disk twice).

On OS/2-based workstations, you'll follow basically the same steps but omit the insertion of the Server disks. For DOS or DOS-and-Windows PCs, you'll use the DOS LAN Services distribution disks to install the network software.

The following sections describe these steps in detail.

■ Installing the LAN Hardware

Before you begin installing network hardware components, you should have had your LAN cables installed. The person who set up your LAN cables should have tested the cables to make sure they are working properly. The usual tool for this test is a Time Domain Reflectometer, or TDR. The TDR operates on a principle somewhat similar to sonar; it sends a signal through each cable, detects the electrical reflections, interprets them, and reports the result. TDRs are common tools of network cable installers.

With the LAN cables already in place, you're ready to insert the network adapters in the workstations and locate the other connectivity components (such as hubs, MSAUs, repeaters, and transceivers). As you connect each workstation to the LAN, you should verify the connection with the diagnostic software provided by the vendor of the network adapter or hub.

The next few sections explain the steps you take to open the computer, configure the adapter, insert the adapter, close up the computer, and test the connection. First, however, here are some basic things you should know:

- You don't have to power off all the computers at the same time; you can take one computer apart while other people continue to work.

- You can start with the least-used PC in the office; the first installation you do will likely take longer (you might go so far as to schedule the work for an evening or on a weekend).

- You'll need a small flat-blade and a Phillips-head screwdriver, and you may also need a screwdriver with a larger handle in case some of the screws are tight.

- Even in a brightly lit office, you may need to use a flashlight as you explore the interior of the PC.

- In addition to this book, you'll need the documentation that came with the network adapter and you may also need the documentation that came with the computer and any other adapters already in the PC.

- It's a good idea to have paper and pencil with you, to make notes as you work; a roll of masking tape may also come in handy.

Opening the Computer

Clear a space around the computer you're working on, especially at the rear of the PC. Save any files and quit any applications that are running. Power the computer off and disconnect all the wires from the back of the machine. You may want to write notes on strips of masking tape that you attach to the wires; these notes will help you reconnect things later.

Many computers have five screws at the sides and the upper back of the PC that hold the cover securely closed. Some PCs have six such screws, while others have a single white plastic hold-down that you turn to release the cover. Still others have a single screw plus two plastic tabs that you depress to remove the cover. If you have trouble finding the exact fastening method for the cover (I often do), consult the documentation that came with the PC. If you've lost the documentation, don't remove all the screws from the back of the PC; only look for the ones that would hold the cover on. Set the screws aside in a safe place. Carefully slide the cover off the computer and set it aside. Now touch the metal case of the computer to get rid of any static electricity your body may have built up. Repeat this step once in a while as you work, especially if you walk away from the PC and come back later.

The Network Adapter

If your network adapter has no jumpers or switches, and if the adapter's configuration utility can automatically determine which settings to use, skip this step. However, even for an adapter that features software configuration, you may need to analyze the settings of the other adapters in your PC to know what values to enter when you run the software configuration. Don't just inspect the card to find out whether you need to set a switch or jumper; read the adapter documentation. Many jumpers and switches are not readily visible on the adapter.

Take the network adapter from its plastic bag (you'll likely see a warning on the bag about avoiding electrostatic charges—now's a good time to touch the metal frame of the PC again). Lay the adapter in front of you on a desk or table, positioned the same as the vendor's drawing (or photograph) of the adapter in the documentation. Take a moment to identify the major components on the adapter, including all the switches and/or jumpers called out by the vendor's documentation. Note the current settings on a sheet of paper. Check if the current settings match the "factory default" settings mentioned in the vendor's documentation, but don't change anything yet if the settings are different.

Microchannel and EISA Bus Adapters

To configure a Microchannel (PS/2) adapter, you use the Reference Disk that came with the computer. You may also need the Adapter Disk that came with the adapter card. Most Microchannel adapters have no switches or jumpers, but instead are configured through software. The software is on the Reference Disk. The Adapter Disk may contain a configuration information file (called an Adapter Descriptor File, or ADF) that the Reference Disk software needs. You insert the adapter (as explained later in this chapter), put the cover back on the computer, reconnect the wires, and boot the machine with the Reference Disk. The configuration utility software runs automatically. You're then ready to attach the LAN cable to the computer.

EISA bus adapters use a configuration method similar to that of Microchannel adapters. The computer manufacturer should have supplied you with EISA configuration software for that PC. Run the software to configure an EISA card.

You cannot put an ISA bus adapter in a Microchannel computer. However, you usually can put an ISA bus adapter in an EISA-based computer. If you have an EISA-based computer and an ISA network adapter, you should continue reading the next few sections. The EISA configuration utility isn't much help at configuring ISA-bus cards, so you'll need to set switches or jumpers.

ISA Bus Adapters

You typically set three or four options on an ISA bus network adapter. These options are the IRQ, the memory address, the I/O address, and possibly a network address. The adapter may have other options you'll need to set.

TIP. *ISA bus adapters typically have jumpers and switches. Each time you open the computer to work on an adapter, you have to also retrieve the documentation for the adapter to understand its current settings. Misplacing the documentation means trouble the next time you open the computer because you won't know what the switch and jumper settings mean. It's always a good idea to put the adapter documentation in a safe place, but here's an extra step you can take to help remember the settings of each adapter.*

Record the settings for all the adapters on the inside of the computer cover using a felt-tip marker. Alternatively, write down the settings (perhaps on a photocopy of the appropriate page of the adapter documentation) and tape the note on the inside of the computer's cover. No one but you will ever see the notes you've made, and they'll be readily available when you need them. Keep the record up-to-date. You'll save time and frustration the next time you install or reconfigure adapters.

You can use the same notes to hold other information about your computer, such as the drive type of the hard disk.

NOTE. *Do you want to know what happens if you choose an incorrect setting as you set the IRQ, I/O address, memory address, and network address on the adapter? The answer: the network simply won't work. In rare cases, the workstation will fail to boot. Usually though, the first time you will know something's wrong is when you run software that asks the network adapter to send or receive LAN messages. The network software will display an error on the screen (the wording varies considerably) to notify you of the error.*

Setting the IRQ (ISA)

IRQ stands for Interrupt ReQuest line. When an incoming LAN message arrives, the network adapter interrupts the computer's currently running software to notify the network software of the pending message. This process takes only microseconds; you aren't aware your software has been interrupted. But the network adapter and network operating system (LAN Server) both have to know which of several possible interrupt request lines to use. No two adapters should use the same IRQ, so your job is clear: Configure the adapter to use an IRQ that no other adapter is using, then remember the setting for later when you install the software.

How do you know what IRQs the other adapters might be using? You have to examine each adapter and interpret the switch and jumper settings according to the adapter's documentation. In addition to avoiding the IRQs used by other adapters, you must avoid the IRQs in use by the base computer hardware. The following list will help you identify available IRQs.

IRQ	Used by
0	Reserved; do not use
1	Reserved; do not use
2	Used by some EGA and VGA video adapters
3	COM2 or COM4 serial port, if present
4	COM1 or COM3 serial port, if present
5	Sometimes used by second parallel port (LPT2)
6	Disk controller adapter
7	Sometimes used by first parallel port (LPT1)
8	Reserved; do not use
9	A mirror of IRQ 2
13	Math coprocessor, if present
14	Disk controller adapter
15	Sometimes (rarely) used by a second disk controller

As you can see from the list, your choices for the network adapter are IRQ 2/9 (depending on the video adapter), IRQ 3 or IRQ 4 (depending on the presence of serial ports), IRQ 5 or IRQ 7 (depending on the presence of parallel ports), IRQ 13 (depending on the presence of a math coprocessor), or IRQ 15 (again, depending on the presence of a second disk controller). The remainder, IRQ 10, IRQ 11, and IRQ 12, are good candidates if another adapter isn't already using that IRQ.

AT-class (80286 and above) machines have IRQs 0 through 15. Older machines based on the 8088 or 8086 CPUs only have IRQs 0 through 7. Don't set the IRQ on the adapter to a value the machine doesn't support.

Your network adapter may have been set at the factory to use IRQ 3 or perhaps IRQ 2/9 (the mirrored IRQ in the list). You can leave the factory setting alone unless your analysis shows a conflict with another adapter or port.

NOTE. *Even if your network card has no switches or jumpers, you may still need to do the analysis to know which IRQ to use. The configuration software may ask you to assign an IRQ, and you'll need to know what's available.*

Setting the I/O Address (ISA)

When the network software (specifically, the adapter device driver) has a message to send through the LAN cable, the software issues commands to the adapter that cause the adapter to transmit the message. These commands are called I/O instructions. The message, "Output the value 32 to address 201 instruction" might very well send the message on its way—but only if the adapter knows that it should respond to address 201. You tell the adapter what I/O address (or beginning of a range of I/O addresses) to respond to, and you later tell the network software what address you've chosen. As with IRQ lines, it's incorrect for two adapters to try to use the same I/O addresses.

When you tell the network adapter which I/O address to use, make sure no other adapter is using that address, and remember the address value for when you run the network configuration software.

The network adapter documentation typically contains a list of I/O addresses for you to choose from, with one address in the list preset at the factory. Just as with IRQ lines, you must analyze your existing PC hardware to see which of the entries in the list you should choose.

Examine the other adapters already in the computer, referencing as necessary each adapter's documentation, to determine what I/O addresses (or ranges of addresses) are in use. Here are some ranges you'll often find already in use, depending on the hardware options of your computer (hexadecimal values):

I/O Address Range	Used by
200-20F	Game port (joystick)
230-23F	Bus mouse
270-27F	Third parallel port (LPT3)
2F0-2FF	Second serial port (COM2)
320-32F	PS/2 model 30 hard disk controller
330-33F	SCSI adapters; MIDI adapters
370-37F	Second parallel port (LPT2)
3B0-3BF	First parallel port (LPT1)
3C0-3CF	EGA or VGA video adapters
3D0-3DF	Various video adapters (color text modes)
3F0-3FF	First serial port (COM1); floppy disk

Other ranges, such as 210-21F or 290-29F, are likely candidates as you make your selection.

Setting the Memory Address

You just learned that the adapter uses an IRQ line to signal when it has an incoming message to be processed. You also learned that the network software gives a "send message" command by using an I/O address. In both situations, though, where is the message itself? The answer is "at a memory address." The address is the beginning of a range of memory addresses; the memory area holds incoming and outgoing LAN messages. The memory area is sometimes called shared RAM. You set the memory address the adapter and the network software should use. Some adapters, however, contain on-board RAM and do not have a shared RAM address you can set.

The factory default memory address may or may not be available, depending on what memory addresses the other adapters in the PC are using. You need to select a memory address that isn't in use and you need to remember the setting for later, when you tell the network software what memory address to use. The network software will expect to be able to put outgoing (or find incoming) messages at the address you select.

Examine the other adapters in the workstation to determine what memory address ranges they already use. Configure the network adapter as necessary to avoid the addresses in use. Remember the address value for use when you install the LAN Server software.

Setting the Network Address

Fortunately, with most adapters you never change the factory-set network address. This address is the one by which the adapter and the PC are known on the network. It's your "LAN mailing address"; other workstations and the file server can send messages to your PC via this address. (You're a human, and you'll use a name to refer to your computer. However, inside the computer, the network translates your name into the network address for LAN message routing purposes.) For most types of adapters, the manufacturer of the network adapter "burns" a unique network address into the adapter. The network address therefore uniquely identifies the particular workstation in which the adapter is later installed. If your adapter's network address is 10005A 01BF15, and if your workstation has sent a "give me file LETTER.DOC" request to a file server, the file server's response message contains a destination address of 10005A 01BF15. This is how network adapters know which adapter a message is for.

The manufacturer may give you the option of overriding the network address, but—with one exception—you should always use the factory default. The exception is an ARCNET adapter. With ARCNET adapters, you assign a number from 1 to 255 to each workstation and set switches on the adapter to indicate your assignment. Make a note of the numbers you assign (if you've chosen to use ARCNET) so you won't give a future workstation the same number as one that's already in use.

NOTE. *The network adapters you've bought may have other settings besides IRQ, I/O address, memory address, and network address. For example, with adapters that offer two or three cable connector options, you may have to indicate on the adapter, with a jumper or switch, which cable option you've chosen. Refer to the network adapter documentation to set these other options. This chapter doesn't discuss these other options because (1) they vary considerably from adapter to adapter and (2) LAN Server won't ask you to enter information about these other options when you install the software.*

Inserting the Adapter in a Slot

Use a screwdriver to remove the screw holding the bracket at the rear of the slot you've decided to use (8-bit or 16-bit). Be careful to not let the screw drop onto the motherboard. Discard the bracket and save the screw.

Line up the network adapter over the slot. If the manufacturer put the *Tee* connector on the back of the adapter (for Ethernet cards), remove the Tee temporarily so you can install the adapter. Before you push the adapter card into the slot, inspect the card from all angles to make sure nothing's obstructed.

Push the card firmly into the slot. Use just enough force to get the tab (with the gold fingers) on the bottom of the adapter card to go squarely and fully into the slot. If you do this correctly, (1) the top of the bracket will be flush with the shelf of threaded holes from which you removed the original bracket screw, and (2) the PC will boot successfully later, when you reconnect things and power it on. If you don't have the adapter card seated correctly, the PC will not begin to boot or will freeze part way through the boot process.

Sometimes, with non-IBM (clone) computers or with poorly made adapter cards, the bracket won't line up well with the shelf. Even though the card is firmly seated, the top of the bracket may be slightly above the shelf or the hole in the bracket may not line up well with the threaded holes in the shelf. In these cases, do the best you can to fasten the adapter card to the case.

Replace the bracket screw now, if possible. If the adapter card looks like it's seated well but you can't fasten the bracket to the shelf, continue the job but remember to be very gentle when you connect the LAN cable to the adapter. You don't want the adapter to come out of the slot.

Replacing the Cover

Slide the cover of the computer case onto the computer and refasten all the cover screws (but not too tightly). Reconnect the wires to the back of the computer. If you feel confident about your analysis of IRQs and other options, put the monitor back on top of the computer. If you're doubtful, leave the monitor to one side; you may need to take the cover off to reconfigure an adapter.

Attaching the LAN Cable

Before you attach the LAN cable to the appropriate connector on the adapter you've just installed, power the PC on and make sure it goes through its normal boot cycle. If everything works okay (at least so far), power the machine off again and attach the LAN cable to the adapter. If the machine doesn't boot properly, go back to the beginning of this chapter. Retrace your steps and determine what you did wrong.

For Thinnet cable, put the Tee connector on the coaxial connector on the adapter's bracket. Then attach the LAN cable to the Tee connector. If another computer attaches on either side of this PC, connect both LAN cables to the Tee connector. If this is the last computer at the end of a LAN segment, connect the cable to one side of the Tee and then use a terminator to cap the open side of the Tee.

If you're using UTP cable for Ethernet or Token Ring, push the RJ-45 telephone jack connector into the keyed connector on the adapter's bracket.

If you're using Thicknet cable, attach one end of the cable to the 15-pin AUI port on the adapter's bracket and attach the other end of the cable to the external transceiver. (If you have a joystick port—a game port—on the computer, don't confuse the joystick port with the AUI port on the Ethernet card. They look similar.)

Before you make any Token Ring cable connections, be aware that you will likely have to use what IBM calls the Setup Aid to prepare the Multistation Access Unit (MSAU) for use. You can do all the ports on the MSAU at once; you don't have to use the Setup Aid after each network adapter card installation.

For STP Token Ring, connect the 9-pin D-connector to the network adapter's bracket. Connect the genderless data connector at the other end to the wall outlet or directly to the MSAU.

Once you have installed the adapter cards in the workstations and connected the cables, you are ready to check out your installation. (The LAN cable installer should already have connected any backbone cables with repeaters and done whatever else was necessary to make the cabling system ready for use.)

You should find diagnostic software on one of the disks supplied by the manufacturer of the network adapters. Only the poorest quality adapters do not come with such diagnostic software. As soon as you have adapters installed in two workstations, use the diagnostic software, according to the manufacturer's instructions, to make sure the two PCs can communicate across the LAN. Thereafter each time you install a network adapter, use the diagnostic software to check your work.

■ Installing the Server Component

To begin the installation of the software on the PC that will become your file server, insert the Server/Install disk in the A drive of your computer. You can start the installation program in one of two ways:

- Open an OS/2 command line session (windowed or full screen) by double-clicking on the session's icon. The icon is located in the Command Prompts folder, which in turn is the OS/2 System folder. At the command line, type

  A:INSTALL

  and press Enter

- Alternatively, open the Drives folder in the OS/2 System folder with a double-click and then open the Drives object for the A drive. Double-click on the icon labeled INSTALL.CMD.

If you're installing from a CD-ROM disk rather than floppy disks, follow the same steps but use the letter of your CD-ROM drive in place of drive A. For CD-ROM or disk installation, you'll momentarily see the window shown in Figure 4.1 on your screen. Click on the OK button when you see the screen shown in Figure 4.2.

Figure 4.1

The first screen displayed during installation

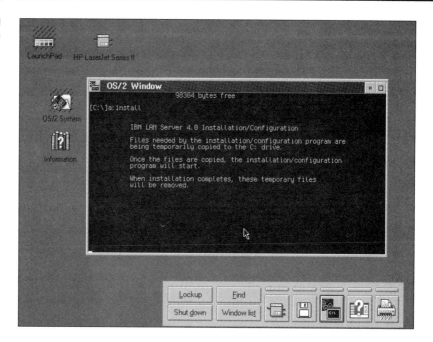

Figure 4.2

The logo screen

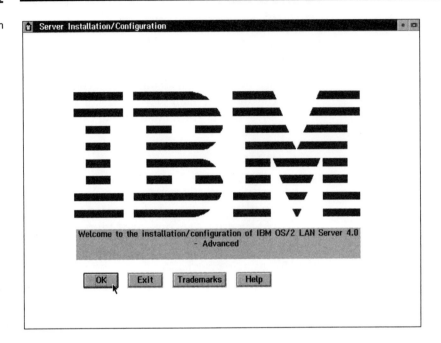

As Figure 4.3 shows, the installation program offers you a choice between easy and tailored (custom) installation paths. If you click on the button labeled Easy, the installation program will ask you to specify a
destination drive letter, name your file server, name your domain, verify
your network adapter, and copy files to the computer's hard disk. The remainder of this chapter explains what happens if you click on the Tailored
button. However, read on even if you choose the Easy installation method;
the screens you'll see during an Easy installation are a subset of the ones
you'd see if you picked the Tailored method.

Why would you pick the Tailored method of installation if clicking on
the Easy button will give you a usable, working file server? The Tailored
method gives you finer control over the installation process, and in particular
lets you do the following:

- Change the server type (change an additional server to a domain controller, for example)

- Change the IBM-supplied installation and configuration parameters

- Choose to use multiple network adapters

- Remove individual components

Figure 4.3

Choosing between Easy
and Tailored installation

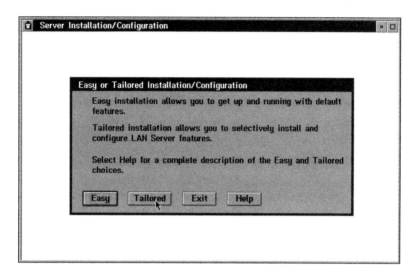

- Create custom disks, create response files, and copy product diskette files for installation on other PCs

- Install, reinstall, or configure a different set of components than the default

    The following list identifies the functions and components you can select with the Tailored method:

- DOS Remote IPL service (lets you boot DOS PCs from images of DOS you store on the server)

- Fault Tolerance (available in LAN Server-Advanced)

- First Failure Support Technology/2 (FFST/2, an error logging function)

- Generic Alerter service (for use with a separate LAN management software product)

- Local Security for 386 HPFS (in LAN Server-Advanced; lets you secure the server's keyboard and monitor)

- Loop-Back Driver (for diagnostic purposes)

- Migration Import Utility (allows you to use logon account lists you've set up under earlier versions of LAN Server)

- OS/2 Remote IPL service (lets you boot OS/2 PCs from images of OS/2 you store on the server)

- Uninterruptible Power Supply (UPS) support

- Virtual DOS LAN API Support

- 386 HPFS (LAN Server-Advanced)

- LAN Server Administration GUI

- LAN Server Applications Development Toolkit

- LAN Services installation/configuration program

- Network DDE and Clipboard

- Network Messaging

On the screen shown in Figure 4.4, you see several options. You can choose to install or configure the workstation (server). You can also create server or requester custom disks; such disks contain configuration information you can transport to other servers or requesters on the LAN. The configurations you build for these custom disks do not affect the configuration of the PC on which you build those disks. You can create server or requester response files; on other PCs, the installation program can play back these response files (they're called scripts) to automate the process of building other servers and requesters. Finally, you can instruct the installation program to copy all the files from the distribution diskettes into a central directory from which you can perform remote installations later. Of these choices, the one you select now is the default: *Install or Configure this Workstation.*

Figure 4.4

Selecting an
installation task

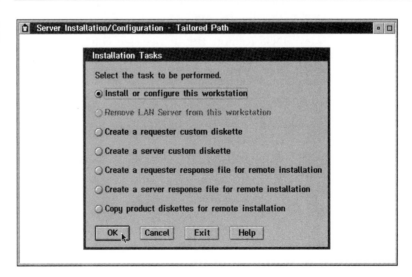

On the next two screens, shown in Figures 4.5 and 4.6, you indicate the drive on which you want to install the LAN Server software if you have more than one partition on your hard disk. You also indicate whether you want this PC to be a domain controller, backup domain controller, or additional server. Recall from the last chapter that you must have at least one domain controller on your LAN, and the domain controller can also be a file server. The domain controller is the file server that holds your list of logon accounts, shared disk drives, shared printers, and other shared resources. A backup domain controller is a file server onto which LAN Server replicates your list of logon accounts and aliases. An additional server is just another file server you add to a group of existing servers.

Figure 4.5

Choosing the drive on which to install LAN Server

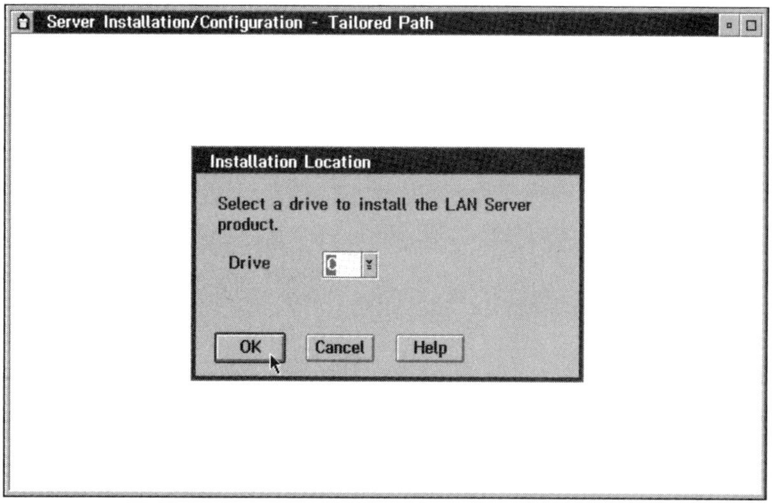

Figure 4.6

Designating domain controller, additional server, or backup domain controller

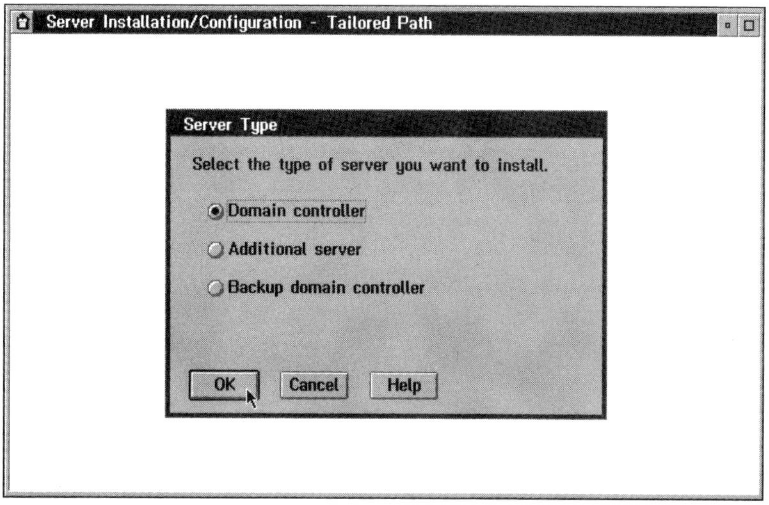

You then use the screen shown in Figure 4.7 to click on Install or remove a component and click the OK button to see a list of LAN Server components.

Figure 4.7

The screen on which you select the installation operation

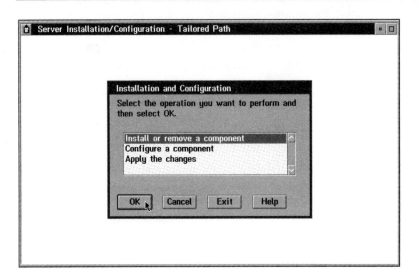

If you've chosen the Tailored method of installation, you can select specific components of LAN Server that you want to install and configure. The screen shown in Figure 4.8 (Install and Remove) lists some of these components along with their installation status and the installation action that you can change. The Server and DOS LAN Services Online Reference components have an installation action of Install (Required), which means these components must be installed. To indicate that you'd like to install a component, highlight it by clicking on the component in the list, then click on the Install button. The Action column changes to reflect your choice.

Once your list of components to be installed is complete, click the OK button on the Install and Remove screen. You next see the screen shown in Figure 4.9, Installation and Configuration. If you highlight the Install or Remove a Component entry and click OK, the installation program will again show the screen in Figure 4.8. If you highlight Apply the Changes and click OK, LAN Server will inform you that some of the components you'd like installed need to be configured prior to installation. Highlighting Configure a Component and clicking OK takes you to the Configure screen, shown in Figure 4.10. To configure an entry, highlight that entry and click on the Configure button. For the Server component, the installation program will ask you to type a server name and a domain name (Figure 4.11). The two names cannot

Figure 4.8

Selecting specific LAN
Server components

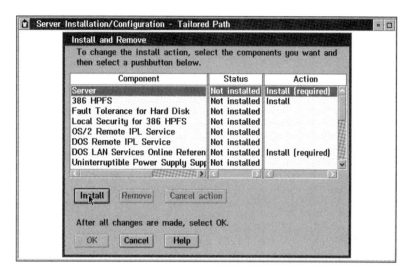

be the same. For server name, you'll want to pick a name that identifies the
file server computer. For domain name, you'll want a name that suggests the
group of people who will be using the file servers in that domain. When you
click on the OK button, the installation program will ask you if you want the
PC to automatically become a file server each time you boot the PC (you normally would answer yes to this question), as shown in Figure 4.12.

Figure 4.9

Choosing to install,
remove, or configure a
component

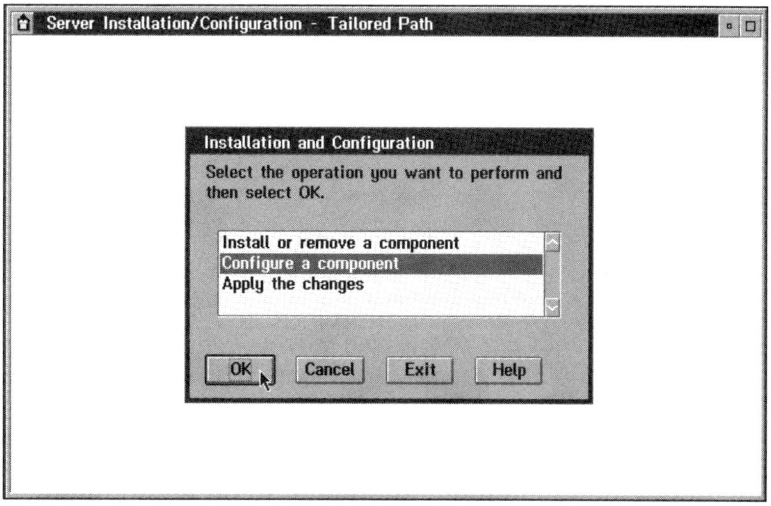

Figure 4.10

The Configure screen

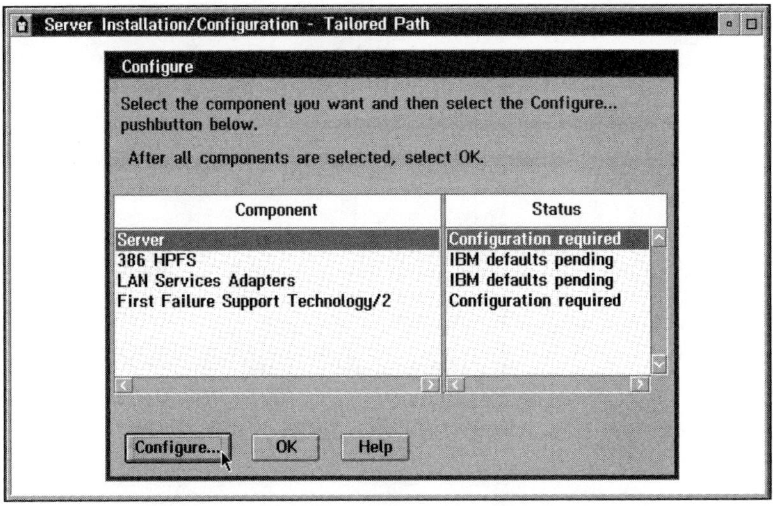

Figure 4.11

Entering your server and
domain names

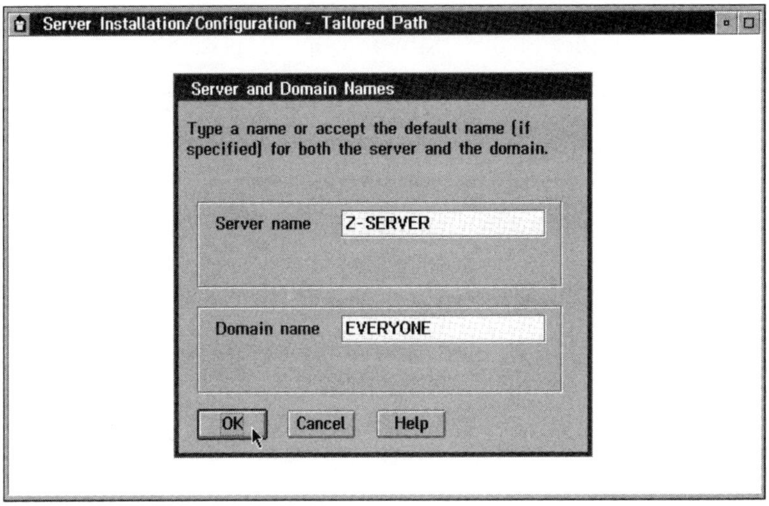

On the next screen (shown in Figure 4.13), you indicate whether your
network adapter can access memory above the 16MB address line. You can
look through the technical documentation that came with your network
adapter to find out its memory access capabilities, or, if you know your network adapter is a 32-bit card, you can simply answer Yes to the question. Answer No if you know your network adapter is an 8-bit or 16-bit card.

Figure 4.12

Starting the server
automatically

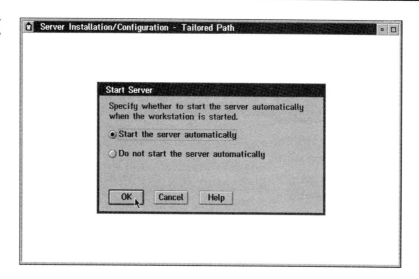

Figure 4.13

The memory addressing
capability of your network
adapter

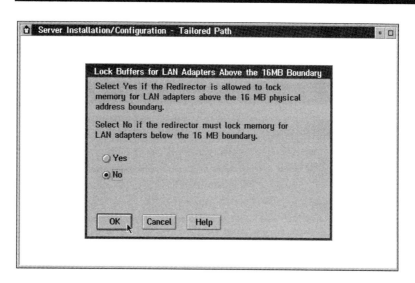

The screen in Figure 4.14 lets you indicate which services of the file server should start automatically when the server itself starts. You should set the Messenger and Netlogon services to have an autostart status of ON. The Messenger service is a kind of e-mail you can use in your office. The Netlogon service is the function that lets workstations log on to the server. You should set the Alerter service to ON if you use a LAN management software

product such as NetView in your organization. Netrun lets you use LAN
Server commands to remotely run programs on the file server computer; set
Netrun to ON if you'd like to have this facility available to you each time the
server starts up. The Replicator service makes backup copies of your list of
logon accounts and shared resources so that if a file server suffers a hardware failure, you can recover from the failure quickly.

Figure 4.14

Setting the autostart
status of server functions

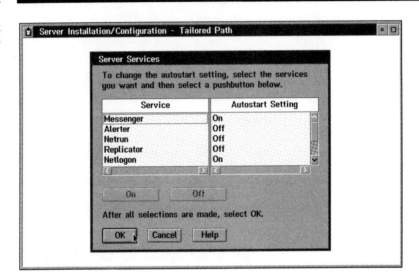

If you're using 386HPFS (in the LAN Server-Advanced package) to
make your file server perform better, you can use the screen shown in Figure
4.15 to control how 386HPFS uses memory for caching (remembering often-
accessed disk files in memory). You can specify the size of the 386HPFS
cache, or you can instruct 386HPFS to determine the size of the cache dynamically, based on the amount of RAM in the server computer. You can
also indicate how you want 386HPFS to manage the cache, and whether
386HPFS should cache write operations as well as read operations. The
screen shown in Figure 4.16, like the one in Figure 4.13, lets you instruct
386HPFS to use memory (RAM) above the 16MB address boundary. You
should answer Yes to this question. In Figure 4.17, you see the screen (Heap
Configuration Option) you use to indicate how much memory the file server
should use. If your plan designates that this file server will not run other programs, but simply act as a file server, you should choose the Workstation Determines Maximum Size option. If on the other hand you'll run other
software programs on this file server, you should specify a maximum size
that leaves enough memory available to run these other programs. Note that

OS/2 can overcommit memory and run programs even when you haven't left sufficient free RAM for them. However, planning ahead and allocating memory wisely will help your programs run faster because OS/2 will need to make less use of its swap file.

Figure 4.15

Controlling 386HPFS

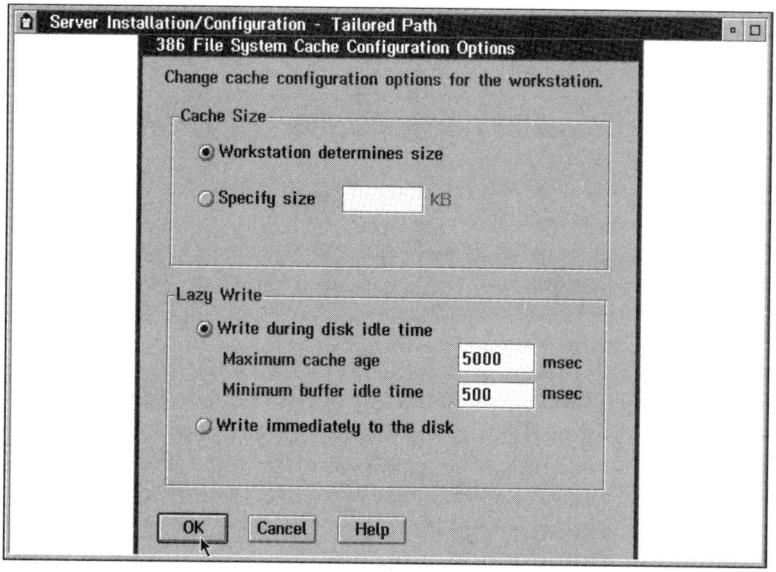

Figure 4.16

Cache location

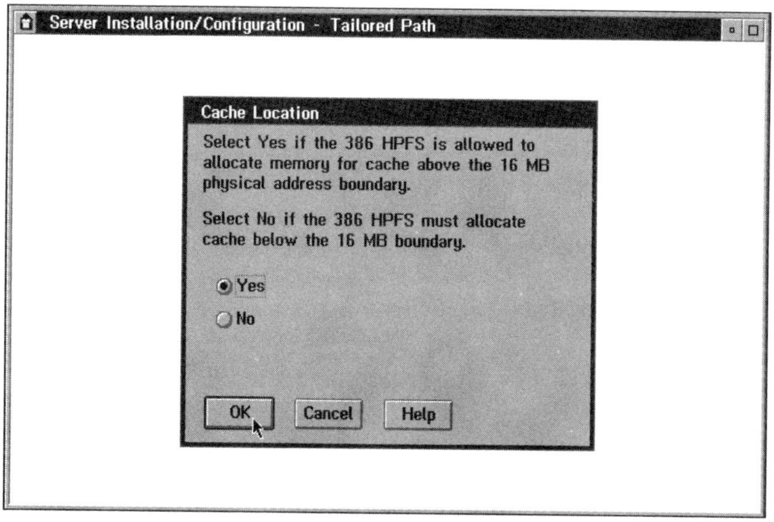

Figure 4.17

Allocating server memory

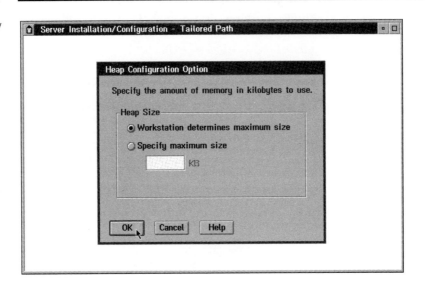

As you move through the Tailored method of installation, you'll see additional screens asking you which of up to four network adapters you're using, whether you want First Failure Support Technology/2 (FFST/2) to start automatically, which directory FFST/2 should use to store system dump files, and how you'd like to identify your file server computer for LAN management purposes. The FFST/2 and server identification questions help LAN Server communicate effectively with a LAN management product such as NetView or LAN Network Manager. If you have one of these products, you should refer to the product's documentation to know how to configure LAN Server. If you don't use a LAN management product that LAN Server can communicate with, you don't need to configure FFST/2.

Once you've selected and successfully configured the server components, you'll see a screen similar to the one in Figure 4.18. Note in the figure that each selected component has a status of "Configured." When you click on OK, you'll return to the screen shown in Figure 4.7. (If you've made configuration errors, the installation program will automatically navigate you to the screen on which you can correct the error. You'll then return to the Figure 4.7 screen after there are no configuration errors.) To proceed with the installation, highlight the Apply the Changes entry and click on the OK button. The installation program will ask you to insert disks (or the program will copy and install files from the CD-ROM drive); depending on your answers to the configuration questions, not all disks may be needed. The program will ask you for Server disks, Requester disks, and AnyNet (network adapter driver) disks.

Figure 4.18

The end of the
configuration phase of
LAN Server installation

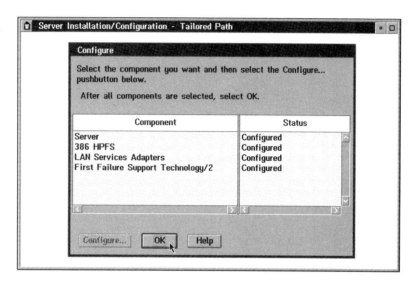

Near the end of the installation, the installation program will notify you
that it has made a backup copy of your CONFIG.SYS file and, if you're using
386HPFS, give you an opportunity to create an emergency startup disk (Figure 4.19). If you'd like to have an emergency boot disk that you can use if
you someday encounter problems with your file server, you'll need to make a
copy of the OS/2 Disk 1 distribution disk that came with OS/2. The LAN
Server installation program will modify the copy of OS/2 Disk 1 to allow you
to boot OS/2 on an emergency basis if, for example, you need to run
CHKDSK on one of your file server hard drives.

■ Installing Network Adapter Support

During the LAN Server installation process, you use Multi-Protocol Transport Services (MPTS) to select your network adapter. Through MPTS, you
inform LAN Server of the IRQ, I/O base address, shared RAM address, and
other network adapter settings you set when you inserted the network
adapter into the PC. You also use MPTS to select the network protocols that
LAN Server should use. On the first MPTS screen, shown in Figure 4.20, you
click on the Install button. Later, you'll return to this same screen to select
the Configure button.

Figure 4.21 is an example of the screen on which you select your network
adapter and protocols. To use the lists of adapters and protocols, you scroll
until you see the entry you want to select. Highlight the entry and click on the

Figure 4.19

Your opportunity to make
an emergency boot disk
for your server

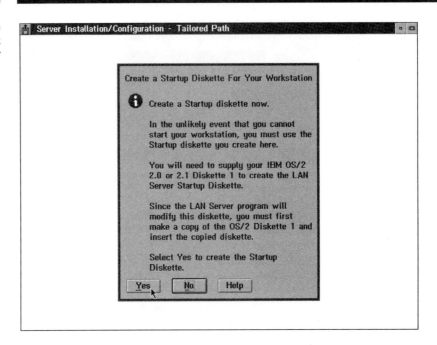

Figure 4.20

The initial MPTS screen

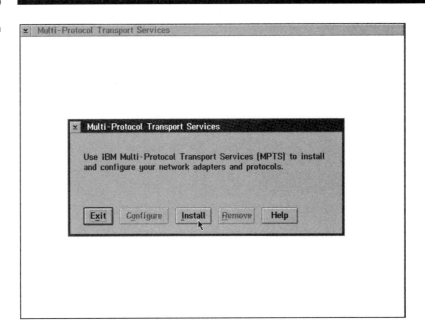

Add button. The installation program adds the selected entry to the Current Configuration list at the bottom of the screen. You should choose one adapter from the left-hand list and one or more protocols from the right-hand list. The button labeled Other Adapters lets you install a network adapter driver supplied by the manufacturer of your adapter, if you can't find that adapter in the on-screen list. Similarly, if your network needs different protocols, the Other Protocols button lets you install other protocols besides those listed on screen. If your organization's network uses protocols not in the on-screen list, your network administration team must supply you with those protocol drivers, but fortunately, you'll rarely need the Other Protocols option.

Figure 4.21

Selecting your network adapter and protocols

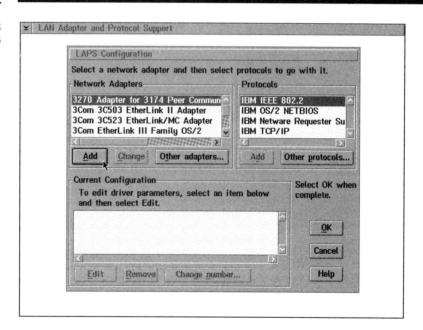

If you only want to use LAN Server on your network's file servers, you should choose the two protocols IBM IEEE 802.2 and IBM OS/2 NETBIOS. On the other hand, if you'd like your LAN Server file server to also act as a workstation on a NetWare LAN, you should additionally select the IBM NetWare Requester Support protocol. To use Netware Requester Support, you should already have installed Novell's NetWare Client for OS/2 (version 2.1 or higher) on the computer. The installation program will configure LAN Server to use the existing NetWare protocols. The NetWare Client for OS/2 documentation explains in detail how to integrate LAN Server into an existing NetWare LAN. Remember to click on the Add button below the list after you highlight each desired entry.

The other protocol option, IBM TCP/IP, is much more complex. TCP/IP is a protocol well-suited to wide area networks (WANs). IBM's NETBIOS protocol, also known as NetBEUI, can be difficult to use in a WAN. You need TCP/IP if you have multiple LANs, perhaps geographically distant ones, that you want to connect. In a wide area network environment, you'll need router or bridge hardware and you'll need to develop conventions for administering the computers on the network. These conventions, which are beyond the scope of this book, give you the parameters and configuration settings you'll need if you select the IBM TCP/IP protocol.

After you've added your network adapter and your protocols to the Current Configuration list at the bottom of the screen shown in Figure 4.21, you highlight each entry and click on the Edit button. When you choose to edit the network adapter configuration, you next see a screen similar to the one in Figure 4.22. This screen lets you specify to LAN Server the jumper or switch settings appropriate for the network adapter you've inserted in the PC. If you select the IBM IEEE 802.2 protocol, the screen shown in Figure 4.23 lets you modify the protocol's configuration. Note that this modification is optional; you should use the default parameters unless your network adapter manufacturer or your organization's network administrators tell you to use different parameters.

Figure 4.22

Specifying your network adapter settings

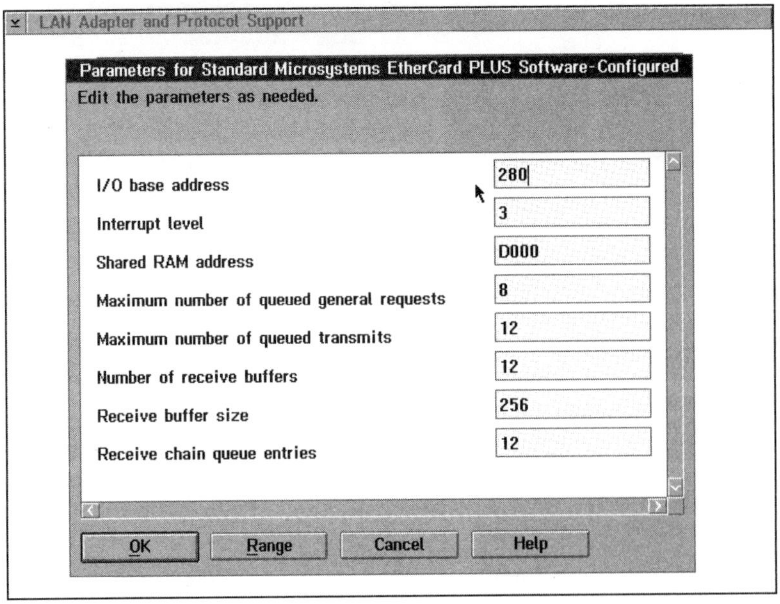

If you choose to edit the parameters for the IBM OS/2 NETBIOS proto-col, you'll see the screen shown in Figure 4.24. This screen, like the previous one, contains default parameters that will work satisfactorily in most environ-ments. However, you'll need to increase the default Maximum sessions, Max-imum commands, and Maximum names parameters if, for example, you will run other NetBIOS-aware software on your file server. IBM's DB2/2 data-base management product is an example of a computer program that re-quires additional NetBIOS sessions, commands, and names.

After configuring LAN Server, configuring MPTS, and inserting disks, you've finished the installation of LAN Server. The installation program cre-ates new folders and program objects on your desktop that you can use to start, stop, and administer the LAN Server product. When you shut down OS/2 and reboot, the PC will be a file server.

NOTE. *If you have OS/2-based PCs on your LAN that you want to use as workstations (rather than servers), you'll run the INSTALL program on the floppy disk labeled Requester Install/Disk 1 instead of the INSTALL program on Server Install/Disk 1. The installation process is similar to the one described for the Server software except that you won't be asked to insert the Server disks during the installation.*

Figure 4.24

Parameters for IBM OS/2 NETBIOS

```
LAN Adapter and Protocol Support
   Parameters for IBM OS/2 NETBIOS
   Edit the parameters as needed.  Except for parameters preceded by "x",
   changes affect all instances of the driver.

      Enable NetBIOS application support          YES
      xNetwork adapter address
      Type of Ethernet driver support             I
      Universally administered address reversed   YES
      NETBIOS trace level                         0
      Maximum sessions                            200
      Maximum commands                            225
      Maximum names                               40
      GDT selectors                               15
      Full buffer datagrams                       NO

      OK        Range        Cancel        Help
```

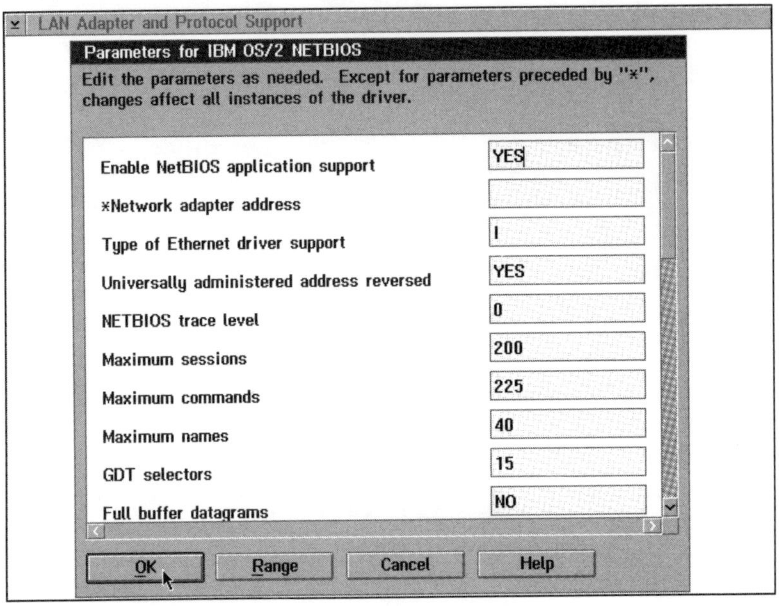

■ DOS LAN Services on Workstations

Installing the requester software on DOS-based PCs is relatively simple. Insert the disk labeled IBM DOS LAN Services Disk 1 in each DOS-based computer that will become a workstation on the LAN and type

A:INSTALL

to begin the installation. After a welcome screen and a screen you use to indicate the drive letter and directory in which the network software should be placed, you see a list of four optional DOS LAN Services components (Figure 4.25). The installation process, by default, installs all four options.

The first option, Graphical User Interface, gives the person using the workstation a point-and-click environment for performing network tasks. These tasks include connecting to shared drives, connecting to shared printers, logging in, and logging out. The person can use the Graphical User Interface if he or she doesn't always use Microsoft Windows on the computer. The Peer Services option lets a workstation act as a simple file server to share its hard disk and printer with other workstations on the network. Using Peer Services consumes more of the workstation's memory, so you should not select Peer Services on workstations that only need to access the LAN Server file server computer's hard disk or printers. If you select the Windows Support

Figure 4.25

The DOS LAN Services
component selection
screen

```
Install for DOS LAN Services
_____


              If all the options are correct, select 'The listed options
              are correct,' and then press Enter. If you want to change
              an option, use the Up Arrow or Down Arrow key to select it. Then
              press Enter to see alternatives for that option.



              Graphical User Interface : Install GUI.
              Peer Services            : Install Peer Services.
              Windows support          : Install Windows support.
              Protocol Driver          : IBM NetBEUI

         The listed options are correct.




         Enter=Continue     F1=Help     F3=Exit
```

option, DOS LAN Services will integrate with Microsoft Windows, if Windows is installed on the workstation. You can install both the Graphical User Interface and Windows support if you want, but be aware that most people will use one or the other interfaces, not both. The fourth option, Protocol Driver, lets you specify the network adapter you inserted into the workstation computer.

On the next screen, shown in Figure 4.26, the DOS LAN Services installation program asks you for this workstation's Machine ID, User name, Domain name, type of network adapter, and other parameters. The installation program contains detection logic to determine the type of network adapter in the computer; you should only have to verify that the listed network card is the type you actually inserted in the PC. Make sure the domain name you enter on this screen is the same domain name you assigned when you installed the LAN Server software on the file server computer.

After you select options and confirm your network parameters, the DOS LAN Services installation process copies files to the workstation's hard disk and modifies the computer's configuration files (AUTOEXEC.BAT, CONFIG.SYS, and possibly some of the Windows INI files).

Figure 4.26

The DOS LAN Services
configuration verification
screen

```
Install for DOS LAN Services
_____


        If all the options are correct, select 'The listed options
        are correct,' and then press Enter. If you want to change
        an option, use the Up Arrow or Down Arrow key to select it. Then
        press Enter to see alternatives for that option.



        Machine ID            : IBMPS
        User name             :
        Domain name           :
        Network adapter       :

    The listed options are correct.



    Enter=Continue      F1=Help      F3=Exit
```

■ Summary

In this chapter, you installed LAN Server. You inserted network adapters into the PCs, connected the LAN cables, and loaded the LAN Server software. You configured your file server and its protocols. You installed Requester software on your workstation computers.

In the next chapter, you begin using your new file server.

- *Learning the Role of the LAN Administrator*
- *Graphical and Command-Line Tools*
- *Starting and Stopping the File Server*
- *Managing Groups and Logon Accounts*
- *Establishing Rights and Permissions*
- *Restricting Access to the Server*

- *Understanding PROTOCOL.INI and IBMLAN.INI*
- *Managing the Network*

5

Administering LAN Server

IN THIS CHAPTER, YOU'LL SEE HOW TO OPERATE LAN SERVER AND
what this network operating system looks like. First we'll cover
LAN Server's graphical user interface, followed by the command
line interface. You'll learn what it means to log in on a LAN
Server network. You'll discover how to assign drive letters, use
files and directories, and print on the LAN. You'll explore how
your computer behaves when it becomes a workstation on a LAN
Server network, and you'll find out about the security features of
your network.

■ Learning the Role of the LAN Administrator

A LAN administrator performs many day-to-day tasks on the network (or perhaps multiple networks) he or she manages. In addition to setting up new logon accounts for new people in the office, the administrator deletes the accounts of people who have left, makes sure that the network's backup procedures are adhered to, modifies rights and permissions to allow only the appropriate people access to files on the file server, and acts as a troubleshooter when problems happen on the LAN. The administrator keeps file servers, workstations, and other network components connected, running, and accessible to the people in the office.

Keeping a LAN up and running is complicated by the dynamic, distributed nature of networks. Many LAN environments intermix PCs, gateways, bridges, routers, minicomputers, and mainframes. The LAN may very well include software systems not originally designed for a large network, and—to further complicate the situation—the LAN may contain components from many different vendors.

To manage a network, you need a plan. The system plan must change and grow as the network changes and grows. The plan must address such issues as cable diagrams, cable layout, network capacity, protocol and equipment standards, security, the addition of new workstations, and new LAN technologies. The plan must also allow you to stay abreast of new network management tools and products. As the administrator, one of most useful and helpful tasks you can perform on behalf of the people who use the network is the ongoing documentation of the sharable resources on the LAN.

On small networks, the LAN administrator's job falls by default to someone already in the office, and is probably a part-time position. On larger systems (20 or more workstations), the administrator's job may be recognized as a full-time position. A LAN with hundreds of workstations typically has several LAN administrators.

Managing a LAN from a centralized location can be a difficult task. As yet, you will not find a complete set of tools offered by vendors to help with all the administrator's tasks. The network administrator typically will have a mixture of software and hardware tools to help get the job done. The administrator has to be an expert in using the available tools, often calling upon his or her own creativity to use the tools at hand to solve unusual problems. The administrator must understand the network's configuration, performance, accounting, planning, security, and applications in order to solve problems as they occur. This chapter discusses the LAN Server software tools you use to administer the LAN, but doesn't explain such tools as protocol analyzers, cable testers (sometimes known as time domain reflectometers, or TDRs), and network monitors. You buy these tools separately from LAN Server if you feel they'll help you with your LAN administration chores.

■ Graphical and Command-Line Tools

LAN Server gives an administrator both graphical, point-and-click tools and command-line tools for managing the LAN. The graphical network administration tools, which use the features of OS/2's Presentation Manager and Workplace Shell, display icons on your screen to represent the different components of your LAN. The text-mode command-line tools, which you run in a full-screen OS/2 command prompt session, let you specify network administration tasks as parameters to the computer program NET.EXE. You can use either the graphical tools or the command-line tools to administer LAN Server.

The Graphical User Interface

Figure 5.1 shows the LAN Server folder, created by the installation program, open on the OS/2 desktop. The icon objects in the LAN Server folder include tools for logging on and off of the network, tuning LAN Server, changing LAN Server's configuration, monitoring the audit trail and error log files, starting LAN Server, and administering LAN Server. Double-clicking the icon labeled *LAN Server Administration* and then closing or minimizing the main LAN Server folder displays a screen similar to the one shown in Figure 5.2. The LAN Server Administation object is the tool you'll use most often in your day-to-day work with LAN Server.

The example folder in Figure 5.2 contains three objects, labeled *Local Workstation Z-SERVER*, *EVERYONE*, and *Shadowed Servers*. The *Z-SERVER* and *EVERYONE* portions of the folder names were assigned by the person who installed the example LAN Server file server. Your names will be different. You'll perform most of your administration of LAN Server by manipulating the objects in the folder with the same name as the server's assigned domain name (*EVERYONE* in this example).

While the IBM documentation that comes with OS/2 explains the features of the Workplace Shell in more detail, the following brief descriptions and definitions will help you with your first few explorations of LAN Server's graphical interface tools.

Icons are graphical representations of objects, and you can do lots of things with them without opening them first. You know how to open a view of an object by double-clicking its icon. This section shows several other things you can do with the icons on the desktop and icons inside folders. IBM's OS/2 documentation calls these actions *direct manipulations* because

Figure 5.1

The LAN Server folder

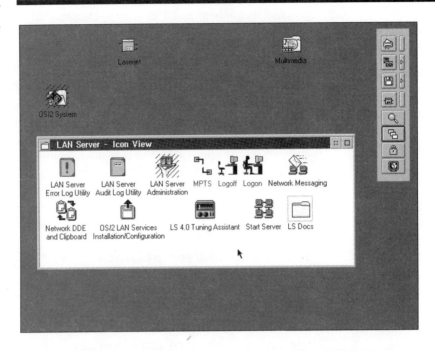

Figure 5.2

An example LAN Server
Administration folder

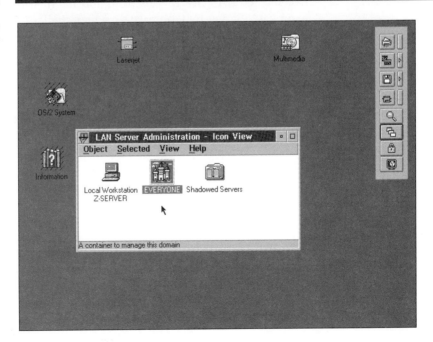

you are dealing directly with the icon instead of going through menus. Each form of direct manipulation gives you a distinctive kind of visual feedback.

Click any icon once to select it. Selecting does not actually do anything to the object. Instead, it means that the next action you take will apply to that object. Pressing Enter, for example, opens any selected object. The Workplace Shell gives you immediate visual feedback by highlighting in gray the icon you select. This is *selection emphasis*. Press Enter to open a view of the currently selected object. Double-clicking mouse button 1 (by default, the left mouse button) on an icon selects and opens the icon. The icon gets *in-use emphasis*—a horizontally shaded pattern that tells you at a glance which objects are open. Clicking mouse button 2 (by default, the right mouse button) on an icon brings up that icon's related system menu. Selecting the icon first isn't necessary.

Moving an Object's Icon

To move an icon, press and hold down mouse button 2 on an icon while you move the mouse. This is called *dragging*. The icon moves on screen with the movement of the mouse cursor. For example, you might drag the LAN Server Adminstration icon to an empty place on the desktop and release the mouse button. The icon moves with the mouse cursor. You can use drag-and-drop to arrange your desktop icons in any way you like.

You also can move objects between folders. For example, you can drag the LAN Server folder icon to an empty spot inside the OS/2 System folder. Drop the icon. The original icon vanishes from the desktop and reappears inside the OS/2 System folder. Similarly, you can move (with drag-and-drop) icon objects to their former locations.

Copying and Shadowing an Icon Object

To copy an object, you perform a drag-and-drop operation while holding down the Ctrl key. First, press the Ctrl key. Then click the object with mouse button 2 and move the mouse cursor to the target location (an empty spot on the OS/2 desktop, for example). Then release the mouse button and the Ctrl key. When you move the icon, the on-screen representation looks dimmer than usual, which gives you visual feedback that a copy is in progress.

A shadow is a great deal like a copy, except that the shadow is just an alias for the original object. Like a reflection in a mirror, the shadow has no independent existence of its own. The advantage of using shadows rather than copies is that these objects don't take disk space, whereas copies do. You can delete a shadow without affecting the original object.

If you want a program object to run (execute) when you boot your computer, you can make a shadow of the object and move the shadow to the Startup folder. You also might put shadows right on your desktop of the objects you open and close frequently during the day. This makes the objects immediately accessible, yet leaves the original in an appropriate folder. You don't have to move such an object onto the desktop, then later move the object back to its proper folder.

You create a shadow the same way you make a copy, but you hold down the Ctrl and Shift keys instead of just the Ctrl key. To help you see the difference between a copy operation and a shadow operation, the Workplace Shell draws a line that connects the original icon to the shadow icon while you move the mouse.

Dropping One Icon on Another

With OS/2's Workplace Shell, you can drop one icon object onto another icon object. The resulting behavior depends on the types of the objects. You can move an object to a folder by dropping the object on the folder's icon. This procedure works even if the folder isn't open. To print an object, you can drop it on the printer object icon. To delete an object, you can drop the object on the Shredder. Within the LAN Server Administration folder

When you try to drop an icon object on another icon that doesn't know what to do with the first icon, you see a circle with a bar through it, similar to a *do not enter* road sign. The *do not enter* symbol tells you that dropping the icon here has no effect.

When dragging an icon, you may change your mind and decide not to complete the operation. Just press the Esc key before you drop the icon.

Changing an Object's Name

You can change the name of any object by typing the new name in the Title box of the General tab of the object's settings notebook. A shortcut is available for mouse users. Hold down Alt and click mouse button 1, either on the icon or on the title bar of an open view. Backspace over the old name, type the new name, and then click the icon or title bar.

The LAN Server Commands

Especially after you have gained some experience with LAN Server, you may feel more comfortable issuing network commands at the DOS command line prompt of your workstation, or at the OS/2 prompt at the file server. You invoke the network commands by running the NET program with command line parameters. The following is a list of NET commands, with frequently used parameters:

NET Command	Function
Net Access	Views permissions
Net Continue	Continues a paused service

NET Command	**Function**
Net Copy	Copies network files
Net Help	Gets help for a command
Net Name	Assigns a computer name
Net Password	Changes your password
Net Pause	Pauses a connection to a network service
Net Print	Displays the print queue or prints a file
Net Start Workstation	Starts the network at a workstation computer
Net Start Server	Starts the network at a file server
Net Time	Synchronizes the workstation's clock with the server's clock
Net Use	Displays shared resources or assigns a drive letter to a shared resource
Net View	Displays a list of servers and server resources
Net Who	Sees who is logged on

In addition to the commands in the list, you use the LOGON command to log on to the network. This command establishes the user ID, password, and domain for a workstation. The user ID and password identify you in a particular domain and grant you access to shared resources. You can use shared resources in other domains once you have logged on. The LOGOFF command terminates your session and your drive mappings. LOGON and LOGOFF are separate computer programs, not parameters you supply to the NET command.

■ Starting and Stopping the File Server

With the graphical interface, you start LAN Server by double-clicking the icon in the LAN Server folder labeled Start Server. You can automate the process by putting a shadow of the Start Server icon in the Startup folder, located in the OS/2 System folder. When it boots, OS/2 loads and starts program objects (or their shadows) in the Startup folder.

If you prefer command line tools, you can start the file server by typing the command

NET START SERVER

at an OS/2 windowed or full-screen prompt. OS/2's command line sessions are icons in the Command Prompts folder, which in turn is in the OS/2 System folder. Automating the command line method of starting the server is also possible; you create a text file named STARTUP.CMD in the root directory of the boot drive (almost always drive C) and insert your NET START command in this batch file program.

With either the graphical or command line method of starting the file server software, you'll see a screen similar to the one shown in Figure 5.3 as the server starts. As LAN Server starts, it automatically establishes the aliases (shared resource names) of the disk directories, printers, and modems you've previously told LAN Server to share.

Figure 5.3

LAN Server's startup
screen

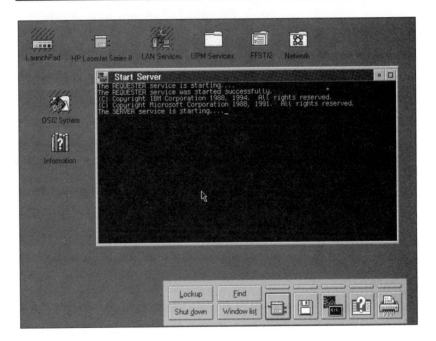

The LAN Server installation process doesn't create an icon that represents the stopping of the server. However, you can make such an icon if you wish. Use a text editor to insert the following command in a batch file program named STOPSVR.CMD:

```
NET STOP SERVER
```

When you run this batch file program, LAN Server will list any currently running services and ask you to confirm you want them stopped. As you'd expect, issuing the command at an OS/2 windowed or full-screen session prompt produces the same confirmation question. To turn your new batch file program into an icon on your OS/2 desktop, follow the directions in the OS/2 documentation for creating a new program object. These directions explain how to use the icon labeled Program in the Templates folder to create new program objects. Type the name of your batch file, STOPSVR.CMD, on the Program page of the settings notebook. Finally, give the new program object an appropriate title, such as Stop Server, and drag the new object into your LAN Server folder.

NOTE. *If you don't stop the file server software before performing a shutdown of OS/2, you'll notice a several-second delay after selecting the Shutdown menu option while the server software terminates itself. The delay is normal. LAN Server takes several moments to stop running.*

■ Managing Groups and Logon Accounts

LAN Server doesn't have command-line equivalents for the graphical tools that let you add, modify, and delete both groups and logon accounts. The graphical tools are the User Accounts and Groups icons in the domain folder. Figure 5.4 shows both the User Accounts folder and Groups folder open, via a double-click, on the OS/2 desktop.

Figure 5.4

The folder of shared objects within a domain

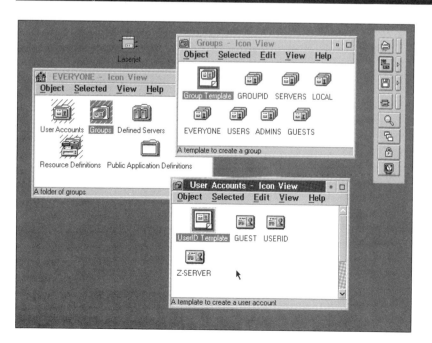

Groups

The first time you use LAN Server, you'll want to set up one or more named groups into which you'll put logon accounts. To create a new group, use mouse button 2 to drag the Group Template icon onto an empty area of the Groups folder. Before manipulating the Group Template icon, you may want to resize the borders of the Groups folder to make room for the new group's icon. When you release the mouse button, the template opens automatically and you see a settings notebook on your screen. Figure 5.5 shows an example of a new group, with the Group name and Description fields filled in. Note that OS/2 and LAN Server give you several ways to accomplish the same operations. In addition to the template method of adding a group, you can use the Create Another menu option that's on an existing group's pop-up menu.

Figure 5.5

The Identity page of a new group's settings notebook

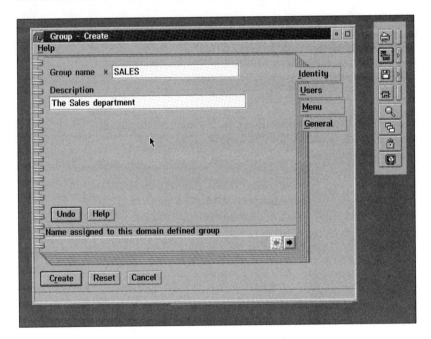

When you want to modify a group, double-clicking on that group's icon also displays the settings notebook shown in Figure 5.5.

The second page of the group's settings notebook, labeled Users, is where you add existing logon accounts to the group, if any. Figure 5.6 shows the Users settings notebook page. Adding logon accounts to a new group is optional. You can add logon accounts later, or, if you wish, you can associate a logon account with a group by modifying the logon account's information or by dragging and dropping a logon account icon onto a group icon. To add a logon account to a group by using the group's settings notebook, click the button labeled Add in Figure 5.6. You see a window titled Add Users to a Group, similar to the one shown in Figure 5.7. Highlight the logon account you want to add to the group and click the window's Add button. Your change is reflected on the Users page of the group's settings notebook. You can additionally give the group a title by using the General settings notebook page. When you're finished specifying information about the group, click the Create button in the lower left corner of the group's settings notebook.

Figure 5.6

The Users page of a
group's settings notebook

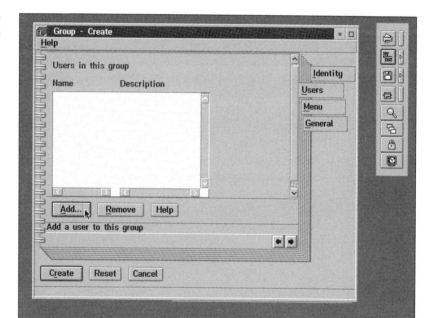

To add a logon account to a existing group through drag-and-drop, arrange your desktop to look like the one shown in Figure 5.4. When the User Accounts folder shows the logon account you want to add and the Groups folder shows the group, use mouse button 2 to drag the logon account to the appropriate group icon. Drop the logon account onto the Group icon, as shown in Figure 5.8. The LAN Server Administration software displays a status window informing you the operation was successful.

You delete a group by using the group's pop-up menu. Click once with mouse button 2 on the group's icon in the Groups folder to see a screen similar to the one shown in Figure 5.9. Choose the Delete menu option and then confirm your deletion on the Group-Delete window that pops up.

Figure 5.7

The Add Users to Group
window

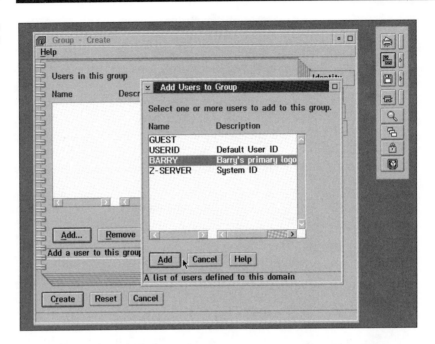

Figure 5.8

Adding a logon account to
a group via drag-and-drop

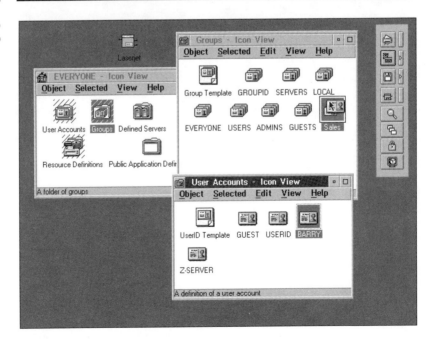

Figure 5.9

Deleting a group

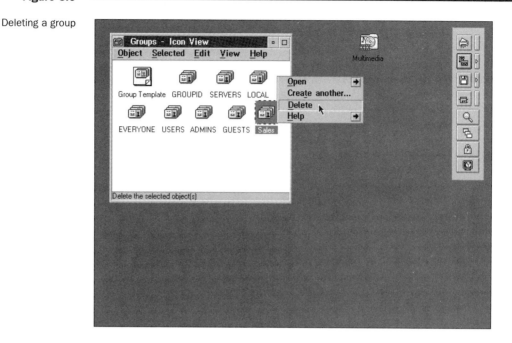

Logon Accounts

The adding, changing, and deleting of logon accounts is similar to the operations you've just learned for groups. When you use mouse button 2 to drag and drop the UserID template onto an empty place in the User Accounts folder, a settings notebook opens and you see the screen shown in Figure 5.10. The tabs on this settings notebook have the labels Identity, Password, Privileges, Home Directory, Account Info, Assignments, Applications, Groups, Menu, and General. Figure 5.10 shows the Identity tab, on which you enter the logon account name and description.

The Password tab has two pages, shown in Figures 5.11 and 5.12. The first page lets you change the password of an existing account, an operation you'd perform for someone who has forgotten his or her password. Administratively setting a new password lets the person use the new password the next time he or she logs on to the network.

NOTE. *After an administrator assigns a new password to a person, that person should change to a new, secret password the next time he or she logs on.*

Figure 5.10

The Identity tab of a
logon account's settings
notebook

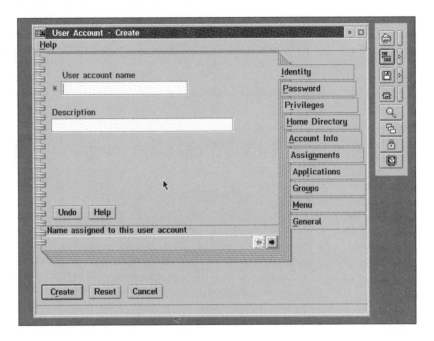

Figure 5.11

The first page of the
Password tab

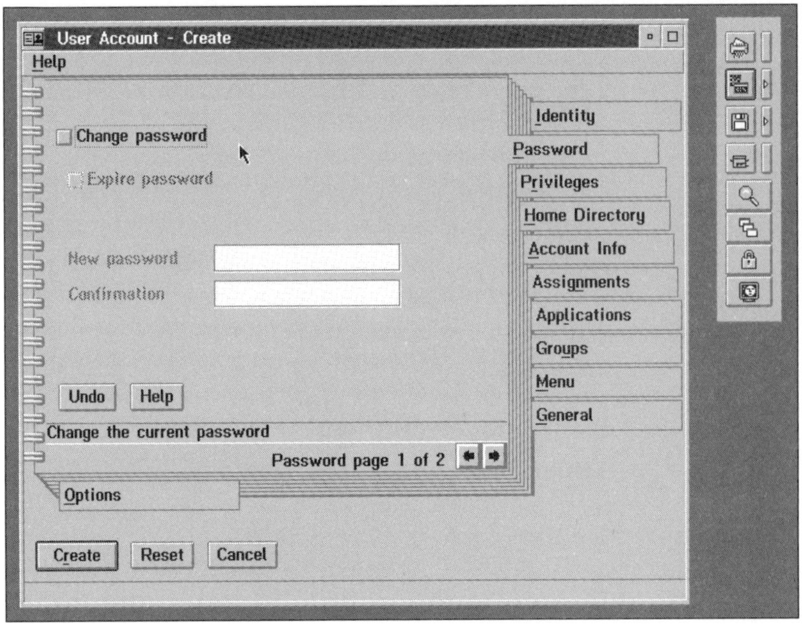

Figure 5.12

Figure 5.12

Administrative control of
passwords on page 2 of
the Password tab

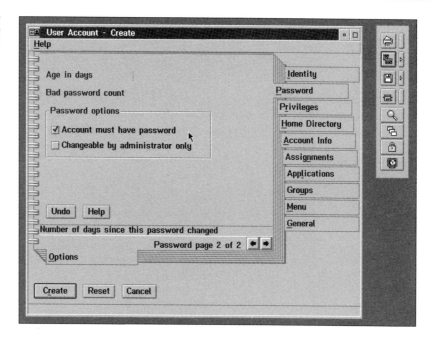

The second page of the Password tab (Figure 5.12) permits an administrator to control how passwords behave for a logon account and to view password information for that account. The adminstrator can designate that the account must use a password and can prevent a person from changing the password.

The Privileges tab of the logon account's settings notebook, shown in Figure 5.13, allows an administrator to designate four attributes for that logon account, as identified in the following list:

- Print—specifies that the logon account can manage print queues.

- Accounts—grants administrative privileges to the logon account.

- Comm—lets a logon account manage shared serial devices, such as modems.

- Server—lets a logon account create, modify, or delete shared resources.

On the Home Directory tab of the settings notebook, illustrated in Figure 5.14, an administrator can allocate a file server directory in which a person can store files. LAN Server creates the directory if it doesn't exist already. The logon account's home directory can be any directory on the server, but you'll likely want to establish a naming convention that helps you easily know which directory belongs to which logon account. You might, for

Figure 5.13

The Privileges tab of a logon account's settings notebook

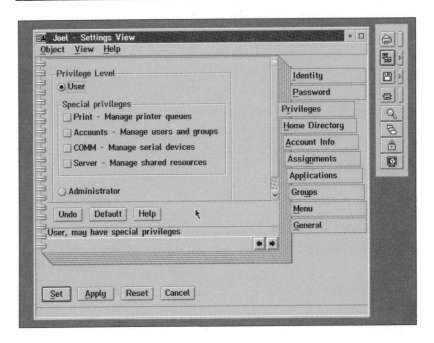

Figure 5.14

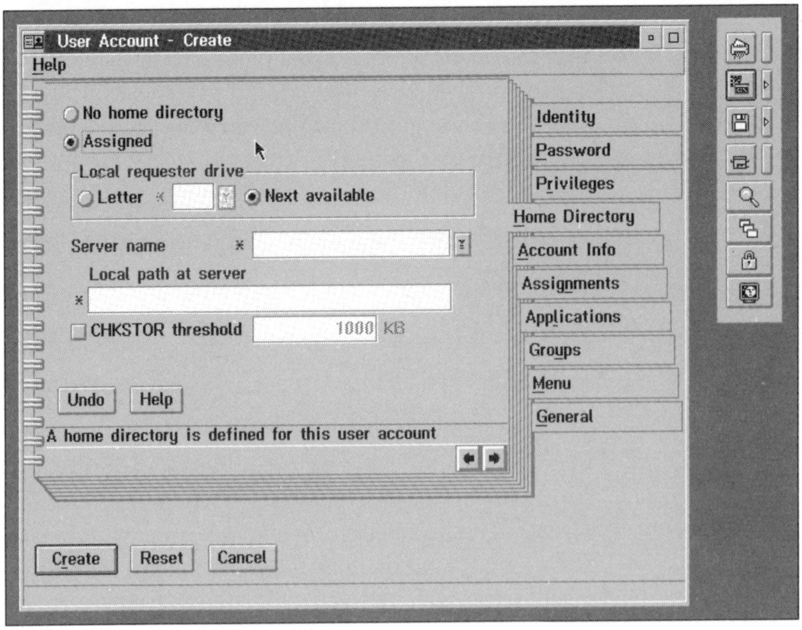

The Home Directory tab of the settings notebook for a logon account

instance, create a directory named HOME or USERS on the server and then create individual directories for each person within HOME (or USERS). The Home Directory tab lets you specify the drive letter the person uses to access his or her home directory.

If the home directory is on a 386HPFS partition of the server and if that partition is not the server's boot drive, you can also specify limits on the disk space consumed within that directory. On the Home Directory tab, click the box labeled CHKSTOR Threshold and enter the maximum amount of disk space, in kilobytes, the logon account can use in that home directory.

The Account Info tab of a logon account's settings notebook has two pages, shown in Figures 5.15 and 5.16. The first page displays the dates the account last logged on and off. The first page also lets an administrator specify whether the account is disabled (that is, temporarily unusable for logging on) and deletable. Clicking the checkboxes sets or unsets these two attributes. The administrator can use the first page of the Account Info tab to give an account an expiration date after which the account can no longer be used. Click the checkbox labeled Specified and use the spin buttons to set the expiration date if you want the logon account to expire on a certain date.

Figure 5.15

The first page of the
Account Info tab

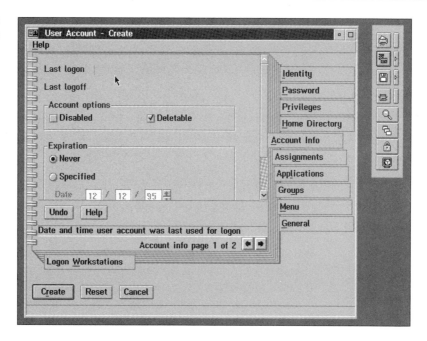

Figure 5.16

The second page of the
Account Info tab

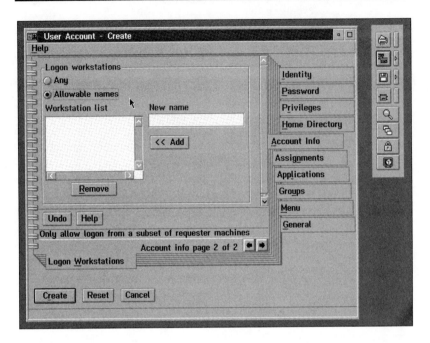

On the second page of Account Info, an administrator can optionally specify which workstations a logon account can use. To identify one or more such
workstations, click the radiobutton labeled Allowable Names and enter a workstation name in the New Name field. Click the Add button to add the workstation to the list. Use the Remove button to delete an entry from the list. Note
that a workstation name you enter here is the name you gave a workstation
when you installed either the DOS LAN Services or OS/2 Requester on a PC.

The Assignments tab lets an administrator name those shared resources
that LAN Server makes available to a logon account. Figure 5.17 shows the
result of clicking on the Assignments tab, clicking the Add button, and then
choosing an alias (shared resource) that the logon account will be able to access. Clicking the OK button in the Logon Assignments window adds that
shared resource to the list for the logon account. Note that you can specify
which drive letter or device name the logon account uses to access the
shared resource. Specifying an asterisk in place of a drive letter name assigns
the next unused drive letter to the account at logon time.

Similarly, the tab labeled Applications is an administrator's means of grant-
ing a logon account access to a public application on the file server. The Groups
tab lets the administrator put a logon account in a named group (every logon account must be in a group). The Menu and General tabs are typical OS/2 settings
notebook pages that an administrator can use to customize the logon account.

Figure 5.17

Allocating shared
resources to a logon
account

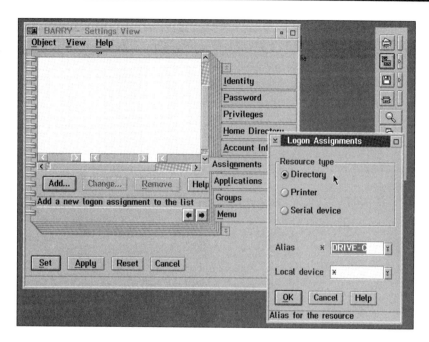

HINT. *While you cannot use a command-line method to configure your network's groups and logon accounts, you can use NET commands to view information about those accounts. For example, you can use the NET WHO command to see who's currently logged on. NET WHO displays a list similar to the following:*

```
Users on Domain EVERYONE

                                Time since
User ID           Requester        logon   Comment
------------------------------------------------------------------------
BARRY             IBMPS          02:33:05   Barry's primary logon acct
USERID            Z-SERVER       05:24:30   Default User ID
The command completed successfully.
```

To modify an existing logon account, simply double-click on that account's icon in the User Accounts folder. To delete an account, use mouse button 2 to display the object's pop-up menu and select the Delete menu item.

Naming and Sharing Resources

With the LAN Server Administration graphical tool shown in Figure 5.2, you can establish named shared resources that workstations on the LAN can access. Double-click on the domain folder (labeled *EVERYONE* in the example) to see a screen similar to the one shown in Figure 5.18. The already-installed objects in the domain folder are templates, in OS/2 terms, and have the titles Printer Template, Serial Device Template, and Directory Template. You create new shared resources by dragging and dropping one of these templates onto an empty area of the folder. Alternatively, you create a new shared resource by choosing the Create Another menu option from an existing resource's pop-up menu.

Figure 5.18

The folder of shared objects within a domain

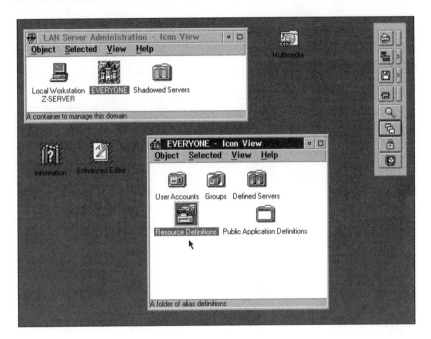

When you use either a shared resource template or the Create Another menu option, a settings notebook opens. Figure 5.19 illustrates the Identity tab of the settings notebook for a shared directory resource with the name DRIVE-C. The other two tabs, Menu and General, offer ways to customize the shared resource object. The Identity tab of the settings notebook for a shared resource is the administrator's primary means of establishing and configuring the resource.

On the Identity tab of a shared directory resource, the administrator specifies the Description, Server Name, and Path (server drive letter and directory name). The administrator can designate whether the resource becomes available at server startup, by administrative action, or only when requested. The administrator can also limit the number of concurrent connections to the shared resource by using the Number of Connections entry on the Identity tab.

Figure 5.19

The Identity tab of a
shared resource's
settings notebook

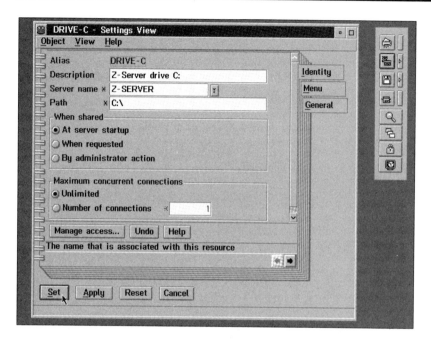

Clicking the Identity tab's Manage Access pushbutton displays the
screen shown in Figure 5.20. On this screen, titled Access Control Profile, an
administrator can grant or restrict access to the shared resource. The next
section discusses the rights and permissions an administrator can specify. The
Auditing tab of the notebook lets an administrator turn auditing on or off for
the shared resource. When auditing is turned on, LAN Server can put entries
in the audit log when access to the resource fails, when access succeeds, or
when any access occurs.

The command line equivalent for establishing or viewing a file server's
shared resources is the NET SHARE command. Typing NET SHARE at a
file server OS/2 prompt, with no other parameters, displays information similar to the following:

```
Netname       Resource                     Remark
---------------------------------------------------------------------------
IPC$                                        Remote IPC
ADMIN$        D:\IBMLAN                     Remote Admin
A$            A:\                           Drive Share for Admin Use
B$            B:\                           Drive Share for Admin Use
C$            C:\                           Drive Share for Admin Use
D$            D:\                           Drive Share for Admin Use
E$            E:\                           Drive Share for Admin Use
F$            F:\                           Drive Share for Admin Use
```

```
G$            G:\                            Drive Share for Admin Use
I$            I:\                            Drive Share for Admin Use
IBMLAN$       D:\IBMLAN                      OS/2 LAN Server root
DRIVE-C       C:\                            Z-Server drive C:
DRIVE-D       D:\                            Z-Server drive D:
DRIVE-E       E:\                            Z-Server drive E:
DRIVE-F       F:\                            Z-Server drive F:
DRIVE-G       G:\                            Z-Server drive G:
DRIVE-I       I:\                            Z-Server drive I:
NETLOGON      D:\IBMLAN\REPL\IMPORT\SCRIPTS  Domain controller share
LASERJET      LPT1                  Spooled  Laserjet printer
The command completed successfully.
```

Figure 5.20

The Access Control
Profile for a shared
resource

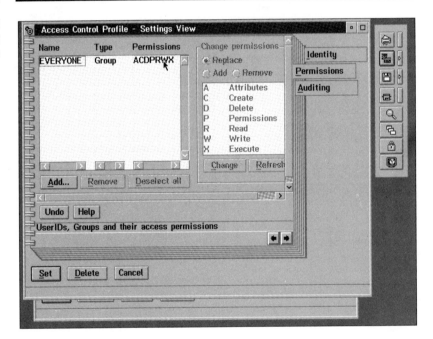

For most uses, the general syntax of the NET SHARE command is

```
NET SHARE <pathname> <alias> <options>
```

where <pathname> is the file server drive letter and directory to be shared, <alias> is the name by which the resource is to be known on the LAN, and <options> consist of password, permissions, or other parameters. The command is a versatile one; please refer to the command reference section of this book for more details. NET SHARE can set up, modify, or delete directory, serial device, or printer resources.

An example of using NET SHARE to make file server Z-SERVER's C drive available on the network as the alias DRIVE-C appears below:

```
net share C: \\Z-SERVER\DRIVE-C
```

You can also use this command, with a /D option, to delete a shared resource, as the following example shows:

```
net share C: /D
```

■ Establishing Rights and Permissions

For a shared resource, Figure 5.20 shows the Access Control Profile, used to grant or restrict access to a directory, printer, or modem. The first line of defense in a network security system is a logon account's password. The second line of defense is the administrator's ability to give files, as appropriate, a read-only attribute (which prevents inadvertent deletion of a file). Another line of defense is the administrator's backup procedure, which should let the administrator restore and recover files. Finally, the administrator can limit access to files and devices with LAN Server's Access Control Profiles.

User-level security on a LAN Server network consists of log-on security and permissions. Each user account has a password; the user specifies a user ID and the password to gain access to the network through a domain. A network administrator can limit a particular user's access to certain times of the day or to certain workstations. Permissions limit the extent to which a user can access shared resources. The network administrator, for example, can create a COMMON directory that everyone can use, and the administrator can create an UPDATE directory with files only certain people can modify but everyone can read.

Through Access Control Profiles, you can assign the following permissions for files and directories:

Permission	Lets a Person Perform This Operation
Change Attributes	Can flag a file as read-only or read/write
Change Permissions	Can grant or revoke access to other people
Create	Can creates files and directories
Delete	Can delete files and remove directories

Permission	Lets a Person Perform This Operation
Execute	Can execute programs (Only workstations running OS/2 or DOS 5 (or later) recognize this permission, which is a restricted version of the read permission)
Read	Can read and copy files, run programs, change from one directory to another, and make use of OS/2's extended attributes for files
Write	Can write to a file

The Access Control Profile screen shown in Figure 5.20 abbreviates these permissions with single letters, as shown in the following list:

Abbreviation	Permission
A	Attributes (can change file attributes)
C	Create files
D	Delete files
P	Permissions (can administer permissions)
R	Read files
W	Write files
X	Execute programs

An administrator can set or change these permissions, either on an individual logon account or group basis, for each shared resource. To give a logon account or entire group access to a shared resource, the administrator uses the screen in Figure 5.20. He or she clicks the Add button to see the Add Access Control Entries screen (Figure 5.21), which shows a list of logon accounts and groups to choose from. On the Add Access Control Entries screen, the administrator highlights the account or group that needs to access the shared resource. The administrator then selects the Permissions to be granted. You can click on the individual permissions, one by one, or you can hold down mouse button 1 while you move the mouse cursor over all (or a range) of Permissions. Clicking OK completes the operation and adds the account or group to the list of entities who can access the shared resource.

Figure 5.21

The Add Access Control
Entries screen

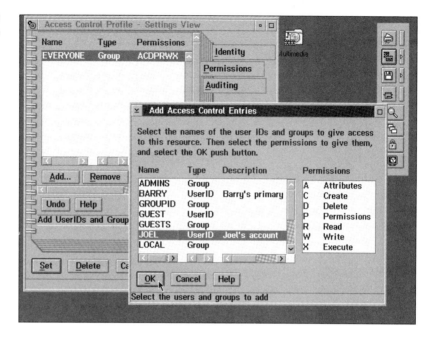

■ **Restricting Access to the Server**

Clearly, physical access to the file server computer by unauthorized people
might result in security and privacy problems in your organization. A person
could view the contents of any file on the server by simply opening a DOS or
OS/2 command-line session and running file browse/view software. You can
administratively take three actions to prevent such access.

First, you can put the file server computer in a room in your office that
has a locked door or that offers a similar measure of security. Next, you can
make sure that you don't leave an account with administrative privileges
logged on while the file server is unattended. Log off before you walk away
from the file server. Finally, LAN Server gives you the ability to control access to the file server's keyboard and computer screen. In a special unattended mode, the file server enables people to view and manage print queues
without enabling them to modify user accounts or other administrative data.
You must specify a password in order to use other screens. You enable this
special unattended mode when you install LAN Server's Local Security for
386HPFS component. Note, however, that this component is available in the
Advanced version of LAN Server but not in the Entry version. Also note

that this component, if installed, implements file server security in a way that makes the later upgrading or configuring of software a difficult process.

■ Understanding PROTOCOL.INI and IBMLAN.INI

At about the same time IBM and Microsoft wrote the Network Driver Interface Specification (NDIS), Novell and Apple created the Open Datalink Interface (ODI). While NDIS and ODI both describe a programming and configuration interface for network adapters, NDIS and ODI are in all other respects quite different. ODI uses the NET.CFG file and NDIS uses the PROTOCOL.INI file to hold configuration information. The format and content of the two files are quite distinct. The IBMLAN.INI file, on the other hand, contains configuration information that LAN Server uses to know which services to offer, which transport layer to use, how much memory to use, and how you want LAN Server to generally behave.

The PROTOCOL.INI File

The LAN Server installation software automatically creates a PROTOCOL.INI file for you. However, you'll often have the opportunity to inspect and perhaps modify the PROTOCOL.INI files on the workstations and at the file server. You might need to increase certain parameters to provide new connectivity for database management software products that you install (more NetBIOS sessions, for example), or you might need to tune the parameters to improve network performance. In general, you should always run MPTS, the OS/2 LAN Services Installation/Configuration utility, or the LS 4.0 Tuning Assistant to make changes to these files. Because the contents of PROTOCOL.INI and IBMLAN.INI are complicated and because these files control the behavior of LAN Server to a significant extent, you should use a text editor only as a last resort.

Breaking a PROTOCOL.INI file by inadvertently inserting bad entries in the file can keep a workstation (or file server) from accessing the network. The most important tip regarding either NET.CFG or PROTOCOL.INI configuration files is this: Always make sure you have a good backup copy of the configuration file before you make any changes.

If you've seen a Microsoft Windows INI file, you'll immediately be at home viewing PROTOCOL.INI files. A simple text file, the PROTO-COL.INI file contains one or more named sections, with each section the module name of a protocol or MAC (Media Access Control) driver. Brackets ([and]) surround the section name. Underneath each section name and indented slightly (usually by three spaces), named configuration entries appear in the format *name = value*. The indentation is optional. Each entry identifies a configuration value or binding instruction for NDIS. For instance, one section of the PROTOCOL.INI file might contain the following entries:

```
[XYZNetBIOS]
  Drivername = NetBIOS$
  Bindings = ETHERFAST
  MaxNCBs = 16
  MaxSessions = 32
  MaxNames = 16
```

PROTOCOL.INI files are never as short as this fragment implies. Listing 5.1 is an example PROTOCOL.INI file for the DOS LAN Requester (DLR) environment, and Listing 5.2 is an example OS/2 LAN Server PROTOCOL.INI file that shows how to use both ODI (for NetWare) and NDIS (for LAN Server) drivers on an OS/2 workstation.

Listing 5.1

A PROTOCOL.INI file for DOS LAN Requester (DLR)

```
[PROTMAN_MOD]
        DriverName = PROTMAN$
[DXMAIDXCFG]
        DXMJØMOD_MOD = DXMJØMOD.NIF
[DXMJØMOD_MOD]
        DriverName = NETBEUI$
        Bindings = IBMTOK_MOD
        NCBS = 15
        ADAPTRATE = 1000
        WINDOWERRORS = 0
        PIGGYBACKACKS = 1
        DATAGRAMPACKETS = 2
        PACKETS = 50
        PIPELINE = 20
        MAXTRANSMITS = 6
        MINTRANSMITS = 2
        LANABASE = 0
        CHAINX5C = 0
[IBMTOK_MOD]
        DriverName = IBMTOK$
        EARLYRELEASE
        MAXTRANSMITS = 6
        RECVBUFS = 2
        RECVBUFSIZE = 256
        XMITBUFS = 1
        XMITBUFSIZE = 2040
```

Listing 5.2

An OS/2 LAN Server
PROTOCOL.INI file for
both ODI and NDIS drivers

```
[PROT_MAN]
    DRIVERNAME = PROTMAN$

[IBMLXCFG]
    IBMTRDB_nif = IBMTRDB.nif
    LANDD_nif = LANDD.NIF
    NETBEUI_nif = NETBEUI.NIF
    ODI2NDI_nif = ODI2NDI.NIF

[LANDD_nif]
    DriverName = LANDD$
    Bindings = IBMTRDB_nif
    ETHERAND_TYPE = "I"
    SYSTEM_KEY = 0x0
    OPEN_OPTIONS = 0x2000
    TRACE = 0x0
    LINKS = 32
    MAX_SAPS = 4
    MAX_G_SAPS = 0
    USERS = 5
    TI_TICK_G1 = 255
    T1_TICK_G1 = 15
    T2_TICK_G1 = 3
    TI_TICK_G2 = 255
    T1_TICK_G2 = 25
    T2_TICK_G2 = 10
    IPACKETS = 250
    UIPACKETS = 100
    MAXTRANSMITS = 6
    MINTRANSMITS = 2
    TCBS = 64
    GDTS = 30
    ELEMENTS = 800

[NETBEUI_nif]
    DriverName = netbeui$
    Bindings = IBMTRDB_nif
    ETHERAND_TYPE = "I"
    USEADDRREV = "YES"
    OS2TRACEMASK = 0x0
    SESSIONS = 184
```

**Listing 5.2
(Continued)**

An OS/2 LAN Server
PROTOCOL.INI file for
both ODI and NDIS drivers

```
    NCBS = 165
    NAMES = 47
    SELECTORS = 5
    USEMAXDATAGRAM = "NO"
    ADAPTRATE = 1000
    WINDOWERRORS = 0
    MAXDATARCV = 4456
    TI = 30000
    T1 = 3000
    T2 = 200
    MAXIN = 1
    MAXOUT = 1
    NETBIOSTIMEOUT = 3000
    NETBIOSRETRIES = 1
    NAMECACHE = 17
    PIGGYBACKACKS = 1
    DATAGRAMPACKETS = 2
    PACKETS = 400
    LOOPPACKETS = 1
    PIPELINE = 5
    MAXTRANSMITS = 6
    MINTRANSMITS = 2
    DLCRETRIES = 5

[ODI2NDI_nif]
    DriverName = odi2ndi$
    Bindings = IBMTRDB_nif
    NETADDRESS = "10005ACC46CE"
    TOKEN-RING = "yes"
    TOKEN-RING_SNAP = "no"
    ETHERNET_802.3 = "no"
    ETHERNET_802.2 = "no"
    ETHERNET_II = "no"
    ETHERNET_SNAP = "no"
    TRACE = 0x0

[IBMTRDB_nif]
    DriverName = IBMTRDB$
```

Listing 5.2
(Continued)

An OS/2 LAN Server
PROTOCOL.INI file for
both ODI and NDIS drivers

```
MaxTransmits = 31
MinRcvBuffs = 20
SizWorkBuf = 2048
MulticastNum = 1
EnableTxEofInt = 1
```

PROTOCOL.INI Rules

NDIS only understands PROTOCOL.INI file entries with a particular syntax. If you follow the NDIS rules as you modify an INI file, you'll be assured that the NDIS Protocol Manager (PROTMAN) and the NDIS driver modules will be able to at least parse your changes. The specific keywords and values you use depend on the drivers you load. You'll need to check the documentation that came with your network adapter (for MAC drivers) or your network operating system (for protocol drivers).

NDIS-compliant driver installation software typically uses NIFs (Network Installation Files) to indicate what entries can legally go into the PROTOCOL.INI file. The installation software reads and uses the NIF to know what configuration choices to present to you at installation time. You can explore the NIF with a file browse utility to better understand the parameters for a driver.

Here are the NDIS rules for constructing a PROTOCOL.INI file:

- The name of each protocol or MAC module must appear in brackets ([XYZNetBIOS] in the earlier example), and the name must contain 15 or fewer characters. You can use upper- and lowercase without worrying about case sensitivity; the Protocol Manager converts all entries to uppercase as PROTMAN reads the file into memory.

- The entry *Drivername* = *<device driver name>* is required in sections that describe device driver modules. The Drivername entry defines the name of the the OS/2 or DOS device driver that contains the module. Each network device driver can ask Protocol Manager to let it view the in-memory version of the PROTOCOL.INI file, and the network device driver finds its module section by searching for the appropriate Drivername entry. NDIS also requires a Drivername entry for DOS dynamic modules such as TSRs. Even though the TSR doesn't represent a device driver, the Drivername entry allows the TSR to find pertinent sections of the PROTOCOL.INI file. Incidentally, it's possible for a single device driver name to appear multiple times in a PROTOCOL.INI file. Such multiple mentions of the name occurs if the device driver contains multiple logical modules.

- Protocol modules (but never MAC modules) can optionally have a *Bindings = <module name>* entry in the INI file. When present, the Bindings entry tells the protocol module how to determine which MAC modules the protocol will bind to. You can use this characteristic to reconfigure a protocol to bind a different MAC module, if your protocol supports it. You don't need the Bindings entry if the protocol driver is preconfigured to bind to a particular MAC module, or if the protocol stack will contain only one MAC module and one static protocol module.

- The remainder of the PROTOCOL.INI file consists of keyword = value pairs, with each keyword being 15 or fewer characters. As with the entries already mentioned, Protocol Manager is not case-sensitive. The keyword = value pairs pertain only to the named section in which they appear. Note that you can put spaces on either side of the equal sign if you find the white space makes the INI file more readable; Protocol Manager removes white space surrounding the equal sign as well as trailing white space on each line of text in the file. White space characters are spaces, tabs, and formfeeds. A carriage return and a line feed mark the end of each line.

- One or more parameters follow the equal sign on each line of text. If an entry has no parameters, the equal sign is optional. If there are multiple parameters, you separate the parameters with spaces, tabs, commas, or semicolons. Note that the Protocol Manager doesn't interpret the parameters; only the protocol or MAC module looks at the values you specify. If a parameter is a number, the parameter is treated as a 32-bit signed quantity. You can express numbers in either decimal or hexadecimal format. To indicate a hexadecimal number, prefix the parameter with either *0X* or *0x*, as in *0x0400*. String parameters can be any length. A string parameter begins with a nonnumeric first character or appears inside quotation marks (").

- Lines that have a semicolon in the first column are comment lines. (Few installation programs insert comment lines to explain what they've created for you, but you can add comments later if you want.) Protocol Manager ignores comment lines and lines that are blank.

When Protocol Manager or one of the drivers detects a syntax error in the PROTOCOL.INI file, NDIS mandates that Protocol Manager or the software driver display an error message detailing the exact syntax problem. If possible, the module finding the error should assume a valid (nonfatal) value for the parameter and continue processing. (Note that not all drivers written by all manufacturers of network adapters comply fully with this mandate. You sometimes find modules that die instantly when they discover errors in the PROTOCOL.INI file.)

The PROTMAN Section

One of the sections you might see in a PROTOCOL.INI file is for the Protocol Manager itself. Under the section heading [PROTMAN], you can find Drivername, Dynamic, Priority, and Bindstatus keywords. The string PROTMAN$ (the parameter for the Drivername entry) lets the Protocol Manager locate this section of the file. Here is a sample PROTMAN section:

```
[PROTMAN]
    Drivername = PROTMAN$
    Dynamic = YES or NO
    Priority = prot1, prot2, ...
    Bindstatus = YES or NO
```

All the keywords in the PROTMAN section of the PROTOCOL.INI file are optional. The Dynamic keyword, which defaults to *NO* if not present, specifies whether the Protocol Manager should operate only in static mode. If the parameter for Dynamic is *YES*, Protocol Manager operates in dynamic mode and can support both static and dynamic binding.

The parameter after the Priority keyword is a list of protocol module names. Putting a module's name first in the list gives that module the highest priority, while putting a module last gives the module the lowest priority. For workstations or file servers containing multiple protocols (that is, that multiplex the packets), the network software first offers an incoming LAN packet to the protocol with the highest priority. Subsequent protocols get to look at the LAN packet only if a higher priority protocol doesn't consume the packet. Protocols not mentioned in the Priority list are the last to get a chance to inspect and perhaps consume a packet.

The Bindstatus keyword specifies whether Protocol Manager can optimize memory and is useful primarily only in DOS environments. If the keyword is absent, Protocol Manager doesn't support Bindstatus.

Processing the PROTOCOL.INI File

Under both DOS and OS/2, the operating system loads and initializes the Protocol Manager during the INIT phase of processing the CONFIG.SYS file. Protocol Manager loads first, before any protocol or MAC driver loads. In the DOS environment, Protocol Manager is a file named PROTMAN.DOS. For OS/2, the file is PROTMAN.OS2. The device name in both environments is PROTMAN$. Under DOS, an auxiliary file named PROTMAN.EXE helps Protocol Manager deal with memory optimization. The Protocol Manager device driver component calls this auxiliary PROTMAN.EXE whenever a module invokes the Protocol Manager NDIS primitives BindAndStart and UnbindAndStop. In static mode, which is the mode that OS/2 and LAN Server use, PROTMAN.EXE remains resident after an invocation of BindAndStart.

The Protocol Manager device driver uses a command line parameter to know what directory contains the PROTOCOL.INI file. This directory is usually LANMAN for Microsoft's LAN Manager product and the IBMCOM directory for IBM's LAN Server product. Protocol Manager reads and parses the PROTOCOL.INI file to create an in-memory image. MAC and protocol drivers can use a programming interface detailed by NDIS to see the in-memory configuration entries and set themselves up according to the keywords and parameters the modules find. In the DOS environment, to conserve memory, Protocol Manager builds the in-memory configuration image at the top of real-mode memory. The image remains in high memory (just below the 640K address point on machines with at least 640K of RAM) while Protocol Manager and the MAC and protocol drivers configure themselves. Once Protocol Manager completes the process of binding the MAC and protocol drivers, the configuration image is no longer needed. Under OS/2, this memory conservation technique is unnecessary; Protocol Manager simply frees the configuration image memory at the completion of the binding step.

Under OS/2 and LAN Server, the Protocol Manager operates in static (rather than dynamic binding) mode. In static mode, protocol drivers load once at system initialization time and remain in memory. In dynamic mode, drivers load at the time they're bound by Protocol Manager and (if they offer a dynamic-unload feature) unload if the network software later unbinds them. Protocol drivers that are static-only load during the CONFIG.SYS INIT phase and remain in memory, even if Protocol Manager is in dynamic mode.

The IBMLAN.INI File

Like the PROTOCOL.INI file, the IBMLAN.INI file is a text file you can edit with a text editor. Before you make any changes to the file, however, ensure that you have backup copies of the file that you can revert to in case your changes don't work. In general, you should always run MPTS, the OS/2 LAN Services Installation/Configuration utility, or the LS 4.0 Tuning Assistant to make changes to the IBMLAN.INI file. Use a text editor as a last resort.

Typical section headings within the IBMLAN.INI file include NETWORKS, REQUESTER, MESSENGER, NETLOGON, REPLICATOR, SERVER, and SERVICES. The following sections of this chapter discuss the basic nature of each of these components of the IBMLAN.INI file. For further detail beyond what this book can provide, you should refer to the Performance Tuning manual that comes with the LAN Server product. Also note that the IBMLAN.INI file on your file server will have different entries and different section headings from those presented in the examples below.

The NETWORKS Section

The NETWORKS section typically contains a single entry expressing the network protocol that LAN Server uses to send information through the LAN cable. In the following example, the protocol is NETBEUI. When it begins executing in the computer, the redirector portion of the LAN Server software uses this entry to configure itself. If you want to change the protocol your LAN uses, you should run MPTS.

```
net1 = NETBEUI$,0,LM10,102,175,14
```

The REQUESTER Section

The REQUESTER section of IBMLAN.INI identifies several parameters that LAN Server uses to manage access to the LAN. These parameters, shown in the following example, include the name of the computer, the name of the domain, and a collection of values that control how the components of LAN Server behave. For example, the useallmem entry determines whether 386HPFS should use memory above 16MB, and the charcount parameter sets the number of characters, in bytes, that the requester stores before sending data to a serial device queue.

REQUESTER entry	Brief Description
COMPUTERNAME= Z-SERVER	Network name of this computer
DOMAIN = EVERYONE	Domain name
charcount = 16	Modem buffer character count
chartime = 250	Milliseconds before emptying modem buffer
charwait = 3600	Seconds to wait for a modem to become available
keepconn = 600	Seconds an inactive shared resource connection lives
keepsearch = 600	Seconds an inactive file search request is maintained
maxcmds = 16	Maximum number of concurrent file service operations
maxerrorlog = 100	Maximum error log entries
maxthreads = 10	Maximum threads LAN Server can start

REQUESTER entry	Brief Description
maxwrkcache = 64	Maximum size (KB) of large-transfer buffers
numworkbuf = 15	Number of file service network message buffers
printbuftime = 90	Seconds before truncating a DOS print job
sesstimeout = 45	Seconds before stopping a non-responsive connection
sizworkbuf = 4096	File service buffer size
useallmem = Yes	Whether 386HPFS should use memory above 16MB

WRKSERVICES = MESSENGER

wrknets = NET1

wrkheuristics = 11111111213111111100010 111201112210012111

The wrkheuristics parameter in the IBMLAN.INI file is a set of one-character options for tuning and controlling LAN Server. Most of the options have a value of either 0 or 1, with 0 signifying "off" and 1 signifying "on." Each character controls a different characteristic of LAN Server. The manual titled *LAN Server Network Administrator Reference Volume 2: Performance Tuning* contains more detail regarding wrkheuristics entries. The following explanation of these entries begins numbering the characters at 1.

- Character 1 is the opportunistic locking of files option (default is 1).

- Character 2 specifies performance optimization for batch (CMD) files (default is 1).

- Character 3 controls asynchronous unlock and asynchronous write-unlock:

  - 0 = never

  - 1 = always (default)

  - 2 = only on a LAN Server virtual circuit

- Character 4 controls asynchronous close and asynchronous write-close:

  - 0 = never

- 1 = always (default)

- 2 = only on a LAN Server virtual circuit

- Character 5 determines whether named pipes and serial devices are buffered (default is 1).

- Character 6 controls combined read-lock and write-unlock:

  - 0 = never

  - 1 = always (default)

  - 2 = only on a LAN Server virtual circuit

- Character 7 specifies open and read optimization (default is 1).

- Character 8 is reserved.

- Character 9 controls the use of the chain-send NETBIOS NCB:

  - 0 = never

  - 1 = when a server's buffer is larger than the workstations buffer

  - 2 = always (default)

- Character 10 indicates whether to buffer small read and write requests until the buffer is full:

  - 0 = never

  - 1 = always (default)

  - 2 = only on a LAN Server virtual circuit

- Character 11 specifies buffer mode:

  - 0 = always read buffer size amount of data if the request is smaller than the buffer size and data is being read sequentially

  - 1 = use full buffer if file is open for reading and writing

  - 2 = use full buffer if reading and writing sequentially

  - 3 = buffer all requests smaller than the buffer size (default)

- Character 12 specifies RAW read and RAW write SMB protocols (default is 1).

- Character 13 specifies RAW read-ahead buffer (default is 1).

- Character 14 specifies RAW write-behind buffer (default is 1).

- Character 15 specifies read multiplexing SMB protocols (default is 1).

- Character 16 specifies write multiplexing SMB protocols (default is 1).

- Character 17 specifies use of big buffers for large (non-RAW) reads (default is 1).

- Character 18 specifies same-size read-ahead or read-to-sector boundary (default is 1).

- Character 19 specifies same-size small record write-behind or write-to-sector boundary (default is 0).

- Character 20 is reserved and must be 0.

- Character 21 specifies how pipes and devices are flushed (emptied) on a DosBufReset or DosClose operation:

    - 0 = flush only files and devices opened by the caller. Wait until flushed. Wait for confirmation before processing with other tasks (default).

    - 1 = flush only files and devices opened by the caller. Flush only once. Do not wait for confirmation.

    - 2 = flush all files and all input and output of short-term pipes and devices. Wait until flushed.

    - 3 = flush all files and all input and output of short-term pipes and devices. Flush only once.

    - 4 = flush all files and all input and output of all pipes and devices. Wait until flushed.

    - 5 = flush all files and all input and output of all pipes and devices. Flush only once.

- Character 22 specifies encryption of passwords (default is 1).

- Character 23 controls log entries for multiple occurrences of an error:

    - 0 = log all occurrences (default)

    - 1–9 = limit occurrences that are logged (1–9 defines size of table used to track errors)

- Character 24 indicates whether to buffer all files opened with deny-write sharing mode (default is 1).

- Character 25 directs LAN Server to buffer all files opened with the read-only attribute set (default is 1).

- Character 26 specifies read-ahead when opening a program file for execution (default is 1).

- Character 27 specifies how to handle the interrupt (Ctrl-C) keypress:
  - 0 = allow no interrupts
  - 1 = allow interrupts only on long-term operations
  - 2 = always allow interrupts (default)
- Character 28 forces correct open mode when creating files on a server (default is 1).
- Character 29 specifies NETBIOS NoAcknowledgement mode:
  - 0 = NoAck disabled
  - 1 = NoAck set on send only (default)
  - 2 = NoAck set on receive only
  - 3 = NoAck set on send and receive
- Character 30 specifies whether to send data along with SMB write-block RAW requests (default is 1).
- Character 31 controls whether LAN Server displays a message when the requester logs an error:
  - 0 = never
  - 1 = on write-fault errors only (no time out) (default)
  - 2 = on write-fault and internal errors only (no time out)
  - 3 = on all errors (no time out)
  - 4 = reserved
  - 5 = on write-fault errors only (time out)
  - 6 = on write-fault and internal errors only (time out)
  - 7 = on all errors (time out)
- Character 32 is reserved.
- Character 33 controls the behavior of DosBufReset on a redirected file (not pipes or devices). DosBufReset handles the data in the buffer as follows:
  - 0 = changed data in the buffer was sent from the requester to the server. The server has written the data to disk.
  - 1 = changed data in the buffer was sent from the requester to the server. The server has not yet written the data to disk.
  - 2 = DosBufReset was ignored (default)

- Character 34 specifies the time interval for performing logon validation from the domain controller:
    - 0 = 5 seconds
    - 1 = 15 seconds (default)
    - 2 = 30 seconds
    - 3 = 45 seconds
    - 4 = 60 seconds
    - 5 = 90 seconds
    - 6 = 2 minutes
    - 7 = 4 minutes
    - 8 = 8 minutes
    - 9 = 15 minutes
- Character 35 controls date validation between workstations and the server:
    - 0 = PC LAN Program date format (default)
    - 1 = MS NET date format
    - 2 = no validation; assume date is correct
- Character 36 determines the free disk space reported to DOS and Windows applications:
    - 0 = return true value (default)
    - 1 = return a value less than two gigabytes
- Character 37 controls time and date synchronization with the domain controller at logon (default is 1).
- Character 38 controls the type of verification for the LAN Server logon:
    - 0 = no verification
    - 1 = verify against local NET.ACC
    - 2 = verify against domain NET.ACC (default)
- Character 39 specifies how LAN Server displays warning messages for a LAN Server logon:
    - 0 = do not display warning messages
    - 1 = display all warning messages (default)

- 2 = do not display LAN Server specific warning messages
- Character 40 specifies how LAN Server buffers files opened in compatibility mode:
  - 0 = buffer only files opened for read access in compatibility mode
  - 1 = buffer all files opened in compatibility mode (default)
- Character 41 allows or disallows multiple logons by a person in the same domain (default is 1).

The MESSENGER Section

The two parameters in the MESSENGER section specify the name of the message log file and the size, in bytes, of the buffer used to receive network messages. The *logfile* parameter specifies a file name within the \IBMLAN\ LOGS subdirectory for the message log. The *sizmessbuf* parameter supplies the size of the buffer.

```
logfile = messages.log
sizmessbuf = 4096
```

The NETLOGON Section

The NETLOGON section provides LAN Server with directions that control how LAN Server makes backup copies of your NET.ACC file. The NET.ACC file contains logon account information, group information, shared resource information, and other important network data.

The *scripts* parameter specifies the path where the Netlogon service searches for the logon scripts. The *update* parameter specifies whether to synchronize the Netlogon service with the primary domain controller at the next pulse. The pulse parameter value gives the number of seconds between backup copy operations.

```
SCRIPTS = D:\IBMLAN\REPL\IMPORT\SCRIPTS
pulse = 60
update = yes
```

The REPLICATOR Section

The REPLICATOR section of the IBMLAN.INI file provides directions to LAN Server that control how often you want LAN Server to automatically make backup copies of your files and directories. LAN Server can replicate files and directories onto another file server or onto a workstation. The server sending the data is an exporter, while the workstation or server receiving the data is an importer. You can have any number of exporters and importers in a domain. A server can be both an exporter and an importer, while a workstation can only be an importer.

In the REPLICATOR section, you designate an export path on the exporter (server) and an import path on the importer. The replicator service within LAN Server monitors the specified export directory. When someone adds, deletes, or changes a directory or file in the export path, the replicator service notifies the importer PC of the operation and sends the importer information that lets the importer PC repeat the operation.

The *replicate* parameter specifies whether the workstation is an importer, an exporter, or both. The parameter can have one of the following values:

- Import

- Export

- Both

If a server is an exporter, the value can be export or both. If a server is an importer, the value can be import or both.

The *importpath* parameter specifies the path of the top-level import directory on the PC acting as importer. LAN Server replicates files into the directory structure underneath the path specified by this parameter. The logon parameter specifies the logon account that the replicator service uses to log on (if no one is already logged on at that machine). The *password* parameter specifies the password that the Replicator service uses to connect to the exporter when no one is logged on at the importer.

The *tryuser* parameter specifies whether the importer should automatically try to log on to the exporter even if a person is already logged on at the workstation. If the parameter is *yes*, the importer tries connecting to the exporter using the logon account and password of the person logged on at the importer PC. The attempt succeeds if the logon account has read and attributes permissions for the directories to be replicated. If the logon attempt fails, no replication takes place until the person logs off.

The *interval* and *pulse* parameters indicate how often the data replication operation should take place.

```
replicate = IMPORT
IMPORTPATH = D:\IBMLAN\REPL\IMPORT
tryuser = yes
logon = GUEST
password =
interval = 5
pulse = 3
```

The SERVER Section

The SERVER section provides parameters and options that control the behavior of the file server component of LAN Server. The entries in this section work in a manner similar to those in the REQUESTER section, discussed earlier in this chapter.

The parameters in the SERVER section establish values that affect the server functions. If these parameters are set too high, the server may fail to start and an error message indicating the possible configuration problems will be displayed. Some of the parameters in the SERVER section of the IBMLAN.INI file work differently for the 386-HPFS server. The descriptions for all the SERVER section parameters are provided in this section. For descriptions of the parameters that function differently for a 386-HPFS server, see Server Section - Advanced Package Function.

NOTE. *When the Advanced server accesses a FAT file system partition, the Advanced server functions like the Entry server.*

The SERVER section parameters that function differently on a server running 386HPFS are maxconnections, maxlocks, maxopens, maxsearches, numbigbuf, and srvheuristics.

SERVER entry	Brief description
alertnames =	Logon accounts to receive server error messages
auditing = no	Which events, if any, to audit
autodisconnect = 120	Minutes before disconnecting inactive workstations
maxusers = 101	Maximum concurrent logons on a 386HPFS server
guestacct = guest	An optional general-usage logon account
accessalert = 5	Alert threshold for resource-access attempts
alertsched = 5	Minutes between checking for alert conditions
diskalert = 5000	Minimum free disk space (K) before alert sent
erroralert = 5	Error count at which server sends an alert message
logonalert = 5	Logon attempt threshold for alert messages
maxauditlog = 100	Maximum size (K) of the audit log file

SERVER entry	**Brief description**
maxchdevjob = 6	Maximum concurrent serial device requests
maxchdevq = 2	Maximum serial device queues
maxchdevs = 2	Maximum shared serial devices
maxconnections = 300	Maximum connections to shared resources
maxlocks = 64	Maximum concurrent file locks
maxopens = 256	Maximum files/devices the server can open
maxsearches = 350	Maximum concurrent directory searches
maxsessopens = 256	Maximum shared resources a requester can use
maxsessreqs = 50	Maximum requests for shared resource operations
maxsessvcs = 1	Maximum virtual circuits a workstation can create
maxshares = 192	Maximum resources the server can share
netioalert = 5	Network error threshold for sending alerts
numbigbuf = 12	Number of 64K buffers for large data requests
numfiletasks = 1	Number of concurrent file/print server processes
numreqbuf = 250	Number of server buffers for workstation requests
sizreqbuf = 4096	Size of each server buffer
srvanndelta = 3000	Milliseconds used to vary handshaking interval
srvannounce = 60	Seconds between server/workstation handshaking
SRVSERVICES = NETLOGON,LS SERVER,ALERTER, GENALERT,NET RUN	
srvnets = NET1	
autopath = D	
srvheuristics = 1111014111131100133 11	

Like the wrkheuristics parameter discussed earlier in this chapter, the srvheuristics parameter sets a variety of server fine-tuning options. Each character of srvheuristics controls a different aspect of LAN Server.

- Character 1, the first digit of srvheuristics, controls opportunistic locking of files (default is 1).

- Character 2 controls read-ahead when the requester is performing sequential access:

  - 0 = do not use read-ahead

  - 1 = use single read-ahead thread (default)

  - 2 = use asynchronous read-ahead thread

- Character 3 specifies write-behind (default is 1).

- Character 4 specifies use of the chain-send NETBIOS NCB (default is 1).

- Character 5 turns on or off checking of incoming SMBs for validity (default is 0).

- Character 6 controls support for FCB opens (default is 1).

- Character 7 sets the priority of server (default is 4); 0 is highest priority, while 9 is lowest priority.

- Character 8 automatically allocates additional memory for directory searches (default is 1).

- Character 9 controls whether audit log records get written on a timed basis (default is 1) by the server watchdog process.

- Character 10 specifies full buffering when a file is opened with deny-write sharing mode (default is 1).

- Character 11 sets the interval for the running of the server watchdog process:

  - 0 = 5 seconds

  - 1 = 10 seconds (default)

  - 2 = 15 seconds

  - 3 = 20 seconds

  - 4 = 25 seconds

  - 5 = 30 seconds

  - 6 = 35 seconds

  - 7 = 40 seconds

- • 8 = 45 seconds

- • 9 = 50 seconds

- Character 12 controls compatibility-mode opens of certain types of files by translating them to sharing mode opens with a mode of deny-none:

  - • 0 = always use compatibility-mode opens

  - • 1 = use deny-none sharing mode for read-only access to programs

  - • 2 = use deny-none sharing mode for read-only access to programs

  - • 3 = use deny-none sharing mode on all compatibility-mode opens (default)

- Character 13 allows or disallows the use of a second NETBIOS session by DOS LAN Services workstations for printer requests (default is 1).

- Character 14 indicates the number of 64K buffers to be used for read-ahead (default is 1).

- Character 15 controls the conversion of incoming path specifications into most basic format (default is 0).

- Character 16 specifies various combinations of Oplock Timeout and NETBIOS Acknowledgment Timeout (default is 0):

  - • 0 = 35 second Oplock Timeout; 34 second NETBIOS Acknowledgment Timeout

  - • 1 = 70 second Oplock Timeout; 69 second NETBIOS Acknowledgment Timeout

  - • 2 = 140 second Oplock Timeout; 127 second NETBIOS Acknowledgment Timeout

  - • 3 = 210 second Oplock Timeout; 127 second NETBIOS Acknowledgment Timeout

  - • 4 = 280 second Oplock Timeout; 127 second NETBIOS Acknowledgment Timeout

  - • 5 = 350 second Oplock Timeout; 127 second NETBIOS Acknowledgment Timeout

  - • 6 = 420 second Oplock Timeout; 127 second NETBIOS Acknowledgment Timeout

  - • 7 = 490 second Oplock Timeout; 127 second NETBIOS Acknowledgment Timeout

- - 8 = 560 second Oplock Timeout; 127 second NETBIOS Acknowledgment Timeout
  - 9 = 640 second Oplock Timeout; no NETBIOS Acknowledgment Timeout
- Character 17 controls the validation of IOCTL API calls (default is 1).
- Character 18 specifies how long the server maintains unused, dynamic big buffers before freeing the buffer memory:
  - 0 = 0 seconds
  - 1 = 1 second
  - 2 = 10 seconds
  - 3 = 1 minute (default)
  - 4 = 5 minutes
  - 5 = 10 minutes
  - 6 = 20 minutes
  - 7 = 40 minutes
  - 8 = 1 hour
  - 9 = indefinitely
- Character 19 specifies how long the server waits after failing to allocate a big buffer before trying again:
  - 0 = 0 seconds
  - 1 = 1 second
  - 2 = 10 seconds
  - 3 = 1 minute (default)
  - 4 = 5 minutes
  - 5 = 10 minutes
- Character 20 controls the use of RAW read and RAW write SMB protocols (default is 1).
- Character 21 specifies whether the server responds to announcement requests (default is 1).

The SERVICES Section

The SERVICES section identifies the location of the LAN Server program files that provide the various services on the file server. Each entry gives the path of the executable program file for that named service.

```
alerter = services\alerter.exe
  dcdbrepl = services\dcdbrepl.exe
  genalert = services\genalert.exe
  lsserver = services\lsserver.exe
  messenger = services\msrvinit.exe
  netlogon = services\netlogon.exe
  netrun = services\runservr.exe
  replicator = services\replicat.exe
  requester = services\wksta.exe
  server = services\netsvini.exe
  timesource = services\timesrc.exe
```

■ Managing the Network

This chapter began by discussing some of the difficulties a LAN administrator faces as he or she works to keep LAN hardware and software running smoothly. A LAN administrator might use a cable tester to determine why a workstation can't connect to a file server. A protocol analyzer can produce LAN traffic statistics to help solve performance and other problems. However, LAN Server includes some tools the administrator can use to determine the nature of LAN problems. These tools can form the administrator's first line of defense against network failures.

Monitoring Logons, Resources, and Connections

Various versions of the NET command—NET WHO, NET SHARE, NET FILE, NET STATUS, and NET STATISTICS—can help you easily monitor the health of your LAN Server network. The NET WHO command displays a list of logon accounts currently connected to a file server. NET SHARE shows the resources a server is currently sharing. NET FILE reveals which files the server has currently open on behalf of the workstations on the LAN. NET STATUS and NET STATISTICS provide information about how the server is configured and how much work the server has performed.

You can type these commands at an OS/2 command line prompt; or, if you prefer, you can create program object icons on your OS/2 desktop that let you run these commands by double-clicking the mouse. To automate the NET WHO command, you can use the Program template in the Templates folder to create a program object that executes a batch file program. You might name the batch file NETWHO.CMD. Use a text editor to insert the following lines of text in the NETWHO.CMD file:

```
@echo off
NET WHO
pause
```

Each time you double-click your new Net Who program object, you'll see a display similar to the following:

```
Users on Domain EVERYONE

                                    Time since
User ID              Requester      logon    Comment
-----------------------------------------------------------------------
BARRY                IBMPS          02:33:05  Barry's primary logon acct
USERID               Z-SERVER       05:24:30  Default User ID
The command completed successfully.
```

Similarly, you can construct a program object that runs the following batch file program, which you might name NETSHARE.CMD:

```
@echo off
NET SHARE
pause
```

Typing NET SHARE at an OS/2 command prompt (or double-clicking on the program object that runs your new NETSHARE.CMD batch file program) gives you a list of shared resource assignments at the file server computer:

```
Netname      Resource                      Remark
----------------------------------------------------------------------
IPC$                                       Remote IPC
ADMIN$       D:\IBMLAN                      Remote Admin
A$           A:\                            Drive Share for Admin Use
B$           B:\                            Drive Share for Admin Use
C$           C:\                            Drive Share for Admin Use
D$           D:\                            Drive Share for Admin Use
E$           E:\                            Drive Share for Admin Use
F$           F:\                            Drive Share for Admin Use
G$           G:\                            Drive Share for Admin Use
I$           I:\                            Drive Share for Admin Use
IBMLAN$      D:\IBMLAN                      OS/2 LAN Server root
DRIVE-C      C:\                            Z-Server drive C:
DRIVE-D      D:\                            Z-Server drive D:
DRIVE-E      E:\                            Z-Server drive E:
DRIVE-F      F:\                            Z-Server drive F:
DRIVE-G      G:\                            Z-Server drive G:
DRIVE-I      I:\                            Z-Server drive I:
NETLOGON     D:\IBMLAN\REPL\IMPORT\SCRIPTS  Domain controller share
```

```
LASERJET     LPT1                      Spooled  Laserjet printer
The command completed successfully.
The batch file program you might want to create to run the NET FILE command
should contain the following lines of text:
@echo off
:again
NET FILE
goto again
```

Double-clicking the NET FILE program object will repeatedly produce a display similar to the following:

```
ID        Path                              UserID          # Locks
- - - - - - - - - - - - - - - - - - - - - - - - - - - - - - - - - - - - - - - - - - - - - -
1         I:\TEMP\PLAN-A.DOC                BARRY           0
The command completed successfully.
```

Each time the batch file program issues the NET FILE command, NET FILE shows which files are currently open. The display will change from time to time as workstations open and close different files on the file server. You can press Ctrl-C to end the running of the batch file program.

You might also create a batch file program that runs the NET STATUS command. When you or your batch file program issue NET STATUS, the command produces a display similar to the following:

```
Server Name                    \\Z-SERVER
Server Comment
Send admin alerts to

Software version               IBM Server 4.00
Server Level                   Unlimited Server
Server is active on            NET1 (002009102F05)
OS/2 LAN Server root           D:\IBMLAN

Server hidden                  No


Auditing enabled               No

Max. Logged On Users           101
Max. resources shared          204
Max. connections to resources  300
Max. open files on server      256
Max. open files per session    256
Max. file locks                64

Access checking interval (min) 5
Access thresholds
Network I/O errors             5
Password violations            5
Access violations              5
```

```
System error                 5
Disk error (K)               5000

Idle session time (min)      120
Max. audit-log size (K)      100

Number of network buffers    250
Network buffer size          4096
Number of big buffers        12
```

```
Netname    Resource                      Remark
--------------------------------------------------------------------
IPC$                                     Remote IPC
ADMIN$     D:\IBMLAN                      Remote Admin
A$         A:\                            Drive Share for Admin Use
B$         B:\                            Drive Share for Admin Use
C$         C:\                            Drive Share for Admin Use
D$         D:\                            Drive Share for Admin Use
E$         E:\                            Drive Share for Admin Use
F$         F:\                            Drive Share for Admin Use
G$         G:\                            Drive Share for Admin Use
I$         I:\                            Drive Share for Admin Use
IBMLAN$    D:\IBMLAN                      OS/2 LAN Server root
DRIVE-C    C:\                            Z-Server drive C:
DRIVE-D    D:\                            Z-Server drive D:
DRIVE-E    E:\                            Z-Server drive E:
DRIVE-F    F:\                            Z-Server drive F:
DRIVE-G    G:\                            Z-Server drive G:
DRIVE-I    I:\                            Z-Server drive I:
NETLOGON   D:\IBMLAN\REPL\IMPORT\SCRIPTS  Domain controller share
LASERJET   LPT1                  Spooled  Laserjet printer
The command completed successfully.
```

The NET STATISTICS SERVER command, which you can also use to monitor the ongoing health of your file server, displays information similar to the following:

```
Server Statistics for \\Z-SERVER

Statistics since 12-11-94 05:10pm

Sessions accepted          2
Sessions timed-out         0
Sessions errored-out       0

Kilobytes sent             582
Kilobytes received         217

Mean response time (msec)  1874
```

```
System errors                     Ø
Permission violations             Ø
Password violations               Ø

Files accessed                    37
Comm devices accessed             Ø
Print jobs spooled                2

Times buffers exhausted
   Big buffers                    Ø
   Request buffers                Ø
The command completed successfully.
```

Inspecting Log Files

You have two already created program objects in your LAN Server folder
for monitoring the log files that LAN Server maintains. The LAN Server
Audit Log Utility, shown in Figure 5.22, produces a nicely formatted list of
the entries in your file server's audit log. Note that the list will be empty if
you haven't turned auditing on for any of the file server's shared resources.
The list shows the User ID (logon account) associated with the audited
event, Event, Date, and Time, where Event is a phrase that identifies the reason the item is in the list.

The LAN Server Error Log Utility, shown in Figure 5.23, displays the
contents of the file server's error log. You should form the habit of inspecting
the error log, either with the Error Log Utility or the NET ERROR command, from time to time. The most recent entries in the error log can help
you pinpoint problems on your network. The Error Log Utility shows col-
umns labeled Program, Date, Time, and Message, where Program is the
LAN Server component that reported the error and Message identifies
which error occurred.

If you prefer LAN Server's command line interface, you might forego
the Error Log Utility and simply type NET ERROR at an OS/2 command
line prompt. The display from the NET ERROR command will resemble the
following sample error log information:

```
REQUESTER          3192                 Ø4-13-94 1Ø:39pm
NET3192:  An SMB error occurred on connection to \\GATEWAY\DRIVE-C.  The SMB
header is the data.
   FF 53 4D 42 81 Ø2 ØØ Ø5 ØØ 88 ØØ ØØ ØØ ØØ ØØ ØØ
   ØØ ØØ ØØ ØØ ØØ ØØ ØØ ØØ Ø2 2Ø 19 ØØ Ø1
   ØØ ØØ ØØ ØØ ØØ ØØ ØØ ØØ ØØ ØØ ØØ Ø
REQUESTER          319Ø                 Ø4-18-94 Ø9:Ø6pm
NET319Ø:  A NetWksta internal error has occurred:
```

Figure 5.22

The Audit Log Utility

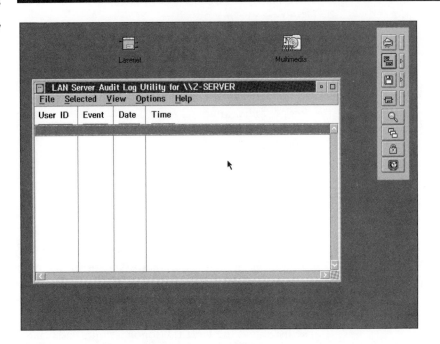

Figure 5.23

The Error Log Utility

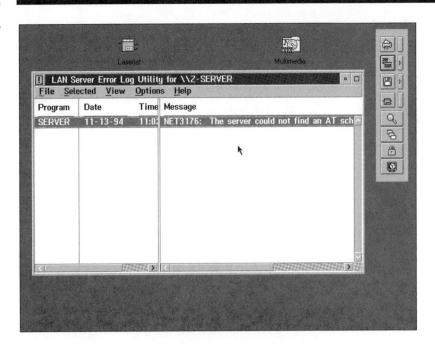

```
  CloseRef: ActiveCnt going negative!.
    CØ Ø6                                                         ..
REQUESTER              3114                 Ø4-18-94 Ø9:Ø6pm
NET3114:  Some entries in the error log were lost because of a buffer
overflow.
REQUESTER              3191                 Ø5-Ø4-94 Ø8:57pm
NET3191:  The redirector is out of a resource:  SMB(NumWorkBuf).
    ØØ 12 ØØ 12 Ø4 ØØ ØC 11 ØØ ØØ ØØ ØØ ØØ ØØ Ø
    ØØ ØØ B4 FF ØØ ØØ Ø1 ØØ Ø1 ØØ                            ..........
REQUESTER              3191                 Ø5-Ø4-94 Ø8:57pm
NET3191:  The redirector is out of a resource:  maxcmds.
    34 38                                                    48
REQUESTER              3193                 Ø6-Ø6-94 Ø2:24am
NET3193:  A virtual circuit error occurred on the session to GATEWAY
The NCB command and return code are the data.
    96 18                                                       ..
REQUESTER              3194                 Ø8-2Ø-94 1Ø:25am
NET3194:  A stalled session to GATEWAY        is being disconnected.
The command completed successfully.
```

Tuning and Configuring LAN Server

The LAN Server 4.0 Tuning Assistant can help you make adjustments to your LAN Server configuration (including the IBMLAN.INI file). When you double-click on the Tuning Assistant program object in the LAN Server folder, you see the settings notebook illustrated in Figure 5.24. The first tab, labeled Server, displays information about the file server. You see Server Name, Domain Name, Server Type, Server Software Package Type, File System Type, and Server Hardware data. You can click the Setting, Supports, and Application tabs across the bottom of the settings notebook to reveal more information. The tabs across the bottom are subcategories of the main Server tab (which appears on the right).

Figure 5.25 shows the display when you choose the Setting subcategory tab. On the Setting subcategory page, you can specify such information as the number of DOS LAN Requesters that connect to this file server, the number of DOS LAN Requesters with Windows that connect to the server, the number of OS/2 Requesters, the number of home directories, the count of directory and printer shared resources, the number of additional servers in the domain, and the number of LAN-attached printers.

Part 3 of the Assumptions tab, shown in Figure 5.26, contains parameters you can adjust to reflect your best estimate of the file server's computer resources that workstations consume. These parameters include NetBIOS command counts, the maximum number of file lock operations as a fraction of the number of file open operations, the number of file opens per DOS LAN Requester, the number of file opens per DOS LAN Requester with Windows, and the maximum number of file opens per OS/2 Requester.

Figure 5.24

The Server tab of the
Tuning Assistant settings
notebook

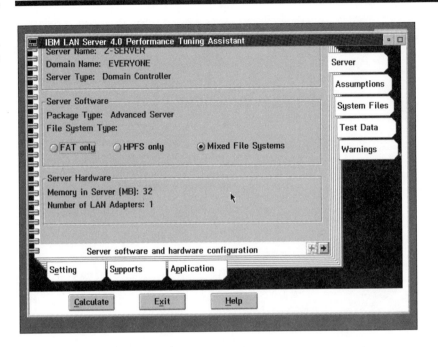

Figure 5.25

The Setting subcategory
for the Server tab

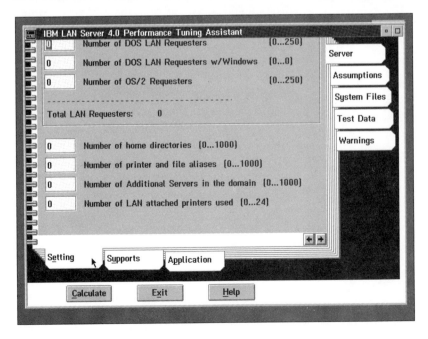

Figure 5.26

Part 3 of the
Assumptions tab of the
Tuning Assistant settings
notebook

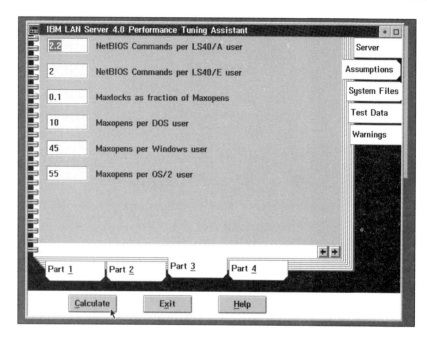

When you've entered information onto the different tabs and subcategories of the Tuning Assistant's settings notebook, you can click the Calculate button at the bottom of the settings notebook to cause Tuning Assistant to modify the file server's CONFIG.SYS, IBMLAN.INI, PROTOCOL.INI, and HPFS386.INI files. For safety's sake, Tuning Assistant puts backup copies of these files in the IBMLAN\BACKUP directory. Note also that you can view both the current contents of and Tuning Assistant's proposed changes to these files by clicking the System Files tab of the notebook. After you use the Calculate button, you'll need to stop LAN Server, shut down OS/2, and reboot your file server computer for the changes to take effect.

■ Summary

This chapter helped you understand how to set up and administer LAN Server at the file server computer. You learned how to manage logon accounts, groups, and shared resources. You explored rights and permissions. You covered the PROTOCOL.INI and IBMLAN.INI files. And you considered ways to manage a LAN Server network.

In the next chapter, we'll turn our attention to accessing the network from a workstation computer.

- *Sharing Applications, Files, Modems, and Printers
- LAN Server Commands
- Using DOS Workstations
- Running Windows on Workstations
- Using OS/2 Workstations

6

Working with LAN Server

IN THIS CHAPTER, YOU BEGIN USING YOUR NETWORK TO SHARE resources. You learn how your PC behaves differently on the network, as a workstation. Whether your workstation runs DOS, DOS-and-Windows, or OS/2, this chapter explains how to log on, log off, assign drive letters to shared drives, run network commands, and share a printer.

DOS-based computers constitute the majority of workstations on local area networks. Much of the LAN Server designers' efforts have gone into making DOS-based access of file servers as transparent as possible. However, if you use Microsoft Windows on your DOS-based computer, your view of the LAN will be different. If you use OS/2's capability to give you both multiple DOS and multiple OS/2 sessions, your view also will be different. This chapter explains how to access LAN Server from various kinds of workstations.

■ Sharing Applications, Files, Modems, and Printers

Once you log on to a LAN Server domain, you use NET USE, or LAN Server's graphical interface, to assign drive letters to shared resources. Depending on how the network administrator has set up the file server's shared resources, you may find that your workstation's new drive letter refers to an entire server disk drive or only a directory. The administrator decides the extent to which the file server's resources are shared. The distinction between sharing an entire disk drive and just a directory is invisible from a workstation.

NOTE. *Many LAN administrators set up aliases at the file server and then configure workstations to automatically connect to those aliases. You may find your workstation connects to the file server when you log on, without your having to establish connections yourself. Check with your administrator.*

The following is an example of a NET USE command that sets up drive F. The network administrator has published the shared resource with the name NORTHEAST on the server named \\SALES.

```
NET USE F: \\SALES\NORTHEAST
```

You also issue a form of the NET USE command to delete, or cancel, the use of a drive letter. The same NET USE command that sets up your network drive letters also redirects your printed output to the LAN printer. In the following two examples, the first establishes a connection to a shared printer resource and the second deletes that connection. The name of the shared printer resource is LASERJET on the file server named Z-SERVER.

```
NET USE LPT1 \\Z-SERVER\LASERJET
NET USE LPT1 /D
```

After you establish the network drive letters your workstation can use, you work with your applications as you ordinarily would. Files on the LAN now are available to the computer programs you run, as long as you have permission to use those files. If you do not have permission to even read a particular file, you cannot access that file at all. Be aware that you may have read permission but not write permission on some files. This means that you cannot save new data in that file. If you encounter strange error messages from the applications you run, you may want to visit your network administrator to make sure that your permissions are correct and appropriate.

A DOS or DOS-plus-Windows workstation can access shared server's hard disks, printers, and CD-ROM drives. An OS/2 workstation, running a native OS/2 communications program, can additionally access shared modems.

■ LAN Server Commands

Whether you're using DOS or OS/2, you can view or change your workstation's relationship to the network by running the NET command with parameters at a command line prompt. The following NET command parameters work at a DOS prompt, a DOS session prompt from within Windows, and an OS/2 command line session (windowed or full-screen) from within OS/2.

NET ADMIN	Begins remote execution of a command (or starts a command line session) on a file server. Your privilege level at the server must be "administrator" to use this command.
NET ALIAS	Shows aliases for a particular domain, or displays information about a particular network alias.
NET CONFIG	Reveals your current requester settings.
NET DASD	Shows disk space directory limits, if the LAN administrator imposed such limits.
NET HELP	Supplies information about commands and error messages.
NET LOG	Begins or ends the sending of a message to a file or printer; also can display information on messaging logging.
NET LOGOFF	Terminates your file server session(s) in a domain.
NET LOGON	Creates a session between you and the file servers in a domain.

NET NAME	Adds or deletes a message name; shows a list of message names.
NET PASS-WORD	Lets you choose a new password.
NET PRINT	Shows jobs in print queues and lets you control those print jobs.
NET SEPA-RATOR	Displays separator page information, or lets you change the separator page configuration.
NET SEND	Sends messages to other workstations on the network.
NET START	Starts the Requester, Peer, Messenger, or Netpopup service on your workstation.
NET STOP	Stops a Requester, Peer, Messenger, or Netpopup service on your workstation.
NET TIME	Sets your workstation's clock according to the clock of a file server running LAN Server's Time service.
NET USE	Connects to or disconnects from a shared resource; displays information about current connections to shared resources.
NET VER	Displays the requester version.
NET VIEW	Displays a list of file server computers; lists shared resources for a specific file server.
NET WHO	Lists accounts logged on in a domain; displays information about accounts.

■ Using DOS Workstations

LAN Server gives a DOS-based workstation two ways to view and modify its network configuration: the command-line NET utility and a NETGUI utility. NETGUI provides a graphical user interface similar to that of Windows, but without the need to run Windows. You run the non-Windows graphical interface by typing NETGUI at a DOS prompt, and you work with NETGUI in much the same way as explained for Windows in the section entitled "Using Windows to Access the LAN" later in this chapter.

Your DOS-based computer can access extra drive letters and print to the LAN printer. In addition, you have new commands and utilities you can run. Some of the DOS commands behave differently on a LAN. Your applications may have less memory in which to run. The DOS PATH statement for your computer almost certainly will change as a result of your connection to the LAN. The LAN Server installation process inserted and changed entries in your CONFIG.SYS file because your computer is attached to the LAN.

The next sections of this chapter address these and other issues for DOS-based computers.

Drive Letters

At boot time, DOS assigns drive letters whose values depend on the number of floppy-disk drives, number of hard-disk drives, and number of DOS-formatted partitions on those hard-disk drives. DOS always reserves drives A and B for floppies, even if you do not have a drive B. DOS assigns drive C to your first hard disk. DOS uses drive D, E, and other drive letters to refer to your second hard disk, your additional DOS partitions, and your additional floppy-disk drives.

The network operating system (NOS) also assigns drive letters, but not until you perform the login sequence. The LASTDRIVE parameter, which you may place in your CONFIG.SYS file, influences how some network operating systems assign drive letters. In LAN Server, LASTDRIVE encompasses both local and network drives. You typically see an entry such as the following in the CONFIG.SYS file of a DOS workstation on a LAN Server network:

```
LASTDRIVE=Z
```

You may have applications that write to the root directory of the current drive. On a LAN, you may not have sufficient rights to the root directory of the file server's disk to run such applications (not to mention the confusion that would reign if the application put such files in the root directory for every person on the LAN).

NOTE. *With some network operating systems, you can assign a drive letter to a file server disk drive that is the same as that of a local disk drive. If you do this, your local disk drive becomes "invisible," and you cannot use the files on that disk drive until you undo the overlapped drive letter mapping.*

The LAN Printer

In Chapter 2, "Looking at Local Area Networks," you learned the basics of LAN printer sharing. From your workstation's point of view, you print to the LAN printer in almost the same way you would have printed to a locally attached printer. Your computer's printer ports are LPT1, LPT2, and LPT3. If you have a locally attached printer, it probably uses LPT1. In this case, you can assign (redirect) LPT2 to the LAN printer. If you do not have a locally attached printer, you can assign LPT1 to the LAN printer. With most network operating systems, you can assign all three printer ports to one or more LAN printers. You do not have to have a physical parallel printer port on your computer to use the LAN printer. The network operating system enables you to pretend that you have an LPT1 port.

With LAN Server, you use the NET USE command to share a networked printer. The printer redirection command makes your applications think they are printing to a real printer. The application software does not know that the print data becomes LAN messages that transfer to the server, into the print queue, before the server's spooler modules print the data. The following is an example of a LAN Server printer redirection command:

```
NET USE LPT1 \\Z-SERVER\LASERJET
```

where LPT1 is the printer port to assign, Z-SERVER names the file server to which the printer is attached, and LASERJET specifies the shared printer.

Once you have sent a printout to the LAN printer, you have not lost control of the data. With LAN Server, before the print queue entry actually prints, you can manipulate the queue entry. You can delete (cancel) the entry, or you can hold it for later processing. You can modify some of the characteristics of the queue entry, such as how many copies you want printed. You cannot change the contents of the printout, however.

NOTE. *Just as with drive letter assignments, you can tell the network operating system to override the printer port assignments that DOS uses. If you have a locally attached printer on LPT1 and you assign LPT1 to the LAN printer, you lose the use of your local printer until you undo the assignments.*

DOS Utilities

The DOS TSR program SHARE.EXE is especially important on a LAN. The SHARE command enables file sharing. You should run SHARE immediately after logging in. You probably will want to make SHARE part of the BAT file that loads the network software.

As Chapter 2, "Looking at Local Area Networks" points out, the following DOS commands do not work on a file server hard disk across the LAN:

ASSIGN
CHKDSK
DISKCOMP
DISKCOPY
FDISK
FORMAT
LABEL
RECOVER
SYS
UNDELETE
UNFORMAT

The following DOS commands, however, operate on a file server disk just as well as they do on your local hard disk:

ATTRIB
BACKUP
COMP
COPY
FC
RESTORE
SORT
TREE
XCOPY

Memory Constraints

The network software that loads at your workstation is usually a TSR program, or a combination of device drivers (SYS files loaded by statements in the CONFIG.SYS file) and TSRs. If your workstation's CPU chip is an 8088, 8086, or 80286 model, you probably will find that the network software takes up some portion of the 640K of conventional memory in your computer, which leaves less memory in which you can run your application software.

If your workstation uses an 80386 or 80486 CPU chip and if you have more than 1MB or 2MB of RAM, you usually can use a memory manager to load some or all of the network software into upper memory. For example, DOS Version 5.0 and Version 6.x include HIMEM.SYS and EMM386.SYS, two 80386/80486/Pentium memory-managers. Depending on how much conventional memory you need for your applications, you may be able to use these DOS utilities to load TSRs and device drivers into upper memory on your DOS-based computer and thus increase available conventional memory.

Memory Management Terms

The following list of memory management terms will help you understand the different types of PC memory that applications, utilities, and the network software might access.

Conventional memory   The memory directly addressable by an Intel CPU in real mode. The upper boundary is normally the infamous 640K limit, but some memory managers raise that ceiling.

DOS Protected Mode Interface (DPMI)   Developed by Microsoft, DPMI offers functions similar to VCPI but enforces control over extended memory access. Most DOS applications that access additional memory beyond conventional memory use DPMI.

Expanded memory Invented jointly by Lotus, Intel, and Microsoft, expanded memory enables an application to bank-switch RAM, in 16K blocks, from an EMS memory card into conventional or upper memory. (Bank-switching is the mapping of a given page of memory into an address space the application can reach.) The specification is the Lotus/Intel/Microsoft (LIM) Expanded Memory Specification (EMS). Version 4.0 of the EMS is the most recent. On 80386 and 80486 machines, memory managers can, on demand, transform extended memory into expanded memory.

Extended memory Memory above the 1MB threshold, addressable only in protected mode.

Extended Memory Specification (XMS) Also developed by Lotus/Intel/Microsoft, this standard provides a rudimentary means for DOS applications to use portions of extended memory.

High memory area (HMA) The first 64K of extended memory, minus 16 bytes, beginning at the 1MB threshold. Through a quirk in the design of the 80286, 80386, and 80486 CPU chips, it is possible to address these 65,520 bytes in real mode.

Protected mode The 80286, 80386, and 80486 CPU chips can operate in protected mode or real mode. In protected mode, the CPU can address more than 1MB of memory.

Real mode The default mode of Intel CPU chips; the only mode available for 8088 and 8086 CPU chips. In real mode, the CPU can address only up to 1MB of memory.

Upper memory The memory between 640K and 1MB. Video adapters, ROM BIOS chips, hard disk controller ROMs, and network adapters live in this region, but there are holes—upper memory blocks—that some memory managers can map as regular memory.

Virtual Control Program Interface memory (VCPI) Two companies, Quarterdeck Office Systems and Phar Lap Software, developed the VCPI standard to enable DOS applications to share extended memory cooperatively, without conflict. VCPI allows uncontrolled access to memory by any application or utility.

The DOS PATH Statement

Naturally, you will want to extend your DOS PATH statement to enable you to load applications and utilities from network drives as well as from your local hard disk. The PATH statement functions the same on a network, but be aware that the maximum length of the PATH statement is 128 characters. On a large LAN, it is easy to make the mistake of trying to exceed this limit.

STACKS

With DOS Version 3.2 (released at the same time IBM began offering its Token Ring LAN products), it was necessary to insert a special statement in the CONFIG.SYS file that looked like this:

```
STACKS=128,9
```

With DOS Version 3.3 and later, however, this entry is not necessary. You can save a small amount of conventional memory by inserting the following statement into your CONFIG.SYS file:

```
STACKS=0,0
```

CONFIG.SYS and AUTOEXEC.BAT

The workstation installation program will copy files to your computer's hard disk and put statements in your CONFIG.SYS and AUTOEXEC.BAT files to load the network software when you boot your computer. You can put your NET USE statements into a BAT file so that you do not have to retype them each time you reboot. Alternatively, you can instruct DOS LAN Services to always reestablish your connections to shared resources when you log on to the LAN.

The following shows the contents of a typical CONFIG.SYS file for a DOS-based workstation on a LAN Server LAN:

```
DOS=HIGH,UMB
FILES=60
BUFFERS=30
LASTDRIVE=Z
STACKS=9,256
DEVICE=C:\DOS\HIMEM.SYS
DEVICE=C:\DOS\EMM386.EXE X=D000-D3FF NOEMS
DEVICE=C:\DLS\PROTMAN.DOS /i:C:\DLS
DEVICE=C:\DLS\SMCMAC.DOS
DEVICE=C:\DLS\DLSHELP.SYS
SHELL=C:\DOS\COMMAND.COM C:\DOS\ /P
```

The LAN Server installation program inserted the lines that reference PROTMAN.DOS, SMCMAC.DOS, and DLSHELP.SYS into the CONFIG.SYS file. These device drivers allow the requester to access the network adapter and the file server.

The following AUTOEXEC.BAT file is a typical example of one modified by the LAN Server installation program:

```
@ECHO OFF
PROMPT $p$g
SET COMSPEC=C:\DOS\COMMAND.COM
PATH=C:\DLS;C:\WINDOWS;C:\EXCEL;C:\WINWORD;C:\DOS;C:\UTILS;
SET TEMP=C:\TEMP
SET DIRCMD=/OD
SHARE
C:\DLS\NET START
```

The NET START entry, along with the first directory in the PATH statement, are from the LAN Server installation.

The LAN Server installation process installed new files on your workstation, one of which defines the protocols the workstation uses to communicate with the file server. A typical PROTOCOL.INI file, which LAN Server installs in the DLS directory, appears in the following:

```
[network.setup]
version=0x3100
netcard=ibm$w13ew,1,IBM$W13EW
transport=ibm$netbeui,IBM$NETBEUI
lana0=ibm$w13ew,1,ibm$netbeui

[protman]
DriverName=PROTMAN$
PRIORITY=ibm$NETBEUI

[IBM$W13EW]
DriverName=SMCMAC$

[SMC8000W]
Adapters=MS$W13EW
irq=3
iobase=0x280
ramaddress=0xD000

[IBM$NETBEUI]
DriverName=netbeui$
SESSIONS=6
NCBS=12
BINDINGS=IBM$W13EW
LANABASE=0
```

The previous chapter, "Administering LAN Server," contains an explanation of PROTOCOL.INI file entries.

In the DLS directory, LAN Server also installs a NETWORK.INI file that contains information about you and your workstation. The entries in the following example NETWORK.INI file expresses the workstation's computer name, the directory in which DOS LAN Services is installed, your logon account name, your domain, whether you want DOS LAN Services to automatically reestablish your connections to shared resources when you log on, and other information about your network configuration.

```
[network]
computername=IBMPS
lanroot=C:\DLS
autostart=netbeui
guiconfig=0,0,1
username=BARRY
domain=EVERYONE
lslogon=yes
reconnect=yes
passwordcaching=yes

[Password Lists]
BARRY=C:\DLS\BARRY.PWL
```

■ Running Windows on Workstations

Because Windows is an operating environment that you run after you load DOS at your workstation, the information in this chapter about accessing the network from DOS applies equally well to workstations running Windows. Additionally, you need to consider whether you'll install the Windows files on a file server, how to share Windows on a server, printing to a shared printer from within Windows, how Windows behaves differently on a LAN, and other issues.

Installing Windows on a File Server

Windows cannot actually run on the server, but you can store some of its files there. Windows (through the network operating system) transfers these files into local workstation memory as needed. On a LAN, you can store the files that Windows reads (but not the ones it writes to) in a central, public directory on the file server. These files include the executables, fonts, DLLs, and help files. You should store each user's initialization and customization files (the INI files, for example) on the personal computer's local hard disk, or perhaps in a private server directory for each user.

If you have used Microsoft Windows, you know that it requires comput-ers and adapter cards that are extremely compatible with the IBM PC stan-dard. You also know that Windows requires a computer with a certain amount of speed and internal memory. These requirements become key is-sues if you want to integrate Windows with your network.

Keep in mind that Windows executes in the workstation, not in the server. You cannot improve the performance of Windows on a slower per-sonal computer by installing Windows on a high-performance file server. The server only acts as a place to store the files that make up the Windows environment.

Sharing Windows from a Server

Windows reads and writes each user's initialization and customization files frequently as it runs. You can save some local workstation hard-disk space by putting these files on the file server, but performance will suffer. When Win-dows accesses files on the server, the Windows file requests must be redi-rected across the LAN like all other such file requests.

As the LAN becomes easier for people to use, the network administra-tor's job gets harder. This is doubly true for Microsoft Windows on a LAN. If you are (or become) a network administrator, you should document and keep detailed records of the Windows configurations on the LAN.

If you plan to install and run Windows from a shared directory on the LAN, be sure to give all files in this directory a read-only attribute so that every user can access but not write to the files. You can do this with the Win-dows File Manager or with the ATTRIB command at a command line prompt. Most Windows applications files must have read-only status before they can be shared.

Using Windows to Access the LAN

On workstations running Windows, the LAN Server installation process cre-ates a program group named IBM DOS LAN Services, as shown in Figure 6.1. The group contains a DOS LAN Services program, logon and logoff pro-grams, a WinPopup program for receiving messages from other people on the LAN, and other program icons.

If you used the NET LOGON command to log on before starting Win-dows, or if you configured your workstation to log on each time you boot your workstation, you don't need to use the LOGON and LOGOFF programs in the DOS LAN Services program group. If you wish to use the Windows-based LOGON and LOGOFF programs, however, double-click the LOGON icon and enter your logon account name and password, as shown in Figure 6.2. Double-clicking the LOGOFF icon terminates your session with the file server.

Figure 6.1

The DOS LAN Services
program group

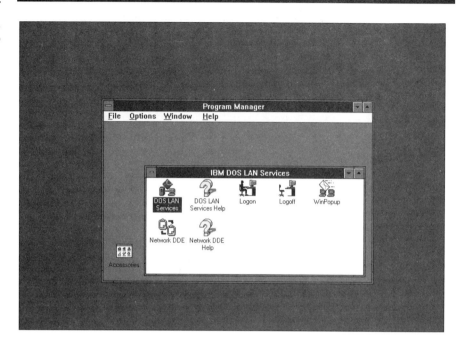

Figure 6.2

Using Windows to log on

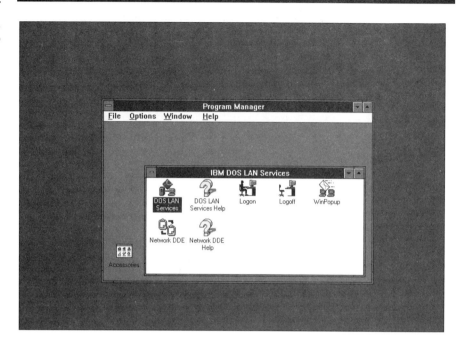

To assign drives to the aliases that the file server makes available to workstations (if the LAN administrator hasn't configured your workstation to automatically connect to those aliases), you use the Drive Connections window shown in Figure 6.3. You open the Drive Connections window by double-clicking the DOS LAN Services program icon and choosing the Connections menu item in the Drives menu. Among other items, the Drive Connections window has a Drive drop-down list box and Network Path text entry box; the Find button next to Network Path allows you to browse a list of network aliases as you assign drive letters. Once you type the name of the alias in the Network Path text entry box or use the Find button, click the Connect button to establish the connection. If you wish to always connect to the shared resource, click Reconnect at Logon before clicking the Connect button.

Figure 6.3

Establishing connections
to shared resources from
within Windows

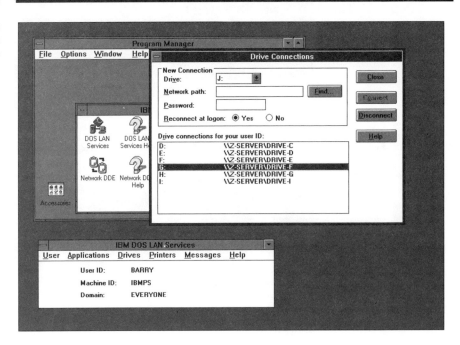

Printing with Windows on a LAN

With Windows Version 3, you can access network queues directly from within the Windows Print Manager. You can see which print jobs are in the queue, delete print jobs, and reselect printers easily. You should set your LAN printer defaults by running the printer redirection command (NET USE) before starting Windows.

If you wish to connect to a shared printer from within Windows, you use the Printer Connections window shown in Figure 6.4. This window works much the same as the Drive Connections window. You choose a DOS printer port name (LPT1, LPT2, or LPT3) in the Device box and assign that printer port to a shared printer resource by entering the name of the resource in the Network Path box. If you don't know the name, you can use the Find button to browse a list of shared printer resources. Click the Reconnect at Logon button if you want to access the shared printer every time you use your PC. Click the Connect button to establish the connection.

Figure 6.4

Connecting to a shared printer from within Windows

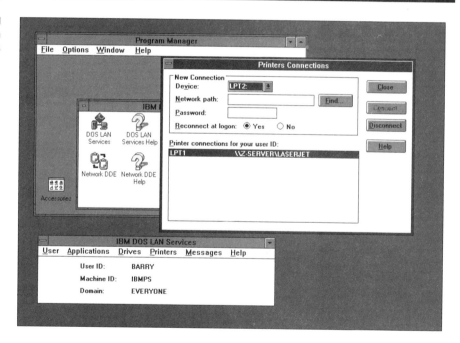

If you have a large LAN, you probably have several LAN printers that people share. When you print from within Windows, you choose a printer from the list of configured printer devices. Such lists can sometimes be un-wieldy. You should set up and configure Windows for those printers that are used most often. Most people do not like to scroll through multiple printer selections to find the one they want to use.

Identifying Problems with Windows on a LAN

Sometimes, when you load network operating system software into upper memory, Windows fails to start or behaves strangely. If this happens, try loading the network software in conventional memory (the first 640K bytes).

The Windows SETUP program modifies the PATH statement in your AUTOEXEC.BAT file. You should review SETUP's modifications to make sure that the PATH statement appears before the statements that load the network software. Also, make sure that your network drives are mapped properly for your Windows environment. Changing the drive letter mappings may require that the administrator make changes to the Windows customization and initialization files for each logon account.

If SETUP has problems running on a workstation, try specifying SETUP /I when you run SETUP. The /I parameter disables SETUP's hardware detection. You may need to do this on an ARCnet LAN, for example. The SETUP program tries to detect an IBM 8514 video adapter by using certain machine instructions. Because these instructions use addresses that also exist on an ARCnet network adapter, SETUP becomes confused.

If any of the Windows INI files seem to become corrupted when people access Windows from the file server, make sure that each person uses a unique, user-specific directory (or local hard disk) to store his or her customization and initialization files.

Configuring Windows on a LAN

You should create a different SYSTEM.INI file for each Windows user, putting the file in a personal Windows directory unique to that user. This means that you will have to change many separate files when you need to modify configuration settings, but Windows will not operate properly otherwise. To save time and effort, you may want to create a template SYSTEM.INI file first, and then customize this file for each user. As you create the template file, you need to know the configuration parameters that the network uses. These network-related parameters are as follows:

AllVMsExclusive=   A Boolean setting that controls whether a DOS application can run in a window or must run in exclusive full-screen mode, regardless of the settings in the program information file. The default setting is FALSE. If the setting is TRUE, network users will see an increase in the time it takes for Windows sessions to be completed.

Network.drv=   Specifies the network driver file name you are using; the default is none. Most network driver choices are available using SETUP. You modify this setting by choosing the SETUP icon located in the Main group window and modifying your network choice. If you want to install a network driver not provided with Windows, you need to run SETUP again.

FileSysChange=   A Boolean setting that controls whether the File Manager automatically receives messages from non-Windows applications when those applications create, delete, or rename files. If the setting is FALSE, a virtual machine can perform file manipulation while running independently of the File Manager. If it is TRUE, all messages automatically go to the File Manager, and system performance is degraded.

InDOSPolling=   A Boolean setting that determines whether other applications can run when memory-resident software has the InDOS flag set. The default setting is No. You must change the setting to Yes if your memory-resident software needs to be in a critical section to perform operations. When the setting is Yes, system performance is degraded.

INT28Critical=   A Boolean setting that specifies whether a critical section is required to handle INT28h interrupts for a memory-resident software application. The default setting is TRUE. If you do not need a critical section, change this setting to FALSE; this should improve Windows' task switching.

INT28Filter=   A numeric setting that determines the number of INT28 hexadecimal interrupts that are generated to software loaded before Windows while your system is idle. The default value is 10. Increasing the value improves Windows' performance but can cause conflicts with memory-resident software such as network shells. Changing the setting to 0 eliminates the interrupts. Users of communication applications on a network should be aware that the lower the value of INT28Filter, the higher the system overhead, which can cause conflict with the communication application.

NetAsynchSwitching=   Controls whether Windows provides the capability to switch away from an application after it has made an asynchronous NetBIOS call. The default value of 0 indicates that task switching is not available. With a value of 1, task switching is available. Network users should determine whether any of their applications will receive network messages while switched to other applications; if an application does receive messages and you have a setting of 1, your system may fail.

NetHeapSize=   A numeric setting (in kilobytes) that determines the size of the buffer pool allocated in conventional memory (640K bytes) for moving data over a network. The default value is 8, but many networks require a bigger buffer size. The larger the buffer size, the smaller the amount of memory provided to applications.

NetAsynchFallback=   A Boolean setting that can require Windows to try to save a NetBIOS request if it is failing. The default setting is FALSE. Windows has a global network buffer to handle data; if sufficient space is not available in this buffer when an application makes a NetBIOS request, Windows fails the request. If you change this setting to TRUE, Windows tries to save the request by creating a buffer in local memory and preventing all virtual machines from processing until the data has been received properly and the timeout period has passed. The timeout period is controlled by NetAsynchTimeout.

NetAsynchTimeout=   A setting (in seconds to one decimal place) that determines the length of a timeout period if Windows is attempting to save a failing NetBIOS request. The default is 5.0 seconds and applies only if NetAsynchFallback is set to TRUE.

NetDMASize=   Determines the buffer size (in kilobytes) for NetBIOS transport software. The buffer size always represents the largest value established by this setting or the value established by DMABuffersize.

Network=   Represents the 386 enhanced-mode synonym for Device. The default is None and is controlled by SETUP.

PSPIncrement=   A setting (from 2 to 64) that tells Windows to reserve, in 16-byte increments, additional memory for each successive virtual machine if UniqueDOSPSP is TRUE.

ReflectDOSINT2A=   A Boolean setting that tells Windows to run through or reflect DOS INT 2A signals. The default is FALSE, which instructs Windows to run through this type of signal, providing more efficiency. If you have memory-resident software that requires knowledge of INT2A messages, change the setting to TRUE.

TimerCriticalSection=   A setting (in milliseconds) that tells Windows to go into a critical section around any timer interrupt code and use the timeout period specified. A value greater than 0 guarantees that only one virtual machine at a time will receive time interrupts. Some network memory-resident software will fail if a value greater than 0 is not used. System performance slows with the use of this setting.

TokenRingSearch=   A Boolean setting that instructs Windows to look for a Token Ring network adapter on machines with the IBM AT architecture. The default is TRUE. This search can interfere with another device.

UniqueDOSPSP=   A Boolean setting that instructs Windows to start every application at a unique memory address (PSP). The default setting is

FALSE. If the setting is TRUE, each time that Windows creates a new virtual machine to start a new application, a unique amount of memory below the application is reserved. PSPIncrement controls the amount of memory that is reserved. This approach guarantees that applications in different virtual machines will start at different addresses. In some networks, the load address of the application is used to identify each process on the network.

■ Using OS/2 Workstations

People with OS/2-based workstations, like those who run DOS-plus-Windows, can type NET commands in an OS/2 command line session or use LAN Server's graphical user interface. The NET command parameters and their meaning appear earlier in this chapter, in the section entitled "LAN Server Commands."

You log on to the LAN from an OS/2-based workstation with the Logon screen shown in Figure 6.5. Double-click the Logon icon in the LAN Server folder, then enter your logon account and password to obtain access to the LAN.

Figure 6.5

Logging on from an OS/2 workstation

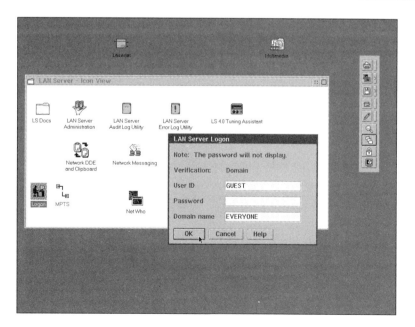

The User Accounts folder enables you to establish, change, or view the drive letter and printer device assignments for your logon account. To open your User Accounts folder, double-click the LAN Server Adminstration folder, then open the domain folder for your domain. The example shown in Figure 6.6 uses a domain name of "EVERYONE." Open (double-click) the User Accounts folder to see your logon account object. In Figure 6.6, the active logon account is "GUEST." When you double-click your logon account object, a settings notebook similar to the one shown in Figure 6.7 (open to the Identity tab) appears.

Figure 6.6

Your logon account object in the User Accounts folder

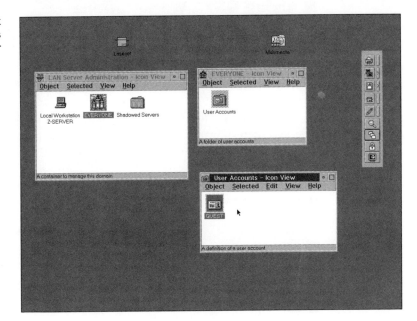

To establish your drive letter assignments, click the Assignments tab of the logon account settings notebook. Click the Add button to see a screen similar to Figure 6.8. First, click the Directory, Printer, or Serial Device button to indicate the type of share resource. For shared resources that are file server directories, choose a shared network resource, by alias name, and select a drive letter in the Local Device drop-down list box. For printers or serial devices, you follow the same steps but assign the printer or serial device shared resource to a local device name on your computer. When you have finished creating connections to shared resources, click the Set button at the bottom of the settings notebook.

Figure 6.7

The settings notebook for
your logon account object

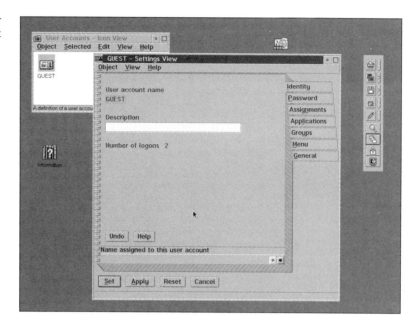

Figure 6.8

The Logon Assignments
window of the logon
account object's settings
notebook

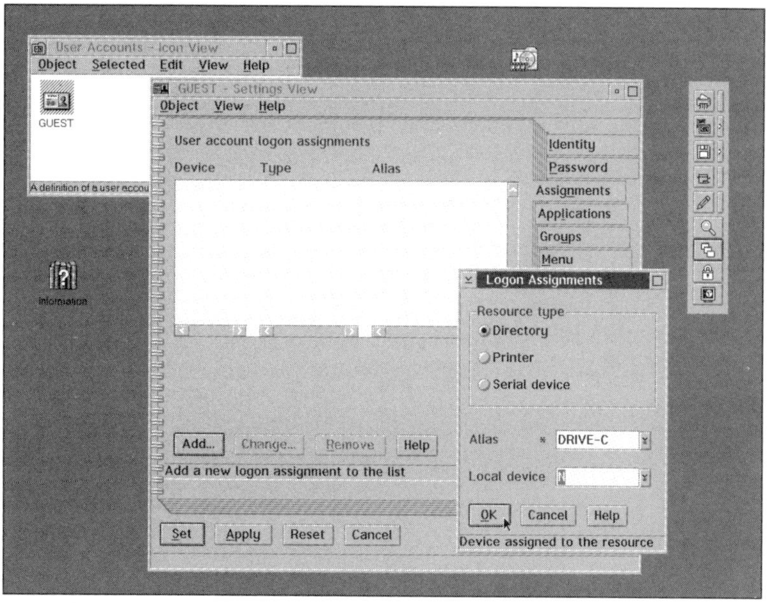

■ Summary

In this chapter, you've learned how to log on, log off, create connections to shared resources, and generally access the LAN. You know how to use network commands and graphical interfaces to manage your LAN sessions. And you understand how to cause your connections to reestablish themselves each time you log on.

In the next chapter, you look at what can go wrong on your LAN Server network.

- *Looking at Network Errors*
- *Understanding First Failure Support Technology*
- *Isolating the Causes of Network Problems*
- *Desktop Management Interface*
- *Using Network Management Tools*
- *Improving Network Performance*

C H A P T E R

7

Troubleshooting LAN Server

THIS CHAPTER LOOKS AT PROBLEMS YOU MIGHT ENCOUNTER WITH
your LAN Server network. You'll find information that will help you
with LAN Server problems as well as general network problems.

Problems related strictly to LAN Server can often be corrected through configuration changes. Most network problems, however, are not caused by the network operating system itself. Hardware malfunctions, for instance, are a frequent cause of network downtime. In addition to exploring LAN Server problems and LAN Server diagnostic tools, this chapter also covers other types of network problems and network tools.

■ Looking at Network Errors

Knowing when a problem relates to LAN Server or the network in general can sometimes be difficult to determine. Examples of problems that are easy to attribute to the network include LAN Server error messages, dropped connections, and a lack of available disk space on a file server. Problems that can be difficult to pin on the network include workstation out of memory conditions, applications that behave incorrectly, and garbled printouts. Observing whether the problem recurs when the network isn't active is one of the first steps you can take to pinpoint the problem.

Discovering Problems

The LAN Server software records problems (events) related to network adapters, cables, and other LAN components. When an error such as a failed network adapter occurs, LAN Server inserts an entry in a log file. You can use the NET ERROR command or the log-viewing utilities discussed in Chapter 5, Administering LAN Server, to see these entries. If the error isn't self-explanatory, you would then look up the error message in the LAN Server Problem Determination Guide reference manual. You can also review error and informational messages in two text files in the \OS2\IN-STALL directory. These files are IBMLANER.LOG and IBMLSHST.LOG.

You use the SYSLOG utility to suspend or resume system logging, redirect error logging data from one file to another, format the contents of error log files, specify the size of the error log files, and print their formatted contents. To start the SYSLOG utility, type the following command at a windowed or full-screen OS/2 command prompt:

```
SYSLOG
```

In the OS/2 Error Log Formatter window, you use menu selections to perform the following tasks:

- Open a system log file

- Print a system log file

- Redirect a system log file

- Refresh the log buffer

- Display file header information

- Display the error logging summary

- Display options for the system log file

- Suspend or resume system logging

To use the SYSLOG utility, you must include the following statements in the CONFIG.SYS file:

```
RUN=C:\OS2\SYSTEM\LOGDAEM.EXE
DEVICE=C:\OS2\LOG.SYS
```

First Failure Support Technology/2 (FFST/2) can also reveal the exact nature of a network problem. FFST/2 contains functions for error logging, message logging, creating snapshots of LAN Server memory, and alert building and routing. The next section of this chapter, Understanding First Failure Support Technology, discusses FFST/2 in more detail.

Network Management Software

You may also have a separate network management software product, such as NetView, that helps identify and locate problems. Such software notifies the LAN administrator of errors through alerts displayed on a central workstation. When there is a problem, the software typically alerts the administrator with both an audible alarm and a highlighted indication of the problem on the display. Sophisticated network management products may even suggest alternative solutions to the administrator. The management software can provide facilities for monitoring file server activity, print servers, and gateways.

On a LAN with hundreds of workstations the management software may forward the alert report to a host computer. The central site can use the information to maintain a centralized problem history file for each remote LAN. The alert log can contain vendor contacts for specific problems, generate trouble tickets, and include information about how the problem was resolved.

The management software can log network events—such as peak network utilization times, new network addresses observed on the network, and error conditions—to a disk file or a printer. The administrator may import the logged events into a database for further filtering, reporting, and statistics-gathering. The LAN management software must be capable of writing a file in a format that can be imported into other applications. The software may offer its own facilities for reporting the data. Typically, you can generate reports from the information stored in the event log over a selected period of time. A network administrator, for example, often wants to review network utilization for the past 24 hours, and will want the software to provide that information.

■ Understanding First Failure Support Technology

First Failure Support Technology/2 (FFST/2) is an optional component of LAN Server that you select at installation time. You can later add FFST/2 to your network by running the OS/2 LAN Services Installation/Configuration utility (located in your LAN Server folder). FFST/2 consists of error detection and reporting services. These services include error logging, message logging, alert building and routing, selective dumping of LAN Server memory to a file, and a message display console. The following describes these services more fully.

Error logging: FFST/2 can translate the particulars of a network error into an understandable format and insert an entry in the OS/2 error log.

Message logging: FFST/2 can obtain application-specific messages from OS/2 message files and record these messages in a log file. FFST/2 can also show the messages via its message console. You use the FFST/2 initialization and configuration program to turn message display on or off.

Building and routing alerts: FFST/2 can build and route a software alert to notify a LAN administrator of a detected error condition. The alert, which FFST/2 sends to the administrator's workstation through the LAN cable, contains the same information FFST/2 placed in the error log.

Selective dump: FFST/2 can dump LAN Server memory areas and files (that is, take a snapshot of LAN Server). You'd give the dump to a service technician or IBM support technician for analysis.

Message console services: FFST/2 displays a scrollable Presentation Manager message console that shows all messages logged by FFST/2. A network management product can also use this service to display its messages.

The following statement in the CONFIG.SYS file runs the FFST/2 program automatically each time you boot the computer, and is the recommended method of using FFST/2:

```
RUN=C:OS2\EPW.EXE ON
```

Alternatively if you want to start FFST/2 while the server is running, rather than at boot time, you can run the FFST/2 program in an OS/2 session by typing the following command:

```
EPW ON
```

An error log entry typically includes the following information:

- Record ID, date and time, qualifier, and originator
- Machine type and serial number from the hardware vital product data
- Software program name and version number
- Message ID and text recorded with the error
- Error code (major and minor codes) associated with the error
- Problem ID for the error record
- Primary symptom string (for example, the actual error codes for this error)

    The meaning of acronyms you see in a log entry are the following:

RIDS	Specifies the name of the network service that failed
PRCS	Specifies the OS/2 return code
ADRS	Specifies the specific location of the error
MS	Specifies the error message ID

■ Isolating the Causes of Network Problems

While the exact steps you take to correct a network error will vary from problem to problem, you'll find that the steps fall generally into categories. The diagnostic process consists of four steps you repeat until you find and fix the problem: observing the symptoms, developing a list of possible causes, performing tests to isolate the cause, and analyzing the results.

Observing Symptoms

You first observe the symptoms of the problem. You may be tempted, in the rush to fix the problem, to begin experimenting with solutions before you finish a thorough examination of the symptoms. If you give in to temptation, you probably will wind up spending more time and money to fix the problem than if you had considered all the symptoms and their ramifications.

    The most obvious symptoms are not always the key to understanding the problem. To know why this is true, you have to understand one of the primary characteristics of network protocols. Network protocols are designed to hide network problems, not expose them. Most network protocols incorporate retry logic and other techniques to support automatic recovery from problems. This causes most network problems to display a single obvious symptom: slow response from the network. Although the network's attempts to retry a failing operation increase network reliability, the retries also make network troubleshooting more difficult. You see a common symptom for many problems.

In your analysis of the symptoms, you need to go beyond the slow response symptom. You need to ask yourself questions that help you focus on the behavior of the LAN. Does this problem affect everyone, only those in a given area, or random individuals? What is the percentage of time the problem manifests itself? Is the problem continuous or intermittent? Does it occur regularly? What has changed recently? Has a computer device been added to the network? Have any internetworking devices been reconfigured? Which vendor's products may have failed to produce these symptoms? What are the vendor and version numbers of the computer systems, network adapter cards, hubs, routers, bridges, application software, and network operating system software?

After you gather this information, you can begin the second step in the diagnostic process—the development of a list of possible causes for the symptoms you have observed.

Knowing What Is Normal

You have to sift through the observed symptoms and facts, looking for the cause of a problem. To recognize the symptoms, however, you must know what is normal and what is not normal on your network. The process of determining the normal characteristics of an individual network is called baselining.

Baselining is not one of the four steps in the diagnostic process. You must perform the baselining before the problem occurs. Of course, once the network is in a problem state, it is too late to determine the normal behavior of the network. If you have a clear, complete picture of the normal behavior of your LAN, you can answer the following questions: What is the average network utilization? How does it vary during the business day? What are the primary applications on the network? What protocols are running on the network? What are the performance characteristics of these protocols? Who manufactured the network interface controllers, media attachment units, hubs, and other network connection hardware? What are their performance characteristics? Who manufactured the repeaters, bridges, routers, and gateways on the network? What versions of software and firmware are they running? What are their performance characteristics?

Making a List of Possible Causes

With the baseline information at your fingertips, you can begin to ask how the observed symptoms relate to the normal operation of the network. You can distinguish unusual behavior and look for its cause. Experience and knowledge are your tools in this step.

To develop your list of possible causes, you must know how each network component can fail and what that failure can do to the entire network. As you make your list, visualize the dynamic nature of the LAN. Imagine how each component (network adapter, network operating system, cabling, or other unit) interacts with the rest of the network. Use your knowledge of protocols and network software to see how a network component's failure may cause the problem at hand. Excessive traffic, for example, can cause high collision counts on an EtherNet LAN. But a cable segment that is too long, or a malfunctioning transceiver, also can cause frequent collisions.

Isolating the Cause and Analyzing Results

In the third step, you test the LAN to see which of the items on your list is the culprit. You will use any and perhaps all of the tools covered earlier in this chapter, but you may find that the tool you use most frequently is the network analyzer. The analyzer enables you to monitor the network's behavior interactively, and the analyzer gives you more views of what is happening.

Once you think you have found the failing component, test your hypothesis. You simply may remove the failing component from the network to see if the problem disappears, or you may reconfigure or reset the component. Because diagnosis usually requires 80 percent of the problem-solving effort, and implementing a solution only 20 percent, you probably will find this last step the most straightforward.

Dealing with Common Problems

A typical network administrator spends a great deal of time solving problems and trying to understand the network's performance. Different parts of a network experience different kinds of problems and exhibit different symptoms.

The most frequent network problems occur in the physical layer—the lowest layer of the Open Systems Interconnection model. Because hardware is subject to physical stress, electrical connectivity problems are the most common fault type. These problems include cable breaks, cable shorts, breaks elsewhere in the circuit, and malfunctions in the actual network adapter circuitry.

You can isolate cable problems with a network analyzer or TDR. You often can find problems with hardware circuitry by examining error traffic on the network using a network analyzer. At other times, you must attack these problems using a process of elimination to isolate the cause. A cable-management product can also help you locate the problem, if you have one in your organization.

■ Desktop Management Interface

Promoted by a group called the Desktop Management Task Force, the Desktop Management Interface is a specification with broad support from many vendors of LAN products, both hardware and software. The new specification provides cross-platform rules and guidelines for defining, identifying, describing, querying, and controlling any component of a network, including PCs, network adapters, printers, operating systems, disk drives, applications, network software, and even PC configuration files. The new standard is emerging as this book is being published; you'll soon be able to take advantage of the Desktop Management Interface on your LAN Server network.

You'll use the new specification to solve network problems, keep track of how your PCs are configured, and generally help manage the LAN. Led by Intel, the many vendors who support the Desktop Management Interface (DMI) or who've announced support for the interface will initially supply compatible hardware and software for the OS/2, Windows, and DOS platforms. Once you begin using DMI, administering your LAN will become much easier.

The DMI specification performs the following four services:

- Defines the contents of the Management Information Format (MIF) files produced by the component-level modules

- Describes the Management Interface (MI) through which software can issue commands to query, reset, or control components

- Provides a Service Layer (SL) that implements the Management Interface and which directs the activities of the various DMI modules

- Identifies the Component Interface (CI) that a LAN product vendor can use to provide querying and controlling access to its product. The Component Interface can not only respond to commands but can also generate event notifications (often called alerts in other LAN management products).

The Desktop Management Interface consists of agent software that runs on workstations as well as a standard definition for LAN components. On DOS workstations, the agent software will usually be a set of small Terminate-and-Stay-Resident (TSR) programs. Windows-based computers will run a combination of TSRs and Dynamic Link Libraries (DLLs). Under OS/2, DMI agent software consists of a background program and a DLL.

The DMI TSR software you load at your DOS-based PC will only use an estimated 6K or so of RAM. Within that 6K TSR, component-level modules will load and run in a dynamic overlay area. Manufacturers of LAN hardware and software will provide modules that dynamically plug into and out of the TSR or DLL environment. The base TSR and the dynamic modules will maintain a collection of Management Information Format (MIF) files on your PC, respond to over-the-LAN-cable requests from the LAN administrator, and process commands delivered to the TSR in Management Information Format language. The specification is a practical one that fills a large gap in network management—the ability to query and control desktop computer components from a central LAN management console through an industry-standard mechanism.

When a LAN administrator, sitting at another workstation on the LAN, chooses menu options presented by the management application's console software, the console software will send the appropriate Get and Set MIF commands to the managed workstation to learn how those components are configured and possibly change the configuration. AUTOEXEC.BAT and CONFIG.SYS files could be manageable objects, for instance. One of the overlay modules might be a remote-control text editor the LAN administrator could invoke, from a management console PC, to make network-wide configuration changes that would take effect the next time people booted their PCs. Network adapters are prime candidates for LAN management software. LAN administrators will be able to remotely query the general health of and the traffic statistics for each DMI-aware network adapter on the LAN.

The DMI specification discusses MIF files and component management commands in great detail, but doesn't say how the information and the commands cross the LAN cable. A LAN management software product is free to encapsulate DMI information and commands, for example, inside SNMP-formatted LAN packets and use TCP/IP to route those LAN packets from a central network administration computer to a workstation and back again. Or a LAN management software product might forego SNMP and simply use Novell's IPX to route the packets containing DMI information and commands. The DMI doesn't care how requests and responses get from computer to computer. The entire scope and focus of DMI is the management and control of the desktop machine.

■ Using Network Management Tools

In the following sections of this chapter, you learn about specific tools you can use to help manage your network. Such tools range from time-domain reflectometers (TDRs) to integrated management systems. Some of these tools can be quite expensive. If your network is important to your business, however, you may find these tools a wise investment. You also discover how to use these tools.

Physical-layer tools include time-domain reflectometers (TDRs), oscilloscopes, breakout boxes, power meters, and similar products that find problems such as cable breaks, short circuits, unterminated cables, and bad connections. Tools that operate at a higher level include network monitors and protocol analyzers.

In recent studies, major corporations reported sizable financial losses when problems occurred on their networks. One study calculated the lost productivity resulting from network problems to be more than $3 million per year, on the average. The same study found that the average network is completely or partially disabled about twice a month, and the downtime lasts more than half a business day.

Setting Network-Management Goals

Network management has two goals. First, proper LAN management tries to reduce the number of network problems. If problems do occur, the second goal aims to minimize inconvenience and localize the damage. With these goals in mind, the International Standards Organization (ISO) identified five management categories that a LAN management system should include: fault, configuration, performance, security, and accounting. Descriptions of these management categories follow:

Accounting management	Records and reports network resource utilization data.
Configuration management	Understands and controls the parameters that define the state of the network.
Fault management	Detects, isolates, and controls problems on the network.
Performance management	Analyzes and controls the rate at which the network can process data.
Security management	Controls access to network resources.

Four types of network management products exist to deal with the five ISO categories: physical-layer tools, network monitors, network analyzers, and integrated network management systems. Each kind of product offers different benefits to the people who manage today's heterogeneous networks.

Using the Time-Domain Reflectometer

Years ago, cable testers were bulky, awkward devices. However, microminiaturization has produced relatively inexpensive hand-held devices that you can carry around the office to check individual cables. These small devices sometimes even come with portable printers that you can use to produce a report on the health of each cable in your cabling system. All such devices are battery-powered, and a few use rechargeable NiCad batteries.

A cable tester contains a Time Domain Reflectometer (TDR) and perhaps additional test circuits. A TDR works by sending sonarlike pulses through the LAN cable. The TDR detects the reflections, analyzes them, and displays the result. A cable tester typically can tell you the length of a cable, whether the cable is correctly wired internally (pin-to-pin wire mapping), whether the cable contains a short circuit (wires touching each other through damaged or missing insulation), whether the cable contains a broken wire (an "open"), and whether the cable suffers from electrical crosstalk (interference). Any of these problems can bring down a network.

Short circuits and open connections can happen months or years after installation, especially if cheap insulation dries out, becomes brittle, and cracks. Conversely, a water-soaked cable won't carry LAN traffic very well. During installation, a person sometimes will pull a wire around a corner, and part of the insulation will scrap off (a condition called a shiner). This cable problem might not immediately manifest itself but wait months before causing a network outage.

Some wiring problems happen during cable manufacture and connection. Once in a great while, the factory or the installer will put connectors on the cable with the wrong wire leading to the wrong pin, and the new cable won't work at all. Or the person may mix up the wire pairs by attaching connectors in a way that causes one of the wires to carry a signal that the other wire pair should carry (a condition known as reversed pairs). Even with perfectly manufactured, carefully connected wire, you might inadvertently cause a cable problem. In planning a network installation or enhancement, you might overlook the published limitations of the wiring specification; the result is a LAN segment with cables that are too long or have too many nodes in a segment. It's easy to overlook distance and number-of-nodes limitations when you are concentrating on giving people access to the network.

Before you attach the cable tester to your LAN, you absolutely must know the type of cable your LAN uses. Electricity travels at different speeds in different types of cable. The testing device must know the "nominal velocity of propagation" (NVP) for your cable before the tester can make accurate distance determinations. NVP, expressed as a fraction or sometimes a percentage of the speed of light in a vacuum, can vary from .60 to .90. For example, Level 3 UTP cable has an NVP of .62, Level 5 UTP has an NVP of .72, RG-58 has an NVP of .80, RG-62 has an NVP of .84, and Type 1 has an NVP of .78. The cable tester will display incorrect results if you don't supply the tester with the right information about the cable type. Even the difference between foam and nonfoam insulation in the cable can throw off the tester's results. The first thing that you do with a new cable tester is calibrate the unit in relation to the type of cable you use. The cable tester often comes with a chart or table expressing the NVP for popular cable types. But you'll want to calibrate the tester anyway, in relation to the exact type of cable in your LAN. Calibration is a matter of trying different NVP values until the tester displays the correct cable length for a cable whose length you know because you've measured it.

You also need an up-to-date, accurate diagram of the topology (layout) of your LAN. When you think you've found a wiring fault, you will want to pinpoint the bad cable on your diagram to make sure that you understand how the symptoms of the problem (a particular group of workstations being dropped from the LAN, for example) relate to the wiring fault you've identified.

The basic procedure for using a cable tester is simple. After you detach both ends of the cable from the network, you connect the cable tester to one end and, for unshielded twisted pair (UTP), you connect a loopback device to the other end. The genderless data connector that you usually find on shielded twisted pair (STP) is its own loopback device. You then run through the tester's diagnostic steps to see whether the cable is healthy.

You can and should use a cable tester to check a new LAN cable installation. When you build a new LAN or add a new cable segment to an existing LAN, you'll want to know that the new wires can carry noise-free LAN signals before you try to log on to a file server. If you have a contractor install and maintain your LAN wiring, insist that the contractor perform cable tests during the installation. If you install your own wiring, use a cable tester to check your work.

Using Network Monitors

A network monitor is a computer device that attaches to a network and monitors all or a selected portion of the network traffic. By examining frame-level information in each packet, network monitors can compile statistics on network utilization, packet type, number of packets sent and received by each network node, packet errors, and other significant information.

Network monitors are relatively inexpensive, and you can use several on a large LAN–one for each network segment. You generally would let your network monitors run continuously, allowing them to collect data and search for problems. A network monitor does a reasonably good job of detecting errors, and most such tools can be part of an overall integrated management system. Network monitors cost from several hundred dollars (for software-only products) to about $10,000.

Using Network Analyzers

While network monitors can detect network problems, network analyzers (sometimes called protocol analyzers) can help you track down and fix those problems. Network analyzers contain sophisticated features for real-time traffic analysis, packet capture and decoding, and packet transmission. Some even include troubleshooting expertise in the form of test suites. Network analyzers sometimes feature a built-in TDR. The most sophisticated network analyzers use special-purpose hardware to detect problems not visible to standard network controllers. Recently, manufacturers of network analyzers have begun adding artificial intelligence (AI) to their products.

Network analyzers are complicated, expensive tools for detecting certain kinds of LAN problems. You would use an analyzer to identify a failing device, configuration error, or LAN bottleneck. These tools are more sophisticated than cable testers or software-only network utilities. When you are faced with a problem that requires you to examine the detailed contents of your data frames, you are like a doctor who reaches for a microscope to view cells in a blood sample. The analyzer is the microscope; as the doctor, you have to know what normal cells look like and how many of each type you should see.

Network analyzers passively listen to all the frames flowing across the LAN and give you a picture of their health. The analyzer selects those frames that meet the filtering criteria you set up, captures them in a file, and summarizes the frames or decodes them to show their contents. You can tell a network analyzer to show just error frames, frames from (or to) a certain workstation or server, frames of a certain type or that contain a given pattern of data, or frames that exceed size and frequency thresholds that you establish. Some analyzers enable you to inject extra traffic on the LAN, enabling you to simulate adding more nodes.

Once you know what to look for, a network analyzer can show you exactly which network adapter is causing a broadcast storm, help identify a misconfigured gateway that is causing routing errors, or show you the interpacket arrival rate of those frames involved in a performance problem. The network analyzer does not substitute for your own experience and knowledge. You need to be a networking expert to use a network analyzer well.

Prices for network analyzers start at about $10,000, and they can cost more than $30,000 with support for multiple physical media and protocol decoding. Analyzers are sold as kits or complete products. The kit consists of a network adapter and software that you install in one of your PCs. If you buy the complete product, you get the adapter and software preinstalled in a PC of the vendor's choice. The Sniffer, from Network General, is a popular network analyzer.

■ Improving Network Performance

Network monitors and analyzers enable you to compile statistics on your LAN's message traffic. You can use these figures to understand your LAN's performance as it relates to the traffic. You can view the daily network utilization patterns, identify the heaviest users, determine the various percentages of different protocol traffic, see where network bottlenecks exist, and perhaps even recognize why those bottlenecks exist.

This analysis may suggest to you that you need to partition the network into multiple segments, add file servers, or upgrade your network adapters to obtain better performance. The performance tuning task is not a small one, however. You will need to spend a significant amount of time gathering statistics and relating those statistics to the particular components of your LAN.

Network management is both an art and a science, but finding a bottleneck on a LAN can require the skills of a magician who has a Ph.D. in electrical engineering. You may get advice like "Put a faster hard drive in the server," "Switch to Token Ring," "Switch to Ethernet," "Put more memory in the server," or "Get a server with a faster CPU." What if you take the advice and discover that performance does not change? The part you replaced was not the bottleneck; something else is. To locate a bottleneck, you need to understand how the network operating system functions.

When you run an application that resides on the file server and that in turn reads and writes files on the server, a flurry of activity takes place. First, the operating system looks in each of your PATH directories for the executable file. This searching of server directories causes a dialog of LAN messages. For each directory, your workstation sends a "Find File" request message and the server sends back a response. The executable file loads into your workstation's memory by way of another series of LAN messages, usually in 512-, 1,024-, or 4,096-byte packets (LAN packets have size limits). Once loaded, the application program issues open, read, write, and close requests that become LAN messages sent to the server. The server responds to each request by sending back an "Okay" or a "Here's the data" message. On NETBIOS-based networks, the receiver separately acknowledges each message.

The server has to manage a queue of requests from the many workstations on the LAN, and the queue can get quite long at times. If you use the server for remote printing, two problems can occur. Multiple print jobs may keep the file server busy reading and writing spool files, thus delaying other file-service requests. The file server also has to devote some time and effort to managing the shared printer. In addition, workstation and server messages (both for file service and print spooling) may have to cross one or more bridges, which creates another delay.

The upper layers of the network software filter each file and print request and create one or more message records that it hands to a lower layer. This layer in turn gives the request message to the network device drivers. Through an 8-, 16-, or 32-bit slot, these drivers tell the network adapter to send the request to the server. When it can use the LAN cable, the network card sends the request. At the server, the network support software hands the request up through more layers of support code before the network operating system finally processes it. If the request cannot be satisfied from server memory (the RAM cache), the server waits for the hard disk to rotate into position to access the data. The response travels back to the workstation, through the support software, server network adapter, LAN cable, workstation network adapter, and workstation support software. A 250K executable, using 512-byte message packets, requires the interchange of more than 500 requests and 500 responses just to load the program. (Larger packets cause less server overhead.) When many people try to use the file server at the same time, the server is the Grand Central Station for LAN traffic and file requests.

The network bottleneck may be at the workstation, in the network device drivers, network TSRs, or network adapter. Or the transmission rate of the LAN may be the bottleneck. At the server, you have several suspects to consider. The server CPU may not be executing the network operating system software quickly enough. The network software may not be efficiently coded. Too little RAM in the server for file-caching purposes means that the server frequently must take the time to access the hard disk drive. The server may spend an inordinate amount of time acting as a print server. Perhaps your server's overhead would be less if you could configure it to use larger packets. Could the speed of the bus be holding you back? Or perhaps the server and the network adapter have trouble communicating through a confining 8-bit slot. The network adapter may not contain enough RAM to buffer all the LAN messages. Are your bridges slowing you down? The list of potential bottlenecks is a long one, and the picture is further complicated by the interactions that can occur between the components. As you look for performance bottlenecks on your LAN, you will need to keep these factors in mind.

■ Summary

In this chapter, you explored techniques and strategies for dealing with network problems. You learned about general network problems as well as errors specific to LAN Server. You have guidelines you can follow to solve network errors.

The next chapter provides information on running applications on a LAN Server network.

- *Running Multiuser Software*
- *Sharing Clipboards between Applications*
- *Avoiding DOS Disk Diagnostic Utilities*
- *Working with Word Processors and Spreadsheets*
- *Running Communications Programs*
- *Using Database Managers and Other Client/Server Products*

8

Using Applications on Your LAN

T HE LAN SERVER ENVIRONMENT OF SHARED RESOURCES LETS YOU run applications in ways that are useful and productive, but you need to be aware of how applications can behave differently on a LAN. This chapter reveals the distinctions between single-user and multiuser application software. You learn which utility programs you cannot run on a network, and you consider the issue of software licensing on a LAN. You explore running word processing, spreadsheet, database management, and other software packages—DOS, Windows and OS/2 varieties. You also cover the sharing of clipboard information across the LAN, via NetDDE.

■ Running Multiuser Software

DOS and OS/2 are by themselves single-user operating systems. On a LAN, however, several users usually need to be able to run the same application on different workstations. A multiuser application, through DOS or OS/2 and the network operating system, coordinates the efforts of each user and workstation by understanding and manipulating the environment presented by the LAN. By extending DOS and OS/2, LAN-aware software adds an entirely new dimension to working with personal computers.

SHARE.EXE

SHARE.EXE enables file-sharing on a LAN. SHARE is distributed on the DOS distribution disks and consists of a terminate-and-stay-resident (TSR) program that inserts hooks deep into DOS. These hooks are so deep that you cannot remove SHARE from memory without rebooting the computer.

If SHARE is not loaded, DOS ignores the special file-access modes that a LAN-aware application specifies at the time it opens a file (to acquire exclusive access to a file, for example). In fact, it is possible to corrupt a network disk quite thoroughly if file collisions occur and SHARE is not in effect. This is one of the reasons that, beginning with DOS 4.0, SHARE is loaded automatically by DOS and is no longer something you can forget to run. SHARE is also automatically in effect under OS/2. SHARE is built into the OS/2 operating system, and you do not have to load SHARE if you use OS/2.

The user guide or reference manual that came with your application software probably will remind you to run SHARE before accessing the application. The best time to run SHARE is after you have loaded the network software but before you do any work. It does not matter whether SHARE runs before the login process.

One interesting aspect of SHARE is that it enables file-sharing even on a stand-alone, single-user PC. Because you can have several TSR-type programs loaded underneath an application program running in the foreground, DOS needs to keep separate track of the file I/O performed by each background or foreground program. If SHARE is loaded on a single-user computer, the same file-sharing that occurs across the network can occur between two TSRs, or between a TSR and a foreground application.

If you are a Microsoft Windows user on a LAN, you should make doubly certain to load SHARE before starting Windows. Windows does not enable you to run SHARE in one of its enhanced mode DOS sessions. Windows prevents SHARE from running by pretending that SHARE is already loaded. Windows does this because you can use the DOS EXIT command to end a DOS session, which would remove SHARE from memory. Windows cannot enable this to happen, because SHARE hooks itself into DOS. As an unfortunate side effect, multiuser software that you run in a DOS session will think that file sharing is enabled, when in fact SHARE is not present. File damage and corruption can result.

You'll find it useful to establish guidelines for sharing data among the people on the LAN who use Windows or DOS applications. The guidelines should include a set of directories on the LAN Server file server whose outline structure closely matches the work you do.

A LAN is no faster than its slowest component, but the speed of each component has a different effect on the capacity and performance of the LAN. A faster CPU in a server allows more people to log on and access shared files. For any one person on the LAN, that person's workstation response times depend mostly on the speed of the server's I/O subsystems—the hard disk, hard-disk controller card, disk cache, and network adapter. As these I/O subsystems empty and fill disk cache memory to satisfy workstation requests, a slow disk subsystem causes data to form a long queue. When the queue fills with cached write data, there is less room for data read from the disk into the cache. Cache hit rates decrease, and the operating system has to wait for disk rotations and head movements to satisfy workstation read requests. Overall performance degrades if the disk can't keep up with write requests. A fast file server (one that responds quickly to workstation requests) will have disks and a hard-drive controller that do a good job of quickly writing disk data. A fast file server will also have a fast network adapter. If the server has a fast CPU chip, the server will support a greater number of concurrent requests from a greater number of workstations.

Evaluating Multiuser Software

Most application software products, especially shrink-wrapped software you buy through mail order or at a computer store, are single-user. This means that the programmer designed the software to run on non-networked PCs. The software can access files on the file server and print to the shared printer because the network operating system redirects (maps) the DOS drive letters and printer ports. But single-user software can't access the same file from two different workstations at the same time. The result, if two people on your LAN happen to cause such a file collision, is a corrupted file, a DOS error message ("Access Denied"), or an overlaid file (the second person to save the file overlays the information updated and saved by the first person).

Multiuser software, on the other hand, is LAN-aware. When two or more people run a multiuser application, the software recognizes the possibility that other instances of itself running on other workstations will access the same file. Multiuser software uses file sharing and record locking techniques to manage the concurrent access; this file management preserves the integrity of the application's shared files. A LAN-aware application can gain exclusive use of a file by opening (loading) the file in what programmers call DENY_READ_WRITE mode. This mode, available to applications running on a LAN, denies other workstations the ability to concurrently access a file until the first workstation is finished with the file. DENY_READ_WRITE mode protects the integrity of a file by allowing only one person at a time to update the file.

A multiuser application can allow several workstations to concurrently access a file by using the alternate file-open mode, DENY_NONE. This mode permits different workstations to open (load) the same file at the same time. An application that uses the DENY_NONE mode must issue record locks before writing updated portions of a shared file. The record locks protect the integrity of the file (or of several interrelated files) during the update process. After one workstation updates a portion of a file and unlocks that portion, other workstations are free to view and further update the new contents of that portion of the file. In a shared file environment, it's the responsibility of the network operating system (LAN Server, in this case) to not buffer or cache the file at the workstation. LAN Server always directly accesses the server to retrieve portions of a shared file.

In addition to sharing files, multiuser software allows each person, at each workstation, to have individual configuration files. These are the files that contain the screen color preferences, printer setup strings, and other information particular to a workstation. Single-user software maintains only one set of configuration information. For example, if you install a product such as WordPerfect or Microsoft Word in one file server directory that everyone shares, everyone will use the same screen colors, menu configuration, and printer setups. This will annoy people. Fortunately, you can optionally install these two products in a way that permits people to share some files (the executable program, for instance) from a file server while those people access configuration files from a local hard drive.

WordPerfect and Word allow you to start up the application in a local hard drive directory containing configuration files, yet access some parts of the application from a file server. Other applications go even further toward maintaining separate configurations for each person. The logon account name (network account identification) you use to log on to the LAN uniquely identifies you. A software product can use your logon account name or your computer name as part of the name of the product's configuration file (BARRY.INI and SUSAN.INI, for example). The software can also note your logon account name or computer name in audit trail files or system log files to separately identify application activity on a person-by-person basis.

File Sharing and Record Locking

Every open file on a LAN Server file server is owned by the workstation that opened it. The ownership can be quite possessive or jointly communal. There are gradations between these ownerships. An application specifies how it wants to share a file when the computer program opens the file. Applications use file sharing and record locking to ensure that file updates occur on a consistent basis.

What would happen if two workstations did not pay any attention to file-sharing concepts (did not load SHARE) and just went ahead and tried to change the contents of the same file? If the two workstations open the same file and attempt to update it at the same time, the results can be messy, to say the least. Here is an example of what can happen:

When workstation A reads a file or a portion of a file, the file server transfers the data from the file server hard disk into workstation A's memory for processing. Writing the data transfers it back to the file server. The same holds true, naturally, for workstation B. Suppose that workstation A reads a file and displays the file's data to user A. While user A is looking at his or her screen and keying in changes, workstation B also reads the file into B's memory and displays it to user B. User B types faster than user A, and saves his or her changes first. User A, after pondering a few minutes, saves his or her changes (by writing the data from workstation memory to the file server). Clearly, the changes that user B made now are lost; they've been overwritten by those of the slower typist, user A.

An even more complicated situation arises when several interrelated files need to be updated. Because the contents of one file are supposed to have a certain correspondence to the contents of the other files, a helter-skelter series of updates from multiple workstations would be disastrous. Any relationships that existed before the several updates took place would be quickly destroyed.

File Sharing

At the time an application opens a file located on the file server, the software informs the server of its intention to simply read from the file or perhaps both read and write to the file. The software also can ask the server to deny other workstations access to the file.

If the application signals an intention to only read from the file, and if the file is flagged with a file attribute of read-only, the server enables the application to access the file. If you have used the DOS or OS/2 ATTRIB command to mark a file as read-only and an application indicates that it wants to write to the file, the network operating system will not enable the application to use the file, and will instead cause the application to produce an error message.

An application uses sharing mode to control how other workstations can concurrently open a file. The application specifies sharing mode at the time it opens a file. Sharing mode works by enabling the application at one workstation to restrict (or not restrict) how other workstations can use a file.

Applications express sharing mode in terms of denying certain capabilities to the other workstations that attempt to open the file. The restrictions an application can specify, as defined by the DOS Technical Reference manual the programmers use, are DENY_NONE, DENY_READ, DENY_WRITE, and DENY_READ_WRITE. In addition, there is a special mode called compatibility mode. The names for these modes seem odd because these are the names that programmers actually use as they develop the software. When a programmer instructs the computer program to open a file, he or she considers the file-sharing requirements for that file and chooses an appropriate mode. You will want to be aware of these modes so that you can recognize their behavior in the LAN-aware software you buy and use.

DENY_NONE grants full access to the file by applications at other workstations. In essence, DENY_NONE defers the protection of the file's integrity until later, when the application updates individual records. If a workstation opens a file with a sharing mode of DENY_READ, the network operating system enables other workstations to write to the file but not read it. DENY_WRITE is the opposite; if a workstation opens a file with a sharing mode of DENY_WRITE, the network operating system does not enable other workstations to update the file. The other workstations can, however, read from the file.

DENY_READ_WRITE confers exclusive access to the workstation that opens the file. Attempts by other workstations to open the file (with any value of sharing mode) will fail.

Compatibility mode is the default sharing mode. If an application does not specify otherwise, the network operating system uses compatibility mode to determine how other workstations can open a file. In general, this mode grants exclusive access to an application. Compatibility mode is also in effect for new files the application creates.

Record Locking

Because a file lock affects the entire file and extends from the time a file is opened until the time it's closed, the resulting coarse granularity (the system-wide effect on the group of people who are using the application at that moment) of the lock may be an awkward inconvenience to the people in the office. A lock that lasts for the entire time an application uses a file prevents others from accessing the file. A file lock does not enable file sharing.

A multiuser application uses record locking to protect the integrity of the data files. A record lock lasts only long enough to ensure that consistent data has been written to the file(s), and it usually affects only a small portion of the file.

A record lock specifies a certain region of a file by giving the region's location in the file (its offset) and its size (length). If the specified region cannot be locked successfully (another workstation opened the file in a mode other than DENY_NONE mode, or another workstation has locked the same record), the network operating system informs the application that the record is not available.

The locked region can encompass a portion of a data record, one data record, several physically adjacent data records, or the entire file. The choice is up to the application programmer. If each data record in a file is independent of all the others, the application simply locks the affected data record. However, if relationships exist among the records in a file (perhaps one record contains a pointer to another record, or the updating of the file implies that several records may need to be physically moved in the file), the application may lock the entire file as if it were a single large record. In either case, the record lock usually lasts only a few milliseconds.

Multiuser Printing

You would think that sending print data to a shared network printer would be easy, painless, and not nearly as much trouble as trying to share files and records. Unfortunately, this isn't so.

Suppose that a person on the network is running Lotus 1-2-3 and needs to print a spreadsheet in condensed (small) print because it is several cells wide. The person sends control codes to the printer, prints the spreadsheet, and walks away from the network printer with a nicely formatted printout in hand. The next person on the LAN to print a report receives a printout with data tightly bunched on the left side of the page in small characters. (The previous person's software left the printer in condensed print mode.)

Here is another example: you tell your application to print a lengthy, complex report. To your bewilderment, you find that other people's printouts are intermingled in the pages of your report. The page breaks occur nowhere near where they should. Yet the report prints correctly on a local (non-LAN-attached) printer. (The network software is inserting automatic page breaks and breaking the printout into multiple print jobs. In this example, the application performs lengthy processing steps between sections of the report. The network operating system senses these pauses and, at each pause, thinks the application has finished printing.)

LAN Server tries to detect when an application finishes printing. The workstation can set a time-out value to help the network operating system know when a pause in printing really means the end of a print job. In addition,

LAN Server allows you to press Ctrl-Alt-Print Screen to signal the end of a print job.

You can create a file that LAN Server uses to print job separator pages between printouts. The job separator page supports a wide variety of printer control options, and you can use these options not only to say what the separator page should look like but also to reset the printer to a default mode before each printout is produced. If you do not specify a job separator file, LAN Server uses its DEFAULT.SEP file.

Software Licensing on Networks

Your organization needs to purchase enough software licenses (copies of a software product) to cover all the concurrent uses of that software product. For instance, if a maximum of 10 workstations on a LAN will run WordPerfect at one time, you need to buy ten licenses. To do otherwise is a form of theft known as software piracy. To avoid legal problems, some organizations buy licenses for each and every person on the LAN.

You can often install one copy of the software on a file server and let people run that software at multiple workstations. However, you should still have purchased as many software licenses as there are people who will run the software.

Some vendors of shrink-wrapped software offer "network packs"—you buy a license for concurrent use by up to 5, 10, or more people. Lotus Development sells a network version of 1-2-3 in a network pack. A few vendors offer "site licenses." A site license gives your organization the legal right to run as many concurrent copies of the software as you would like. Site licenses are appropriate for networks of more than 10 people, if you and the seller of the software license can negotiate a mutually satisfactory arrangement for the site license.

■ Sharing Clipboards between Applications

The clipboard sharing and network dynamic data exchange feature of LAN Server lets you exchange information between applications on different workstations, without explicitly copying or sharing a named file on the file server. A destination application can receive the current contents of the clipboard (static sharing) or can receive updates as they occur in the source application (dynamic sharing). The two workstations might be running the same or different applications. However, the application programs must offer a Paste Link function if they are to share data dynamically.

Using NetDDE

When you share data through the clipboard, you transfer the data statically or dynamically, depending on whether you simply copy the data from the clipboard or set up a link to the data. With static transfers, updates to the original information on the source computer don't automatically get reflected in the destination application. You have to reshare the clipboard, and the other person has to connect to the shared clippings and recopy the data, before the destination application gets the latest version of the data.

Establishing dynamic links between workstations is an alternative to sharing and copying static data. Through the clipboards of two workstations, you use Network Dynamic Data Exchange (NetDDE) to cause the information in the destination application to always be up-to-date.

DDE links are sometimes fragile. Renaming, deleting, or moving a file involved in the DDE link can break the link. Not all applications support DDE, and those that claim to support DDE sometimes don't correctly implement the DDE specification. If both workstations involved in the DDE linkage are not up and running at the time the link needs to transfer data, the transfer can't take place. If you want to update the source data, you must run an application on the source workstation; you can't remotely update the data from the destination workstation. If you create a lot of NetDDE links, your computer (and your network) may slow down significantly as it tries to keep up with the NetDDE requests and responses that your PC must process.

The person in your organization who designed the link may go on a long vacation (or even get a different job)—you need to document DDE links to make sure everyone knows which DDE links exist, where the data links from, and where the data links to. DDE links may seem like an easy-to-set-up, fun-to-use technology. But be aware of the extra layer of control and administration that you'll need to impose if you want the right data to always flow to the right application at the right time.

DDE Basics

When you create a dynamic link between two applications, using DDE, your clipboard (for links local to your PC) or your clippings (for over-the-network links) acts as a data transfer agent. You use special Copy and Paste operations to establish the link between the source document and the dependent document.

The classic example of why you'd use DDE is a word processing document that contains regularly updated spreadsheet data. The spreadsheet might be a product of Excel, 1-2-3 for Windows, or Quattro Pro for Windows. You use the Copy command in the spreadsheet program to put a copy of the data into the clipboard. You then choose either Paste or Paste Link in a Windows word processor (perhaps Word for Windows or Ami Pro) to transfer the clipboard data into the document.

If you choose Paste, you'll get an image of the spreadsheet data as it existed the moment the data was copied to the clipboard. Pasting doesn't involve Dynamic Data Exchange. When the spreadsheet changes (when the new sales numbers come in on the second day of the month, for example), you'll need to Copy the spreadsheet data to the clipboard and re-Paste. If you forget to Copy and Paste the new figures, the word processing document will be out of date.

Choosing Paste Link, on the other hand, does not merely copy the clipboard data to the destination document. Paste Link uses the clipboard to tell the source application (the spreadsheet software) what to link. DDE transfers the spreadsheet data to the word processing document. After you choose Paste Link, you see a dialog box asking if you want the link to update anytime the spreadsheet figures change; if you say yes, the spreadsheet software will control when updates happen. If you say no, the word processor will control when updates happen. The next time you load the document in the word processor, the word processor will automatically try to reestablish the link and transfer the (possibly changed) spreadsheet figures.

DDE Clients and Servers

The basic concept behind DDE is that of a conversation. There are two applications: a client and a server. The client initiates and controls the conversation flow, and the server responds to requests from the client. Applications often act as both client and server, carrying on multiple conversations simultaneously. As long as you understand the basic conversation verbs, you can establish communications between applications at will.

Types of DDE Links

DDE is an open-ended, language-independent, message-based protocol that lets applications exchange data or commands in any mutually agreed-on format. In a conversation between client and server, the client is the initiator. The following table identifies the types of messages supported by DDE:

Message	Application	Description
INITIATE	Client	Begins a conversation.
INITIATE	Server	Acknowledges conversation initiation.
REQUEST	Client	Requests data from server.
DATA	Server	Sends data to a client.

Message	Application	Description
EXECUTE	Client	Requests command execution.
ADVISE	Client	Establishes a hot link with a server. The server notifies the client when changes occur.
UNADVISE	Client	Terminates a hot link.
POKE	Client	Sends data to a server.
ACK	Client or server	A positive or negative acknowledgment of a previous request.
TERMINATE	Client or server	Terminates a conversation.

Using DDE Across the Network

When you create a DDE link across the network, you establish a hot link between two applications. The data in the dependent document updates automatically whenever you change the source file. To create the first half of the link—on the source workstation—you select the desired portion of the data to be shared, copy the data to the clipboard, and use the Clipboard Sharing and Network DDE to put the data in a new clipping. You then share the new clipping as a LAN resource.

You complete the creation of the link at the destination workstation. You open the destination workstation's Clipboard Sharing and Network DDE to connect to the source workstation. The source workstation's clippings appear in list form. You click on the name of the clipping containing the data you want to link, to highlight that entry in the list, then copy the clipping to the clipboard. You then run the application that will receive the link and choose Paste Special in that application's Edit menu. After you indicate the type of data you're linking and click on the Paste Link button, the link activates. The destination application now displays the linked data. Changing the data on the source workstation causes the data within the destination workstation to update automatically.

Copying, Cutting, and Pasting a Shared Clipboard

On Windows or OS/2 workstations, the icon labeled Network DDE and Clipboard is the key to sharing data between applications running on separate workstations. When you double-click the icon, you see a window consisting entirely of pushbuttons. These buttons have the labels Copy clipboard, Copy

Clipping, Manage Clippings, Control Access, View Links, Active Workstations, and Clear clipboard.

A clipping is a clipboard that you want to save for later use or transfer to another workstation. To display a window that will allow you to copy data stored in a remotely saved clipping, and view DDE link details about remote clippings, use the Copy Clipping button.

To display a window that will allow you to copy data stored in a remote clipboard to your clipboard, use the Copy Clipboard button. To copy data stored in a remote clipboard, use the Copy Clipboard button.

Use the Manage Clippings button to display a window that will allow you to save the contents of your clipboard as a clipping, rename or delete clippings at your workstation, or view DDE link details about your clippings.

To control network access and remote linking to data stored in your clipboard and saved clippings, use the Control Access button.

To display a window that will show information about your active links, and allow you to close links, use the View Links button.

To determine whether clipboard sharing and network DDE is started on the selected workstation, use the Active Workstations button.

The Clear Clipboard button erases the current contents of the clipboard and leaves the clipboard empty.

■ Avoiding DOS Disk Diagnostic Utilities

For two good reasons, some DOS commands and all of the DOS-based and Windows-based "disk doctor" utility products do not work on network drives. First, in a multiuser environment, the network cannot allow such operations as sorting directories or doctoring the DOS File Allocation Table. The concept of locking a file doesn't extend to locking disk directories or the File Allocation Table. A directory sort or a FAT repair effort from one workstation could "pull the rug out from beneath" the other workstations on the LAN. Secondly, computer programs that operate on disk sectors rather than files cannot access a network drive. LAN Server redirects file operations (open, read, write, close) but does not redirect sector read and sector write operations. CHKDSK performs sector-level reads and writes and is a good example of a DOS command that will not work on a network drive.

You'll also need to be careful about sharing DOS commands across the network. If workstations use different versions of DOS, trying to share commands such as XCOPY, MORE, or BACKUP will result in the message

```
Incorrect DOS version
```

Disk diagnostic and maintenance utilities do not work on file server hard drives. To use one of these products, you need to boot the file server with plain DOS and run the software before you start the network. Recent versions of the most popular DOS-based hard-drive utility, Norton Utilities from Symantec Corporation, detect the presence of the network and provide informative error messages to tell you why Norton Utilities cannot run in the network environment. Other popular hard-drive utilities that don't work on a network drive include PC Tools Deluxe, from Central Point Software; HDTest, from Peter Fletcher; SpinRite, from Gibson Research; OPTune, from Gazelle Systems; and Mace Utilities, from Fifth Generation Systems, Inc.

■ Working with Word Processors and Spreadsheets

People who do word processing on a LAN need to keep track of document files, need to avoid two people editing the same file at the same time, and sometimes need to convert from one word processor file format to another. The directory structure you create on the file server will help manage the document files your team creates. You can design a directory structure in which there's an assigned location for each and every word processing file. Publish the directory structure to the team, perhaps by posting a note on a bulletin board, and make sure everyone knows why it's important to adhere to the established structure. You may even want to consider using a database manager software product to help keep track of document files if you have hundreds or thousands of files.

Avoiding concurrent access of a word processing file is easy if you implement the concept of file ownership. To put this concept into use, you can use naming conventions and your directory structure. Emphasize to the team that files of a certain name pattern or files in a certain directory belong to one person—the person who "owns" those files. People who want to change those files must ask permission of the file's owner. This lets one person have responsibility and authority for knowing which files are being updated. The owner can update one of his or her files at any time, provided someone else hasn't asked permission to update that file.

HINT. *If your team uses a collection of "boilerplate" documents—template files that you customize for individual use—consider putting the template files in a separate directory and giving all the template files an attribute of READ-ONLY. You'll then avoid the problem of people overlaying the templates with other files and you'll avoid file collisions. Files marked READ-ONLY can be concurrently shared by many people without danger of one person overwriting another person's changes.*

TIP. *Perhaps your team uses and updates the same word processing document files or spreadsheet files over and over. Before the LAN, your team easily kept track of who had a particular file—the disk containing that file was only on one person's desk at a given moment. With the LAN, however, you need to find a different way to track possession of a file. You might consider designating each of the frequently accessed files as a resource in Schedule+ and, as described in the previous chapter, scheduling the team's access to those files.*

Some people on the LAN might use WordPerfect, some might use Word for Windows, while others might use AMI Pro. If members of your team use different word processing software products, you'll want to agree on a common file format you can use to share document files. For whatever word processors your team uses, you'll want to examine the import and export capabilities of each software product to determine the "lowest common denominator"—the file format that all the software products can both read and write. Test your software's file conversion functions yourself; don't rely on the vendor's claims of file format compatibility. One of your team members may possibly use a feature of a word processor that some file formats cannot represent.

The same techniques you use to manage and control access to word processing files can be used for spreadsheet (worksheet) files, such as those you would create with Quattro Pro, Excel, or Lotus 1-2-3 for Windows.

■ Running Communications Programs

You can configure your LAN so that people can reach out to other computers from your LAN (bulletin board systems; an information service such as Prodigy, CompuServe, or America Online; or a host computer). And you can set things up so that people outside your office can access your LAN remotely through a communications link. You can also share a fax machine on your LAN.

Sharing a Modem

On a LAN Server network, OS/2-based workstations running native OS/2 communications programs can share modems on the LAN. The LAN administrator creates an alias for a shared modem just as he or she does for a shared disk drive or printer. LAN Server allows OS/2 communications software to access the shared modem. DOS and Windows workstations, on the other hand, need additional products, in addition to LAN Server, to be able to connect to a shared modem.

Remote Access to the LAN

You can access a LAN remotely in one of five ways, and each has its advantages and drawbacks. The simplest, least satisfying way is mere file transfer. If one of the computers on your LAN runs bulletin board software, or if you transfer a file to someone on the LAN through an e-mail service such as MCI Mail, you're in the first category. The second category consists of application-specific access to the LAN, usually for e-mail purposes. Users of cc:Mail Remote are in this second category. Remote control, through which you treat an in-the-office PC as a slave through your modem, is the third category. When you use a product like pcANYWHERE, Close-Up, or Carbon Copy to control another PC by sending the PC your keystrokes and viewing an echo of the PC's screen on your own screen, you're using remote control. Multiuser remote control is yet another, fourth category. An 80386 or better PC in the office, with lots of RAM and several modems attached, can multi-task several concurrent remote control sessions.

The final category is remote access, through which your remote PC actually connects—on a dial-up basis—to the central LAN and becomes just another workstation node. While different implementations of remote access provide varying degrees of emphasis on performance, ease-of-use, interoperability, and security, all remote access products work hard to make you think you're locally attached to your LAN, just as if you were sitting in front of the computer at your desk in the office. Remote access technology turns your modem into a network adapter, figuratively speaking.

A simple way to enable remote access to the LAN is to use remote-control software. The remote user runs one copy of the software on his or her computer; a workstation on the LAN, with a modem attached, runs another copy. The remote user controls the workstation computer remotely, from his or her remote computer. The mirroring of screen and keyboard activity makes the remote user think he or she is logged into the LAN directly. In reality, the LAN workstation does all the work.

The remote-control approach is simple but it has drawbacks. While the remote user is communicating through the LAN workstation, that workstation cannot be used by anyone else. If you do not use fast modems, the remote user experiences slow response time. The remote PC becomes merely a terminal through which the screen and keyboard activity of the LAN-attached computer is mirrored. If an application changes the appearance of the screen frequently, or if the application uses graphics rather than text (as does Microsoft Windows), a remote control product is hard-pressed to keep up with the activity.

IBM's LAN Distance product, for example, implements the remote workstation driver software as an Advanced Network Driver Interface Specification (Advanced NDIS, or just ANDIS) module. Advanced NDIS extends the NDIS standard to encompass such modem-oriented functions as dialing the phone and keeping track of the modem's carrier signal. Advanced NDIS works with modems the same way NDIS works with network adapters, and you can generally use an Advanced NDIS driver in place of a regular network adapter NDIS driver. This degree of interoperability means you can run any NDIS-compliant workstation network software you wish on your remote PC, and you can attach to LAN Server from a remote site. LAN Distance and LAN Server work well together.

Sharing a Fax Machine

Fax machines are essential tools in offices today, just as are networks. The combination of the two is an interesting marriage of technologies. If you do not have a LAN-based fax server, you typically take the following steps to send a document by fax:

- You use a word processor or perhaps other application software to prepare the document you want to send by fax.

- You print out the document pages and you fill out a fax cover page.

- You walk over to the fax machine, punch in the telephone number, and send the document.

When the fax machine prints an incoming document addressed to you, someone in the office may drop it off at your desk or you may have to visit the fax machine periodically to retrieve your fax correspondence.

A LAN-based fax server saves both steps and paper. You can send fax documents directly from your workstation, without printing them first. The LAN-based software prepares much of your cover page for you. The same word processing or other application software creates the document file, but you send the printout to the LAN-based fax server rather than to a printer. Under software control, the document goes into the fax queue to wait its turn for transmission.

For incoming fax documents, the fax server device stores the image in a file on a file server. You or an administrator can route the file to your workstation, where you view the image (the document) at your leisure. If you want to print the fax, you can, but you do not have to.

■ Using Database Managers and Other Client/ Server Products

While word processing and spreadsheet software products are inherently single-user (at least for now), database management products have a natural affinity for multiuser environments. Products such as the Windows-based Access and Paradox for Windows computer programs, the fi-S/2-based DB2/2 and Oracle, and the DOS-based DataEase, dBASE, FoxPro, Paradox, and R:BASE computer programs permit concurrent, shared access to files from multiple workstations. These applications perform file sharing, record locking, and logon account name detection to make it possible for several people to work on the same database of customer records, inventory records, accounting records, or other collections of records at the same time.

You'll want to follow the directions in the reference manual for your database manager closely and carefully. Many will insist you run the DOS SHARE.EXE program before you start the database manager program. You should also ensure that each person on the LAN has a unique logon account name and a unique computer name.

Running a database manager product on a LAN represents a higher level of network usage, compared with word processing or spreadsheet product LAN usage. Even if you only have a few people on the network, running a database manager is a strong criterion for making one of the PCs on the LAN an unattended file server machine. You don't want someone running applications at the file server to cause the server to lock up; if database updates are in progress when the server freezes, the database will likely become corrupted. Even if the server doesn't crash, you don't want the server to provide slow responses to people who are accessing the database.

Database manager software always requires faster, bigger computers than other types of software. This is especially true under Windows. The cost of the software may seem reasonable or even cheap, but don't forget to factor into your budget the cost of larger hard drives and more RAM to enable the database manager software to function.

■ Summary

In this chapter, you explored application software on a LAN Server network. You became familiar with the characteristics of multiuser applications, you learned how to use LAN Server's NetDDE function to share clipboard data, and you gained an understanding of how word processors, spreadsheets, communications programs, and database managers behave on a LAN.

The next chapter introduces you to programming in a LAN Server environment.

- *Nan2702/Index/F1/mdbInformation Processing on*

---

  a LAN
- *Computer Languages*
- *Creating Batch File and REXX Programs*
- *Sharing Files*
- *Working with the LAN Server API*
- *Sending Data with NetBIOS*
- *Testing and Debugging on a LAN*

9

LAN Server Programming

THIS CHAPTER HELPS YOU GET STARTED WITH PROGRAMMING YOUR LAN. If you're a programmer, you'll find information and references on the various APIs available to you in the LAN Server environment, including a detailed look at NetBIOS. If you're not a programmer, this chapter's discussion of client/server technology will help you understand what your LAN is capable of; you'll thus be able to talk effectively with programmers about the levels of automation you'd like to have.

■ Information Processing on a LAN

LAN Server is an excellent environment for client/server computing. It's relatively easy to program an OS/2 computer, even one that is already running as a file server. If you have a staff of programmers, or if the application software you buy already supports it, client/server architecture becomes a possibility. SQL Server, Oracle, and DB2/2 are examples of relational database managers that work well on OS/2-based LANs. LAN Server offers file sharing and printer sharing in an environment that encourages custom programming and efficient use of network resources.

■ Client/Server Advantages

Client/server computing challenges you to inexpensively create business automation systems that are appropriately sized, easy to use, easy to maintain, and distributed across your organization's computers. These criteria apply equally to the smallest and the largest systems that you develop and manage. From the smallest employee badge ID and personnel scheduling systems that you develop to support your company's security department to the largest administration, sales, billing, collection, and statistical systems you develop to support your company's line-of-business, day-to-day core operations, the systems you provide should all—eventually—embrace the advantages and benefits of client/server technology.

Distributing the processing power of your organization's computers onto the desktops of the people who use those computers entails careful design of the distribution of processing power. You want to distribute the application logic in appropriate ways, using technologies that help the system perform more effectively. At the same time, you want to avoid technologies that might prove to be incapable of handling the current and future workload, that might cause developers to have to rethink their design, or that simply might not work for your organization.

■ Distribution of Processing Power

Sometimes called "downsizing," sometimes "rightsizing," the hallmark of distributed systems is the deployment of application logic onto inexpensive desktop computers. Whether your programmers use COBOL, C, C++, REXX, or some other programming language, the desktop computer affords your end users a friendly interface and the ability to accomplish greater amounts of work than if they depended totally on a large-scale computer that might be thousands of miles away. While you might very well use a large-scale computer as a data repository that all your locations reference, the inexpensive desktop computers offload a considerable amount of data collection, editing, and formatting chores from the central computer. Desktop computers, mid-range computers, and large-scale computers can treat each other as peers in your client/server design. With more of the processing occurring inside the desktop computer, you also reduce the computer-to-end-user communications workload and corresponding message traffic.

The trend toward distributed client/server application systems puts computing power close to the people who can make the best use of it. From a practical standpoint, distributing the logic of an application onto desktop computers helps offload data collection, editing, and formatting from a large-scale computer. Distribution of processing also cuts down on the need for extra high-speed communications links between geographically-distant sites. The desktop computer doesn't have to send and receive over-the-wire messages every time a person presses the Enter key. In your organization, you can probably think of many practical benefits to distributing an application onto desktop computers.

Scalability

For some systems you develop, you'll want the ability to run your application software inside the same computer that's acting as a file server or database server. For other systems, your design might call for separate computers to play individual roles as database servers, file servers, and calculation engines. You might very well want to deploy the same application software in two locations, one large and one small, and only vary the mix of computers on which you run the software. Your own analysis of the workload volume at each location will help you decide how many PC configurations you'll need to create.

Implementing Appropriate Systems

It doesn't make sense to try to develop a distributed client/server application system whose size never varies from location to location or from one year to the next. An organization with a large office in New York City and a small office in Cheyenne, Wyoming, will want to implement appropriate systems for each location. If the workload volume at one location increases considerably, you'll want to be able to accommodate that growth with appropriate additional computing power. The ability to incrementally add computers and software to a growing office location will help make that location productive in cost-effective ways.

■ One Size Doesn't Fit All

At a large office site with many employees and a large workload, you easily accept the fact that you'll install multiple file servers and configure several unattended PCs to perform individual tasks. At a small office site, however, you may not have the budget—much less the floor space—to install the same application system configuration you install at the larger site. You may very well want a file server computer to take on additional tasks beyond sharing its files with workstations. These tasks might include calculating results, formatting print streams, or acting as a database server. The combination of OS/2 and LAN Server makes it possible for you to painlessly configure different computers to perform different roles in your system. Other combinations of operating systems and network software either do not permit such consolidation of automation tasks or require such a tremendous amount of PC resources that you might as well have purchased extra computers to play different roles in your system. The network software and your client/server application should cost-effectively support your smallest and largest offices.

LAN Server/400 and LAN Server/6000

Scalability is more than being able to choose the processing power of the PC you'll use as a file server. It's even more than being able to run additional programs inside the file server computer. Scalability also encompasses being able to choose mid-range computers such as an AS/400 or RS/6000 as file servers in those instances when even the fastest PC isn't up to the challenge of running your system. Perhaps the PC doesn't have the horsepower your application requires, or perhaps you have AS/400 or RS/6000 applications you'd like to integrate with your PC-based software.

While LAN Server originated as a PC-only network operating system, IBM has migrated the LAN Server product onto the AS/400 and RS/6000 computers. You can now choose the right type of computer on which to run your network software. From a LAN-aware perspective, the client/server computer programs you develop for the AS/400 or RS/6000 computers can easily take part in your overall distribution of data, business logic, and/or presentation across your organization. These non-PC-based versions of LAN Server offer greater performance than the PC versions and also help you consolidate the administration of your LAN. The storage of mission-critical data on an AS/400 or RS/6000 computer lets you use the mid-range computer's native data backup and restore facilities. When you make backup copies of your AS/400 files, for instance, you're also making backup copies of the data on your file server. The data integrity features of these mid-range computers apply equally to file server data as well as to the other data stored on the computer. And the administration of logon accounts only needs to occur once for both AS/400 (or RS/6000) accounts and LAN Server accounts.

Computer programs running inside the mid-range computer and programs running in the workstations around the LAN can all concurrently access shared files. As with any other LAN-aware application, the programs use record locking to prevent one program from over-writing another program's in-progress updates.

■ The Five Client/Server Models

There are many ways to categorize client/server computing. The three-tier, five-model matrix is an especially useful way to categorize client/server because the matrix helps you visualize at a glance how you can distribute the three tiers of your systems—data, logic, and presentation.

In the Distributed Presentation and Remote Presentation models, the two tiers of data and logic reside at a central site. Only the presentation tier (data collection and viewing functions) exists at the location where people work. These models might, for example, use a mainframe or midrange computer for storage and processing purposes. The distributed portion of this example, the presentation tier, might consist of PCs that display screens and collect data. At the central site, the Distributed Presentation model prepares the screens that people interact with and transmits those screens to the remote location. Distributed Presentation screens are text-mode screens rather than graphical (GUI) screens. The Remote Presentation model allows the remote computers (PCs) to display graphical interface screens, but the business logic that controls the interactive dialogs still remains at the central site.

The Distributed Logic model characterizes systems in which data resides at a central site but some or all business logic and all presentation screens exist at each remote location. Designers often choose this model to balance processor workload and message traffic. Additionally, because developers find programming PCs a relatively easy task, this model is a popular one.

In the Remote Data and Distributed Data models, all three tiers—data, logic, and presentation—are located close or virtually close to the people using the system. The Remote Data model describes a system whose data repository is at a central site but whose software accesses that data as if it existed on the local (in the workplace) system. The software typically uses IBM's Distributed Relational Database Architecture (DRDA) to make the distributed system software believe it's accessing locally-stored data, when in fact the data repository is at the central site. On the other hand, the Distributed Data model stores data locally, in the workplace, and may very well employ a database replication mechanism to also store application system data at a central site. With DRDA, you can easily switch your application from

Remote Data to Distributed Data or (vice versa). You merely copy the database to the appropriate new location and change a system catalog entry to cause your application to use the new client/server model.

■ LAN Server and Programming

Programmability is the biggest reason that people talk about client/server in connection with the OS/2-based network operating system, LAN Server. OS/2 is easily programmed, perhaps even more so than DOS. LAN Server can share the network adapter with other OS/2 application software running on the file server computer. OS/2 *multitasks*, which means that it runs several computer programs concurrently. One such computer program is the network operating system, of course. Another may be a database server application. The workstations can see and use the extra drive letters provided by the network operating system. Your programming staff also may program the workstations to send and receive special requests and responses to and from the file server (or a separate computer, for that matter). These custom-programmed requests and responses may, for example, carry SQL statements and relational database records.

OS/2 provides *named pipes* to programmers. The programmer treats a named pipe almost exactly as he or she would a file, but the named pipe actually contains message records. These message records travel from the workstation to the file server. On the file server, a custom-written application may do some record handling and other processing before returning a response to the workstation through the named pipe.

DB2 for OS/2 is an IBM product that enables programmers to create client/server applications. DB2/2 provides a relational database "engine" that you install on an OS/2 computer on the network. Programmers write workstation software that sends SQL statements to DB2/2. The relational database manager DB2/2 honors each request by sending back the appropriate records from within its database. Some database management products, such as Microsoft's FoxPro and Borland's Paradox, can work with DB2/2 to give you the ability to update and query your data without hiring COBOL or C-language programmers.

LAN Server is an excellent environment for client/server computing. IBM, Borland, Watcom, Metaware, Computer Associates, Microfocus, and many other vendors offer compilers that emit OS/2 programs. In addition, IBM's easy-to-use REXX language, which IBM includes in the base OS/2 product, can access LAN Server functions as well as perform other client/server tasks. If you can use REXX, if you have a staff of programmers, or if the application software you buy already supports it, client/server architecture becomes a possibility. SQL Server, Oracle, and DB2/2 are examples of relational database managers that work well on OS/2-based LANs. OS/2 runs in protected mode in a flat, 32-bit memory model. IBM includes LAN Server programming specifications with LAN Server. OS/2 is an excellent base for advanced, high-end PC networking. It has multi-tasking facilities that makes it a good candidate for distributed processing, it eliminates the memory-crunch problems so often faced on LANs, and it is part of IBM's *System Application Architecture* (SAA) standard.

In addition to providing both real mode and protected mode support for file sharing, printer sharing, and PC-to-PC communications via NetBIOS, OS/2 LAN Server offers built-in support for remote program execution and various kinds/levels of interprocess communications, including APPC and named pipes.

NetBIOS

NetBIOS accepts communications requests from an application program or from LAN Server itself. These requests fall into four categories:

1. *Name Support.* Each workstation on the network is identified by one or more names. These names are maintained by NetBIOS in a table; the first item in the table is automatically the unique, permanently assigned name of the network adapter. Optional user names (such as "AppServer") can be added to the table for the sake of convenient identification of each user. These user-assigned names can be unique, or, in a special case, can refer to a group of users.

2. *Session Support.* A point-to-point connection between two names (workstations) on the network can be opened, managed, and closed under NetBIOS control. One workstation begins by "listening" for a call; the other workstation "calls" the first. The workstations are peers; both can send and receive message data concurrently during the session. At the end, both workstations "hang up" on each other.

3. *Datagram Support.* Message data can be sent to a name, a group of names, or to all names on the network. A point-to-point connection is not established and there is no guarantee that the message data will be received.

4. *Adapter/Session Status.* Information about the local network adapter card, about other network adapter cards, and about any currently active sessions is available from NetBIOS.

Advanced Program-to-Program Communications

APPC is an IBM-designed programmatic interface that fundamentally changes the way PCs communicate with larger computers. It replaces the technique of talking to a host computer through a terminal emulator with a technique that is conversation (peer-to-peer) based. IBM designed APPC to be a programmer's view of the Systems Network Architecture (SNA) standard known as *LU 6.2*. Before LU 6.2, PC/mainframe communications were accomplished by loading a terminal emulator program on the PC and forcing the emulator to pretend each byte of data to be sent was a keypress that had come from the keyboard. Similarly, receiving data from the mainframe involved intercepting 3270 screen data before it reached the terminal emulator screen.

APPC, on the other hand, assumes that two *computers* are talking to each other; both sides of the conversation are allowed to be "smart." APPC dispenses with 3270 keypress and screen-at-a-time transmissions and instead provides that only the LU 6.2 verbs and raw data move through the communications link.

Because of the peer-to-peer nature of LU 6.2 (accessed via APPC), it can be used as the basis for communications between workstations on a LAN as well as between a workstation and a mainframe (in fact, it can be used between any two computers on an SNA network). Application programs are unaware that the communications medium is Token Ring, an SDLC mainframe link, or even a direct computer-to-computer link.

There are two types of conversations possible under LU 6.2, *basic* conversations and *mapped* conversations. With mapped conversations, the protocol takes care of converting the data into a standard *generalized data stream* for sending and converting the data back into its original form upon reception. With basic conversations, the application must handle any necessary conversions. Programs that use basic conversations also have some responsibility for error recovery.

LU 6.2 implements a set of verbs. You can think of these as a programming language for developing the communications aspect of an application. Each verb is a specifically-formatted record with a particular purpose. The major verbs are the following:

ALLOCATE   Initiates a conversation with a remote application. Parameters include LU_NAME, which gives the name of the Logical Unit that represents the remote program; TPN, which gives the name of the remote program; MODE_NAME, which specifies session properties for the conversation; and SYNC_LEVEL, which specifies a synchronization level between the two conversants.

GET_ATTRIBUTES	Returns information such as mode name, partner LU name, and synchronization level about the conversation.
DEALLOCATE	Terminates a conversation.
CONFIRM	Asks the remote computer to confirm successful reception of data.
CONFIRMED	The reply sent in response to a CONFIRM verb.
SEND_DATA	Sends data to the conversation partner.
RECEIVE_AND_WAIT	Used by an application to notify the remote application that it is ready to receive data; waits for a response.

You can see from this description of APPC and LU 6.2 that these are powerful tools. There are costs, however. The PC implementation of APPC takes up a sizable chunk of memory (a resident program that offers a subset of APPC can be as small as 70K to 80K; full APPC takes a little under 200K of resident code) and, under DOS, this is a big concern. Under OS/2, however, such memory constraints are not a consideration. In the OS/2 environment, network software doesn't consume any of the 640k of conventional DOS memory. IBM's Communications Manager/2 (CM/2) product includes an APPC implementation that lets OS/2-based PCs easily send and receive information in the form of message records that flow through LAN cables or other physical media.

In addition, you can achieve platform independence by using the SAA Common Programming Interface-Communications (CPI-C) calling conventions and code libraries to create your LU 6.2-aware programs. A program that uses the CPI-C conventions can compile and run, unmodified, on several different types of computers. The list of these computers includes 370 architecture mainframes, AS/400 mid-range computers, desktop computers, and RS/6000 computers.

■ Computer Languages

If you're accustomed to writing assembler software, you'll be right at home with the services the network provides. The fundamental interface to the network in both the DOS and Windows environments consists of putting certain values in the CPU registers and performing a software interrupt. Within the OS/2 environment, you perform a far call to a function in a DLL. Assembler programmers can easily construct code that invokes these network services.

For any other language besides assembler, you'll need to discover the extent to which your language gives you an ability to either set up CPU registers and perform software interrupts or, for OS/2, call system functions from within your program.

C and C++ programmers who want to develop DOS or Windows software can take advantage of the int86x() function mentioned earlier in this chapter. The int86x() function allows these programmers to set registers and invoke a software interrupt. In addition to offering the int86x() function, the Borland C/C++ compiler for DOS and Windows also offers direct access to CPU registers and a geninterrupt() function for invoking a software interrupt without going through a library call. Furthermore, the calling interface to the network services is one natural to the C language. IBM supplies you with C header files and import libraries that fit right into a C language development environment. If you work in C++, you might even create your own objects for the network services you invoke.

Pascal programmers can also set CPU registers and invoke software interrupts. For instance, Turbo Pascal offers the MsDos() procedure for issuing Interrupt 21h and the Intr() procedure for issuing other interrupts. Turbo Pascal programmers can also write inline assembler statements that invoke network services. If you're a Pascal programmer, however, you'll need to understand enough assembler or C to translate the calling conventions for a particular network service into a form you can easily code in your program.

Similarly, most Basic compilers and Basic development environments supply programmers with intermediate subprograms (in library or DLL form) that the programmer can use to set CPU registers and invoke network services. Basic programmers can adopt the same approach as Pascal programmers to translate the calling conventions into a form they can use in their programs. Unfortunately, Basic compilers don't offer a means to easily code a callback function that network software can invoke when a particular event occurs. In fact, many Basic or similar-to-Basic development environments (such as Visual Basic for Windows, PowerBuilder, and ObjectView) do not compile the Basic statements into executable machine code, but rather provide an interpreter program that uses a tokenized version of the Basic program to know what processing to perform at run-time. To produce NetBIOS-aware computer programs, Basic programmers usually need to develop static library or DLL functions in C or assembler that their Basic programs can use.

■ Creating Batch File and REXX Programs

In DOS, the program COMMAND.COM executes the commands and statements in your batch files. In OS/2 sessions, CMD.EXE executes the commands and statements. COMMAND.COM and CMD.EXE are the same operating system components that process the commands you enter at a command line prompt. COMMAND.COM and CMD.EXE process your batch file commands by simulating keyboard entry of those commands. Because the commands are stored in a text file, however, you don't have to worry about typing errors. This benefit is especially important if you use a long sequence of commands frequently or if one or more of the commands requires command line parameters that are difficult to use.

The command processors in OS/2, for both OS/2 and DOS sessions, execute your batch file programs one line at a time. The command processor begins with the first line of your batch file. Unless you direct otherwise, the statements in your batch file execute one after the other, from the top of the file to the bottom. You can use the GOTO statement to change the order in which the commands and statements execute.

OS/2 batch file programs have an extension of CMD. DOS batch files use BAT. Most commands work the same whether you run the commands in a CMD file in an OS/2 session or run the commands in a BAT file in a DOS session. Some commands behave differently, however, or are not supported in one kind of session or the other. START, for example, is an OS/2-only command; MEM is an example of a DOS-only command. MKDIR, on the other hand, works the same in DOS and OS/2 sessions, assuming that you use the same directory names in each session.

You'll find detailed information on batch file and REXX programming in various technical references, including IBM's online REXX.INF file (use the OS/2 utility VIEW to read the online documentation). However, the following sections of this chapter reveal some of the LAN-oriented tasks you can do with batch file programming and REXX.

■ Saving Your Work

Many office environments use a single tape drive to make backup copies of files on a local area network. To include your files in the office's backup procedure, you must copy files from your PC to the file server. Assuming that your file server is drive F and that you customarily put files in the F:\BACKUP directory so that the LAN tape drive can back up the files, you can automate your daily backup chores with the following batch file program:

```
@echo off
COPY C:\DOC\*.DOC F:\BACKUP
COPY C:\WKS\*.WK1 F:\BACKUP
COPY C:\DATA\*.DAT F:\BACKUP
```

Although you can type each of these commands individually at a command line prompt, you have to wait for one command to finish executing before you type the next command. A batch file accomplishes all of the work of the several commands in one typing operation. You can insert these three lines with a text editor in a DOS batch file (named SAVEWORK.BAT, perhaps) or an OS/2 batch file (named SAVEWORK.CMD).

If you run this three-line batch file program from a DOS-only (non-OS/2-based) workstation and if the files take a long time to copy, you must find something else to do while that computer runs the COPY commands. With OS/2, however, you can start the batch file in one session and continue to work in other sessions.

REXX on a LAN

Your batch file program can execute different commands or programs depending on whether a file exists, but a batch file program cannot prompt the person running the program for information. The batch file program also cannot perform calculations. The next logical step beyond simple batch file programs is REXX, which does provide these capabilities (and more). REXX allows you to embed programming language statements in your batch file programs, along with OS/2 commands and utilities. REXX programming is only slightly more complicated than batch file programming.

A REXX program is an OS/2 batch file with special capabilities. You write a REXX program by using a text editor to create a text file with an extension of CMD, and you make the first line a REXX comment line. A REXX comment starts with the two characters /* and ends with the two characters */.

NOTE. *The first line of a REXX program must contain /* */. If the REXX comment line is the second line of the text file (perhaps you left the first line blank), OS/2 will not treat the file as a REXX program. Also, you may need to install REXX support, via OS/2's selective install facility, before you can run your REXX programs.*

On your LAN Server file server, in the IBMLAN\NETPROG directory, you'll find some REXX programs that can help you administer your LAN. The DSPDOMDF.CMD program, for example, displays information about domains, logon accounts, and shared resources.

You can make one system login script for all users, and that script can be a REXX program. While the standard utilities require you to specify the login script for each user individually, you can modify your LAN Server environment to have the same script used by all logon accounts.

To make the same script work for all accounts, you write a REXX script to execute at the server. This script takes the output of the NET USERS command and executes the NET USER username /SCRIPT:scriptname for each user on the server.

If you leave the extension off of the script, you can have a LOGON.CMD and a LOGON.BAT file so that DOS and OS/2 users have the same script name. If a same user logs in from an OS/2 machine, they'll run LOGON.CMD, and if the same user logs in from a DOS machine, they'll run LOGON.BAT. Put the script in the \ibmlan\repl\import\scripts directory on the domain controller. To enable it for a logon account, use the NET USER acctname /script:cmdfile command where acctname is the logon account name and cmdfile is the script's base name.

■ Sharing Files

How your programs manage files in a LAN Server environment depends on the extent to which you want (or expect) multiple workstations to access those files at the same time. You can control access at the level of the entire file or, with finer control, at the level of specific records within a file. The following discussions apply to high-level languages in general (COBOL, Basic, C, and Pascal, for instance), but the emphasis is on C.

File Ownership

At the time an application opens a file, it specifies three things to DOS or OS/2: *Access Mode*, *Sharing Mode*, and *Inheritance*. How the file is handled by the network also depends on whether the file has an attribute of Read-Only.

You can set the Inheritance flag to "File is Inheritable" if you are spawning one or more child processes that need to have access to a file opened by the main program. Setting this flag allows the child process to use the same file handle issued to the main program by the *open()* call.

Access Mode indicates whether you intend to write to the file. You should use this flag conservatively; if you only need to read from a file, open it with an Access Mode of *Read-Only*. This gives you a better chance of successfully opening the file, because the network software allows multiple readers of a file but rejects a *Read-Write* open if others already have the file open in *Read-Only* mode. Similarly, if a workstation has opened a file for *Read-Write* access and subsequent attempts are made by other workstations to open the file for *Read-Only* access, the subsequent attempts will fail.

The value of Sharing Mode lets you control how other workstations can open the file once it's opened successfully by your workstation. Sharing Mode is expressed in terms of denying certain capabilities to the other workstations that attempt to open the file. The restrictions you can specify are

DENY_NONE, *DENY_READ*, *DENY_WRITE*, and *DENY_READ_WRITE*. In addition, there is a special mode called *Compatibility Mode*.

DENY_READ_WRITE Mode (Exclusive Access)

When you open a file in *DENY_READ_WRITE* mode, you gain exclusive access to the file. While you have the file open, no other workstation can read from the file or write to it. The file belongs to you until it's closed. By the same token, however, your open attempt will fail if another workstation already has the file open in any other mode.

DENY_WRITE Mode

Opening a file in *DENY_WRITE* mode allows other workstations to open and read from the file, but not to write to it. The other workstations must open the file for Read-Only access in *DENY_NONE* mode, or else their open attempts will fail. Likewise, an attempt to open a file in *DENY_WRITE* mode will fail if any other workstation has the file open in a *DENY_WRITE* or *DENY_READ_WRITE* (exclusive) mode.

DENY_READ Mode

You can cause other workstations to fail to open a file for reading if you open it first in *DENY_READ* mode. Strangely, this mode allows multiple workstations to write to a file but not to read from it. It is perhaps a less useful mode than the others, at least in common practice.

DENY_NONE Mode

This mode, *DENY_NONE*, represents the "joint, communal ownership" situation mentioned earlier. It allows multiple workstations to open a file for read/write access, and it defers control of concurrent reads and writes to the record locking functions described below.

Compatibility Mode

Compatibility Mode, generally, is an exclusive mode. It's set automatically when a file is created (as opposed to opened) or when you use File Control Blocks—FCBs—instead of File Handles. You should avoid this mode when you open a file, and you should also avoid using FCBs in LAN-Aware software. FCBs are a holdover from DOS 1.X, and they continue to be supported by DOS only so that users can run "old" programs. (That's where this mode got its name). Compatibility Mode is also in effect when you open a file with a call to *fopen()* rather than the more explicit *open()*.

In certain cases, DOS changes *Compatibility Mode* to a different file sharing mode during the process of opening the file. If a file has an attribute of Read-Only (as indicated by its directory entry), DOS replaces *Compatibility Mode* with *DENY_WRITE*. If other workstations attempt to open the file, access is allowed or denied based on the rules given under *DENY_WRITE*.

Since a newly created file falls into the *Compatibility Mode* category, which gives the creating workstation exclusive control of the file, how can you change the mode so that the new file can be shared with other workstations? Unfortunately, there is no mechanism for changing Sharing Mode on the fly; you have to close the file and then open it with a suitable Sharing Mode.

Record Locking

Since a file lock (opening a file for exclusive access) affects the entire file and, under DOS and OS/2, extends from the time a file is opened until the time it's closed, the resulting "coarse granularity" of the lock may be an awkward inconvenience to the users of your application. It also may very well not suit the design of your application. You can choose instead to implement locking at the record level; a record lock lasts only long enough to ensure that consistent data has been written to the file(s), and it (usually) affects only a small portion of the file.

A record lock specifies a certain region of a file by giving the region's location in the file (its offset) and its size (length). If the specified region cannot be successfully locked (another workstation opened the file in other than *DENY_NONE* mode, or another workstation has locked the same record), an error is returned to your program. The locked region can encompass a portion of a data record, one data record, several physically adjacent data records, or the entire file. If each data record in a file is independent of all the others, it's appropriate to simply lock the affected data record. However, if there are relationships among the records in a file (perhaps one record contains a pointer to another, or the updating of the file implies that several records may need to be physically moved in the file), the correct approach is to lock the entire file as if it were a single large record.

Don't forget to unlock the record when you're through using the record.

DOS Function Call 0x5C, *Lock/Unlock File Access*, is used to lock or unlock a range of bytes in a file. All workstations using the file should have opened it in *DENY_NONE* mode. If DOS cannot acquire the lock, it returns an error to your program. If another workstation tries to read from or write to a locked region, DOS generates a critical error situation by invoking Interrupt 24 (hex), the Critical Error Handler (which produces an "Abort, Retry, Ignore, or Fail?" message at that other workstation). In the OS/2 environment, you call DosSetFileLocks() to either lock or unlock a region of a file.

As mentioned in the DOS Technical Reference manual, it's expected that the record lock will last for only a brief duration of time. If your program needs to make sure that a portion of the file remains untouched while it interacts with the user, you should consider implementing the Library Card scheme discussed earlier.

Also note that it's incorrect for a program to discover that a region of the file is locked by attempting to write a record and noticing that a critical error has occurred. You must first issue the lock request and, if it is successful, proceed then to write the record.

OS/2 File Sharing

Borland and IBM offer 32-bit compilers for the OS/2 2.x environment, and you can use Microsoft C 5.1 or 6.0 to create 16-bit OS/2 software. For Microsoft C, the functions *open()* and *sopen()* are also applicable to the OS/2 environment. If you want even more control over the way a file is opened, however, you can call the *DosOpen()* kernel API function directly, using any one of the three vendors' compilers:

```
char            filename[80];   /* drive, path, name      */
unsigned        handle;         /* returned file handle   */
unsigned        action;         /* action that OS/2 took  */
unsigned long   filesize;       /* file's new size in bytes */
unsigned        file_attribute; /* used when creating file */
unsigned        flag;           /* action to take         */
unsigned        open_mode;      /* Sharing Mode; Access Mode*/
unsigned long   reserved;
unsigned        return_code; /* returns 0 if successful   */

strcpy(filename, "SHARED.OS2");
filesize       = 01;
file_attribute = 0;
flag           = 0x0001;
open_mode      = 0x0042;
reserved       = 01;

return_code = DosOpen  (filename,
                        &handle,
                        &action,
                        filesize,
                        file_attribute,
                        flag,
                        open_mode,
                        reserved);
```

This example does not create a new file and so the file_attribute and filesize items are set to 0. The flag value of 0x0001 signifies that the action to take if the file exists is simply to open it and that the action to take if the file doesn't exist is to fail the call (return an error). The open_mode informs OS/2 that the file should be opened for *Read/Write* access in *Deny_None* mode. If the file is successfully opened, OS/2 returns a file handle in the handle field and sets the action field to 1 if the file exists, 2 if it was created, and 3 if the file was replaced.

■ Working with the LAN Server API

Unlike some other network operating system products, LAN Server comes with online documentation (IBM can provide you with printed versions, if you wish) to help programmers understand the intricacies of LAN programming. The online documentation is in the file A3A4AM02.INF, which the installation process copies into the IBMLAN\BOOKS directory. You can use the OS/2 utility VIEW.EXE to read the documentation. Before you delve into the details of the various APIs LAN Server offers, you'll want to read the following sections of this chapter. They provide basic information about the LAN Server programming environment. You'll also find a list of frequently-used APIs in the LAN Server API Reference Section of this book.

Workstation Identification

LAN Server and the DOS LAN Requester use Machine Names automatically. The *Net Start* command that loads and runs DLR requires a Machine Name be present in an INI file. The DOSLAN.INI and IBMLAN.INI configuration files contain machine name entries on machines running DLR and LAN Server, important because NetBIOS is a name-oriented PC-to-PC communications service. The DOS LAN Requester and OS/2 LAN Requester use NetBIOS to send file data requests and responses back and forth to the file server. The Machine Names used by DOS LAN Requester and OS/2 LAN Requester are always present and always unique.

DOS LAN Requester uses the Multiplex Interrupt 0x2F. The Multiplex Number for both products is B8 (hex), and both PCLP and DLR support the same Get Installed State call as SHARE does. If the AL register remains 0 after the call to Interrupt 2F (hex), DLR is not loaded. The following code fragment shows how to detect the presence of DLR.

```
if (_os_major < 3)
   {
   printf("Can't check for DLR.\n");
   exit(1);
   }
else
   {
   regs.h.ah = 0xB8;
```

```
regs.h.al = Ø;
int86(Øx2f, &regs, &regs);
if (regs.h.al == Ø)
      {
      printf("DLR is not running.\n");
      exit(1);
      }
}
```

Machine Name

The DOS *Get Machine Name* function call, hex 5E00, returns a 16-byte Machine Name. The name is padded on the right with spaces and is null-terminated in the 16th byte (in other words, it is an ordinary C string). This function also returns *NetBIOS Name Number*, which is really only meaningful on NetBIOS-based LANs. It is a number assigned by NetBIOS when you do either of the NetBIOS functions *Add Name* or *Add Group Name*. This function returns a 0 in the CH register if Machine Name is not defined. An example of the function follows.

```
char              machine_name[16];
unsigned char     netbios_name_number;

regs.x.dx = FP_OFF( (void far *) machine_name);
sregs.ds  = FP_SEG( (void far *) machine_name);
regs.x.ax = Øx5EØØ;
int86x(Øx21, &regs, &regs, &sregs);
if (regs.h.ch == Ø)
  {
  printf("ERROR.  Machine name not set.\n");
  exit(1);
  }

netbios_name_number = regs.h.cl;

/* If you want to use Machine Name as part of a */
/* filename, you should remove the spaces.      */

i = strlen(machine_name) - 1;
while (i > Ø && machine_name[i] == ' ')
  {
  machine_name[i] = '\Ø';
  i--;
  }
```

Logon Account Name

Your program can ask DOS LAN Requester for the name of the person logged in at a workstation. The API returns the name or an indication that no one is currently logged in. To use this service, you invoke interrupt 2Ah after setting the AX CPU register to 0x7802 and setting the ES:DI register pair to point to a 9-byte area of memory. After the call, the AL register will be zero if no one is logged in. If they set AL to a non-zero value, DLR puts the logon name in the area of memory pointed to by the far pointer in ES:DI. The resulting name is blank-padded and the last byte contains a null value.

The following get_logon_id() example is a function you can call from within your program. The function obtains logon name and status information from DLR and returns the information via the function's parameters.

```
void    get_logon_id(char *logon_name, int *status_ptr)
   {
   union REGS regs;
   struct SREGS sregs;

   regs.x.ax = 0x7802;
   regs.x.di = FP_OFF( (void far *) logon_name );
   sregs.es  = FP_SEG( (void far *) logon_name );
   int86x(0x2A, &regs, &regs, &sregs);
   *status_ptr = (int) regs.h.al;
   }
```

Named Pipes

A pipe is a stream of data between two programs. One program opens the pipe and writes data into it; the other opens the pipe and reads the data from the first program. Sound easy, and simple to program? It is. A Named Pipe is a file whose name has a particular format:

```
\PIPE\path\name.ext
```

OS/2 provides a set of functions for opening, using, and closing Named Pipes. The application that wants to create the pipe (called the *server*, but don't confuse this with a file server) does so by calling *DosMakeNmPipe*. It can then use *DosConnectNmPipe* to wait until another application (called the *client*) has opened the pipe with *DosOpen*. Both the *server* and the *client* can use a simple *DosWrite* to put data into the pipe or *DosRead* to get data from the pipe. *DosPeekNmPipe* can be used to inspect data in the pipe without removing it. Finally, the server can close the pipe and destroy it with *DosDisConnectNmPipe*.

Named Pipes can be treated as simple data streams or, if the programmer desires, as message pipes. In the latter case, each call to *DosRead* fetches one message at a time from the pipe.

Since Named Pipes do so much work yet only require a programmer to code a few simple program statements, Named Pipes are extremely popular on OS/2 LANs.

Using NetBIOS

From DOS-based, Windows-based, and OS/2-based workstations, you can use the NetBIOS API to send and receive data messages. You don't have to store the data as a file on the file server for multiple workstations to share. The following sections explain using NetBIOS in the DOS and OS/2 environments. NetBIOS in a Windows environment is virtually the same as for DOS. However, you have to be keenly aware of how Windows manages memory to use NetBIOS within a Windows program.

NetBIOS and DOS

To invoke a NetBIOS function within DOS, you set up a Network Control Block (NCB), put a far pointer to the NCB in the ES:BX register pair, and execute Interrupt 0x5C:

```
void    NetBIOS (NCB far *ncb_ptr)
  {
  struct SREGS sregs;
  union  REGS regs;

  sregs.es  = FP_SEG(ncb_ptr);
  regs.x.bx = FP_OFF(ncb_ptr);
  int86x(0x5C, &regs, &regs, &sregs);
  }
```

Network Control Block

An NCB is a self-contained vehicle, telling NetBIOS all it needs to know about each particular operation. The NCB itself does not get transmitted across the network. NetBIOS just uses it as a set of directions about what you want done. You should use/declare a separate NCB for each operation; you'll find this easier to manage than using one or two generic NCBs for multiple purposes. Here is a typedef'd struct that shows the layout of the NCB:

```
typedef unsigned char byte;
typedef unsigned int  word;
```

```
/* Network Control Block (NCB)   */
typedef struct
    {
    byte NCB_COMMAND;
    byte NCB_RETCODE;
    byte NCB_LSN;
    byte NCB_NUM;
    void far *NCB_BUFFER_PTR;
    word NCB_LENGTH;
    byte NCB_CALLNAME[16];
    byte NCB_NAME[16];
    byte NCB_RTO;
    byte NCB_STO;
    void interrupt (*POST_FUNC)(void);
    byte NCB_LANA_NUM;
    byte NCB_CMD_CPLT;
    byte NCB_RESERVE[14];
    }
    NCB;
```

The following gives a brief definition of each field:

NCB_COMMAND	Command id
NCB_RETCODE	Immediate return code
NCB_LSN	Local session number
NCB_NUM.	Network name number
NCB_BUFFER_PTR	Far pointer to message packet
NCB_LENGTH	Length of message packet
NCB_CALLNAME	Name of the other computer
NCB_NAME	Our network name
NCB_RTO	Receive time-out, in 500 ms. increments
NCB_STO	Send time-out, in 500 ms. increments
POST_FUNC	Far (function) pointer to POST routine
NCB_LANA_NUM	Adapter number (0 or 1)
NCB_CMD_CPLT	Final return code

NetBIOS Commands

There are two types of NetBIOS commands, *wait* and *no-wait*. When you use the wait option, control does not return to your program until the operation completes. In contrast, the no-wait option tells NetBIOS to start the operation in the background and return immediately to your program. You can give NetBIOS a pointer to a function in your program (a POST routine) which NetBIOS will call upon event completion, or you can poll for the completion of the event by looping until the NCB_CMD_CPLT field changes from 0xFF to an actual return code. You might want to include the following list of symbolically-defined NetBIOS commands in your program:

#define RESET	0x32
#define CANCEL	0x35
#define STATUS	0xb3
#define STATUS_WAIT	0x33
#define UNLINK	0x70
#define ADD_NAME	0xb0
#define ADD_NAME_WAIT	0x30
#define ADD_GROUP_NAME	0xb6
#define ADD_GROUP_NAME_WAIT	0x36
#define DELETE_NAME	0xb1
#define DELETE_NAME_WAIT	0x31
#define CALL	0x90
#define CALL_WAIT	0x10
#define LISTEN	0x91
#define LISTEN_WAIT	0x11
#define HANG_UP	0x92
#define HANG_UP_WAIT	0x12
#define SEND	0x94
#define SEND_WAIT	0x14
#define SEND_NO_ACK	0xf1
#define SEND_NO_ACK_WAIT	0x71
#define CHAIN_SEND	0x97

#define CHAIN_SEND_WAIT	0x17
#define CHAIN_SEND_NO_ACK	0xf2
#define CHAIN_SEND_NO_ACK_WAIT	0x72
#define RECEIVE	0x95
#define RECEIVE_WAIT	0x15
#define RECEIVE_ANY	0x96
#define RECEIVE_ANY_WAIT	0x16
#define SESSION_STATUS	0xb4
#define SESSION_STATUS_WAIT	0x34
#define SEND_DATAGRAM	0xa0
#define SEND_DATAGRAM_WAIT	0x20
#define SEND_BCST_DATAGRAM	0xa2
#define SEND_BCST_DATAGRAM_WAIT	0x22
#define RECEIVE_DATAGRAM	0xa1
#define RECEIVE_DATAGRAM_WAIT	0x21
#define RECEIVE_BCST_DATAGRAM	0xa3
#define RECEIVE_BCST_DATAGRAM_WAIT	0x23

NetBIOS passes back both an immediate return code (NCB_RETCODE) and a final return code (NCB_CMD_CPLT) to your program. If you use the wait option for a command, or if you use a command that does not have a no-wait option, you should look at the NCB_RETCODE field to find out if it was successful. If you use the no-wait option, however, NetBIOS sets the NCB_CMD_CPLT field to a value of 0xFF while the operation is underway. Only upon completion does NetBIOS put an actual, final return code in NCB_CMD_CPLT.

NetBIOS POST Function

If you don't want to have a POST routine associated with a particular NCB, just set the POST_FUNC pointer to NULL. If you're executing a no-wait command, your program should then loop on NCB_CMD_CPLT until it changes from 0xFF to a real return code.

For a no-wait command, you can code a function that will be called by NetBIOS when the operation completes. Place the address of the routine in POST_FUNC, as a pointer to a function. The POST routine should be coded to execute as quickly as possible. At its completion, an IRET machine in-struction must be used to exit the routine. The IRET is automatically gener-ated by the compiler as one of the side effects of using the *interrupt* keyword. A simple POST routine, coded in Borland C (note the direct reference to CPU registers, as well as the *interrupt* keyword), looks like this:

```
/*  Borland C POST routine */

unsigned es_reg, bx_reg;
unsigned msg_received_flag;
NCB far *posted_ncb_ptr;

void interrupt post(void)
  {
  es_reg  = _ES;
  bx_reg  = _BX;
  posted_ncb_ptr = MK_FP(es_reg, bx_reg);
  msg_received_flag = TRUE;
  }
```

NetBIOS Names

The fields in an NCB that relate to NetBIOS name management are NCB_NAME, NCB_CALLNAME, NCB_LSN, and NCB_NUM. NCB_NAME represents the name you're inserting into the local name table (for an Add Name call) or the name by which you want to be known (for a Listen or Call command). NCB_CALLNAME, on the other hand, ex-presses the name of the other (remote) workstation. Except when you're performing an Add Name or Add Group Name command, NCB_NAME should already exist in the local name table. The name you add with an Add Name command must be unique on the network. Group names, on the other hand, do not have to be unique, but must not already be on the net-work as a regular name.

Each workstation is "pre-identified" by a permanent node name. This workstation id is constructed by obtaining the 6-byte identification number that is "burned into" the network adapter and prefixing it with 10 bytes of bi-nary zeros. The name thus formed is always unique on the network and al-ways available to you in your software. You cannot add or delete the name, but you may use it to establish sessions with other workstations, if you want. The 6-byte ID number of the network adapter is returned by the Adapter Status call (described below). Be careful in your handling of the permanent node name; it is not a normal, null-terminated C string.

NCB_LSN is the Local Session Number that is returned from a successful Listen or Call command, and it represents an established session. Use it in subsequent calls to Send, Receive, and Hang Up to refer to this session. NCB_NUM is the network name number returned by an Add Name or Add Group Name command. Use the value in NCB_NUM when sending datagrams to other workstations.

Each name that you add to the local name table should be "filtered" to ensure that it is both a normal C string that you can easily manipulate in your program and a proper name entry for the table. This means that the name should be 15 bytes in length, with a null byte after the last string character. For example:

```
char netbios_name[16];

struct SREGS sregs;
union  REGS  regs;

NCB     add_name_ncb;

strcpy(netbios_name, "BARRY");
while (strlen(netbios_name) < 15)
  strcat(netbios_name, " ");
```

To add the above name to the local name table as a unique name, follow these steps:

```
memset(&add_name_ncb, 0, sizeof(NCB));
add_name_ncb.NCB_COMMAND = ADD_NAME;
strcpy(add_name_ncb.NCB_NAME, netbios_name);

sregs.es  = FP_SEG( (void far *) &add_name_ncb);
regs.x.bx = FP_OFF( (void far *) &add_name_ncb);
int86x(0x5C, &regs, &regs, &sregs);

while (add_name_ncb.NCB_CMD_CPLT == 0xFF)
  ;

if (add_name_ncb.NCB_CMD_CPLT != 0)
  {
  printf("Error.  Could not add name %s\n",
            netbios_name);
  exit(1);
  }
```

NetBIOS Datagrams

Assuming that the above Add Name operation completed successfully, you would find that NetBIOS had assigned a name number and placed it in *add_name_ncb.NCB_NUM*. You use this name number to identify the local workstation when you issue datagram commands. The destination of a datagram is specified simply as a name (or a group name) in the NCB_CALLNAME field.

Datagrams can be sent on a point-to-point basis (Send Datagram; Receive Datagram) or broadcast throughout the network (Send Broadcast Datagram; Receive Broadcast Datagram).

Establishing a Session

If the dialog you've designed is going to be more prolonged than the above example, you may want to consider establishing a session between the two workstations. Basically, you create a session by having one workstation issue a Listen command and subsequently causing another workstation to issue a Call command. The Listen NCB that you construct and give to NetBIOS can specify "listen for a call from anyone" or, if your design dictates, "listen for a call from a specific name." In the first case, you put an asterisk ("*") in the first byte of the NCB_CALLNAME field. When listening for a call from a specific name, that name goes into the NCB_CALLNAME field. Note that the names (caller and who-can-call) must match on all 16 bytes; this is where the convention I mentioned earlier regarding the padding of the name with spaces can come in handy.

Once the Listen command completes on the first workstation, NetBIOS returns a Local Session Number (LSN) that you use in the Send and Receive NCB's to refer to that session. On the other workstation, the same thing happens once the Call command completes. Additionally, if you are listening for a call from anyone, the caller's name is returned in the NCB_CALLNAME field. At either workstation (Listener or Caller), you can begin sending/receiving messages just as soon as the Listen (or Call) command finishes.

When you fill out the Listen NCB, you specify NCB_CALLNAME as the name to listen for ("*" = anyone) and NCB_NAME as the name in the local name table you want to be known by. You also specify the timeout intervals that will be used by NetBIOS for the Send and Receive commands issued in this session. NCB_RTO is the Receive Time Out and NCB_STO is the Send Time Out. Both are expressed in 500 millisecond ($^1/_2$ second) intervals. If you use a value of zero in either field, no timeout will be signaled by NetBIOS for that command.

Note that the Listen command itself does not time out (use the "wait" option carefully!). A Call command will time out after a few retries; this indicates that the remote workstation has not issued a Listen command.

Also note that the occurrence of a timeout during a Send operation will abort the session, while the occurrence of a timeout for a Receive operation will merely invalidate that particular NCB, allowing you to re-issue the Receive command if that suits your design. The following is an example use of the Listen function:

```
/* - - - - - - - - - - - - - - - - - - - - - - - - - */
/*
 *    Build the 'listen' NCB and send it out
 *    across the network.  Set the POST address to
 *    point to a 'background' routine to handle a caller.
 */
void    net_listen_post(char *caller, char *us,
                            void interrupt (*post_function)(),
                            unsigned char rto, unsigned char sto)
        {
        memset(&listen_ncb, 0, sizeof(NCB));
        listen_ncb.NCB_COMMAND = LISTEN;
        strcpy(listen_ncb.NCB_NAME,      us);
        strcpy(listen_ncb.NCB_CALLNAME, caller);
        listen_ncb.POST_FUNC = post_function;
        listen_ncb.NCB_RTO = rto;
        listen_ncb.NCB_STO = sto;
        sregs.es  = FP_SEG( (void far *) &listen_ncb);
        regs.x.bx = FP_OFF( (void far *) &listen_ncb);
        int86x(0x5C, &regs, &regs, &sregs);
        }
```

The calling workstation ("BARRY") would construct and issue an NCB in this manner:

```
/* - - - - - - - - - - - - - - - - - - - - - - - - - */
/*
 *  "Call" another workstation.
 */
void    net_call(char *who, char *us,
              unsigned char rto, unsigned char sto)
        {
        memset(&call_ncb, 0, sizeof(NCB));
        call_ncb.NCB_COMMAND = CALL;
        memcpy(call_ncb.NCB_NAME,      us,   16);
        strcpy(call_ncb.NCB_CALLNAME, who);
        call_ncb.NCB_RTO = rto;
        call_ncb.NCB_STO = sto;
        sregs.es  = FP_SEG( (void far *) &call_ncb);
```

```
            regs.x.bx = FP_OFF( (void far *) &call_ncb);
            int86x(0x5C, &regs, &regs, &sregs);
            }
```
...with the call to this function, elsewhere in the program,
coded:
```
net_call("DATABASE_ENGINE", "BARRY          ", 20, 20);

while (call_ncb.NCB_CMD_CPLT == 0xFF)
  ;

if (call_ncb.NCB_CMD_CPLT == 0)
  local_session_number = call_ncb.NCB_LSN;
else
  abort("Call was unsuccessful.");
```

Sending and Receiving Session Messages

While a session is underway, you can issue Send and Receive commands
(NCBs) to transfer information back and forth. In fact, you have a choice of
NetBIOS commands—Send, Chain Send, or Send No ACK—for sending
data. The Send command can be used for data packets up to 65,535 bytes in
length, while the Chain Send command concatenates two send buffers that
you specify into a message that can be up to 131,070 bytes in size. The Send
No ACK command is coded just like a Send command, but behaves something like a datagram; no (internal) acknowledgement is sent between Net-
BIOS on the two workstations. I discuss the plain Send and Receive
commands here; please refer to the Reference section of this book for descriptions of the Chain Send and Send No ACK commands.

To construct an NCB that causes data to be sent to the other session part-
ner, you fill in the NCB_LSN field to identify the session and you fill in the
NCB_BUFFER_PTR and NCB_LENGTH fields to describe the data message you want sent. Here is an example of a function that performs a Net-
BIOS Send:

```
/* - - - - - - - - - - - - - - - - - - - - - - - */
/*
 *     Build the 'send' NCB and send it out
 *     across the network.
 *
 */
void    net_send(unsigned char lsn,
               void far *packet_ptr, int packet_len)
            {
            memset(&send_ncb, 0, sizeof(NCB));
```

```
    send_ncb.NCB_COMMAND = SEND;
    send_ncb.NCB_LSN = lsn;
    send_ncb.NCB_LENGTH = packet_len;
    send_ncb.NCB_BUFFER_PTR = packet_ptr;
    sregs.es  = FP_SEG( (void far *) &send_ncb);
    regs.x.bx = FP_OFF( (void far *) &send_ncb);
    int86x(0x5C, &regs, &regs, &sregs);
    }
```
You might call the *net_send()* function with these parameters:
```
net_send(local_session_number,
    &aircraft_age_rcd, sizeof(struct AGE_RECORD));
while (send_ncb.NCB_CMD_CPLT == 0xFF)
    ;
```

The Receive command also makes use of the local session number to refer to the session. This example additionally shows how a POST routine can be specified at the time the Receive is issued:

```
/* - - - - - - - - - - - - - - - - - - - - - - - - - */
/*
 *    Build the 'receive' NCB and send it out
 *    across the network.  When the operation completes,
 *    let NetBIOS call the POST routine to handle it.
 */
void    net_receive_post(unsigned char lsn,
                         void interrupt (*post_function)(),
                         void *packet_ptr, int packet_len)
        {
        memset(&receive_ncb, 0, sizeof(NCB));
        receive_ncb.NCB_COMMAND = RECEIVE;
        receive_ncb.NCB_LSN = lsn;
        receive_ncb.NCB_LENGTH = packet_len;
        receive_ncb.NCB_BUFFER_PTR = packet_ptr;
        receive_ncb.POST_FUNC = post_function;
        sregs.es  = FP_SEG( (void far *) &receive_ncb);
        regs.x.bx = FP_OFF( (void far *) &receive_ncb);
        int86x(0x5C, &regs, &regs, &sregs);
        }
```

At the point in your program at which you want to let NetBIOS know you're ready to receive some data, you would invoke net_receive_post() in this way:

```
net_receive_post(local_session_number,
    post_handler, &input_buff, sizeof(input_buff));
```

Session Termination

When the exchange of data messages is complete, both session partners issue a Hang Up command to end the session. All you need to specify when hanging up on a session is the Local Session Number. The Hang Up command that both session partners should execute looks like the following example:

```
/*
 *    Build and issue a 'hang up' NCB
 *
*/
void    net_hangup(unsigned char lsn)
        {
        memset(&hangup_ncb, 0, sizeof(NCB));
        hangup_ncb.NCB_COMMAND = HANG_UP;
        hangup_ncb.NCB_LSN = lsn;
        sregs.es  = FP_SEG( (void far *) &hangup_ncb);
        regs.x.bx = FP_OFF( (void far *) &hangup_ncb);
        int86x(0x5C, &regs, &regs, &sregs);
        }
```

Deleting NetBIOS Names

When you're done sending/receiving datagrams, or after you've closed a session by cancelling any outstanding commands and performing a Hang Up, you should delete the name(s) you added to the local name table. This leaves things neat and tidy; it also prevents your user from encountering the error "Duplicate Name" if he/she runs your software again without rebooting the workstation (since the name is still in the local name table when your software issues its Add Name command). An example of Delete Name follows:

```
/*
 *    Build the 'delete_name' NCB and issue it
 *
*/
void    net_delete_name(char *name)
        {
        memset(&delete_name_ncb, 0, sizeof(NCB));
        delete_name_ncb.NCB_COMMAND = DELETE_NAME;
        strcpy(delete_name_ncb.NCB_NAME, name);
        sregs.es  = FP_SEG((void far *) &delete_name_ncb);
        regs.x.bx = FP_OFF((void far *) &delete_name_ncb);
        int86x(0x5C, &regs, &regs, &sregs);
        }
```

■ NetBIOS and OS/2

Programming NetBIOS in the 32-bit OS/2 environment is only slightly different from programming NetBIOS for DOS. You use a calling interface, Net-
BiosSubmit(), rather than Interrupt 5Ch to invoke NetBIOS. You use an OS/2
semaphore to handle POST processing, rather than have NetBIOS call one
of your program's functions. You're free to poll for the completion of a Net-
BIOS event, instead of using a POST routine, but you should consider using
a separate OS/2 thread for receiving and processing incoming NetBIOS messages. The formats of the NetBIOS data structures, including the NCB, are
similar to the data structures you'd use in a DOS program. In all other respects, the principles and concepts you learned earlier in this chapter apply
equally to both the DOS and OS/2 environments.

NOTE. *If you use the OS/2 LAN Server Requester to connect to a LAN Server
file server, you can run NetBIOS-aware DOS programs in OS/2's virtual DOS
sessions. You first must make sure that the Virtual DOS API Support
component is installed on the workstation, however.*

From within an OS/2 program, you call NetBIOS functions in a DLL;
the DLL comes with the requester that allows the workstation to access
the file server. The NetBIOS function you'll use most often is NetBios-
Submit(). This function lets your program give an NCB to NetBIOS for
processing.

Most implementations of NetBIOS for OS/2 are 16-bit device drivers.
This means you need to pass 16-bit pointers to the functions in the NetBIOS
DLL. The following prototype shows one way to tell the IBM C Set/2 or
C/C++ Tools compiler to emit the proper 16-bit code for the NetBiosSubmit()
function:

```
extern unsigned short _Far16 Pascal NetBiosSubmit(short, short, void * _Seg16);
```

The _Far16 keyword informs the compiler to emit a 16-bit call to
NetBiosSubmit() in your program, and the _Seg16 keyword instructs the
compiler to pass the pointer to the NCB as a 16-bit entity.

To add a name to the NetBIOS name table from within an OS/2 program, you can use the following code fragment:

```
memset(&ncb, Ø, sizeof(struct network_control_block));
ncb.ncb_command  = NB_ADD_NAME_WAIT;
ncb.ncb_lana_num = Ø;
memcpy(ncb.ncb_name, name, 16);
NetBiosSubmit(Ø, Ø, &ncb);
```

The following code fragment receives a datagram packet; note how the address of the field rcv_buffer is cast into a 16-bit pointer:

```
memset(&recv_ncb, Ø, sizeof(struct network_control_block) );
recv_ncb.ncb_command = NB_RECEIVE_DATAGRAM_WAIT;
recv_ncb.ncb_lana_num = Ø;
recv_ncb.ncb_num = namenum;
recv_ncb.ncb_length = bufsiz;
recv_ncb.ncb_buffer_address = (char * _Seg16) rcv_buffer;
NetBiosSubmit(Ø, Ø, &recv_ncb);
```

The following code fragment deletes a name from the NetBIOS name table:

```
memset(&ncb, Ø, sizeof(struct network_control_block) );
ncb.ncb_command  = NB_DELETE_NAME_WAIT;
ncb.ncb_lana_num = adapter;
memcpy( ncb.ncb_name, name, 16);
NetBiosSubmit(Ø, Ø, &ncb);
```

You can use the following code fragment to send a datagram message packet:

```
memset(&ncb, Ø, sizeof(struct network_control_block) );
ncb.ncb_command = NB_SEND_DATAGRAM_WAIT;
memcpy(ncb.ncb_callname, callname, 16);
ncb.ncb_lana_num = adapter;
ncb.ncb_num = namnum;
ncb.ncb_buffer_address = (char * _Seg16) buffer;
ncb.ncb_length = bufsiz;
NetBiosSubmit(Ø, Ø, &ncb);
```

You should use the following definition of an NCB in your OS/2 programs:

```
struct    network_control_block
{
  byte      ncb_command;          /* Netbios command code     */
  byte      ncb_retcode;          /* Return code              */
  byte      ncb_lsn;              /* Local session number     */
  byte      ncb_num;              /* Number of application name*/
  address   ncb_buffer_address;   /* Address of message buffer */
  word      ncb_length;           /* length of message buffer  */
  byte      ncb_callname[16];     /* Destination name         */
  byte      ncb_name[16];         /* Source name              */
  byte      ncb_rto;              /* Receive timeout          */
  byte      ncb_sto;              /* Send timeout             */
  ulong     ncb_post_sem_handle;  /* Semaphore handle         */
  byte      ncb_lana_num;         /* Adapter number           */
  byte      ncb_cmd_cplt;         /* Final command status     */
  byte      ncb_reserve[14];      /* Reserved                 */
};
```

The following defines the structure of data returned by NetBIOS when you use the adapter status NetBIOS command:

```
struct        ncb_status_information
{
  byte        burned_in_addr[6];         /* Adapter's burned in addr  */
  byte        reserved1[2];              /* RESERVED always X'0000'    */
  word        software_level_number;     /* X'FFnn' - nn is level num */
  word        reporting_period;          /* reporting period (minutes)*/
  word        frmr_frames_received;      /* Number of FRMR received    */
  word        frmr_frames_sent;          /* Number of FRMR sent        */
  word        bad_iframes_received;      /* # bad Iframes received     */
  word        aborted_transmissions;     /* # aborted transmits        */
  dword       packets_transmitted;       /* # Successfully transmitted*/
  dword       packets_received;          /* # Successfully received    */
  word        bad_iframes_transmitted;   /* # bad Iframes transmitted */
  word        lost_data_count;           /* Lost SAP buffer data cnt   */
  word        t1_expiration_count;       /* Number of T1 expirations   */
  word        ti_expiration_count;       /* Number of Ti expirations   */
  address     extended_status_table;     /* Address of extended status*/
  word        number_of_free_ncbs;       /* Number of NCBs available   */
  word        max_configured_ncbs;       /* Configured NCB maximum     */
  word        max_allowed_ncbs;          /* Maximum NCBs (always 255) */
  word        busy_condition_count;      /* Local station busy count   */
  word        max_datagram_size;         /* Maximum datagram packet    */
  word        pending_sessions;          /* Number of pending sessions*/
  word        max_configured_sessions;   /* Configured session maximum*/
  word        max_allowed_sessions;      /* Maximum sessions (254)     */
  word        max_data_packet_size;      /* Maximum session packet     */
  word        number_of_names_present;   /* Number of names in table   */
};
```

The following data structure defines the area of memory NetBIOS fills with information when you use the session status NetBIOS command:

```
struct        ncb_session_status
{
  byte        name_number_of_sessions;   /* Name number for sessions   */
  byte        sessions_using_name;       /* # of sessions using name   */
  byte        active_rcv_datagrams;      /* # of receive datagrams out*/
  byte        active_receive_anys;       /* # of RECEIVE.ANY cmnds out*/
  byte        local_session_number;      /* Local session number       */
  byte        session_state;             /* State of session           */
  byte        local_name[16];            /* Local name                 */
  byte        remote_name[16];           /* Remote name                */
  byte        active_receives;           /* # of RECEIVE cmnds out     */
  byte        active_sends;              /* # of SEND, CHAIN.SEND out */
};
```

The OS/2 NetBIOS reset command accepts a specially-formatted NCB containing information about the NetBIOS environment, as shown in the following definition:

```
struct     ncb_reset
{
  byte       ncb_command;            /* Netbios command code      */
  byte       ncb_retcode;            /* Return code               */
  byte       ncb_lsn;                /* Local session number      */
  byte       ncb_num;                /* Number of application name*/
  address    dd_name_address;        /* Device drive name address */
  byte       not_used1[2];           /* Not used                  */
  byte       req_sessions;           /* # of sessions requested   */
  byte       req_commands;           /* # of commands requested   */
  byte       req_names;              /* # of names requested      */
  byte       req_name_one;           /* Name number one request   */
  byte       not_used2[12];          /* Not used                  */
  byte       act_sessions;           /* # of sessions obtained    */
  byte       act_commands;           /* # of commands obtained    */
  byte       act_names;              /* # of names obtained       */
  byte       act_name_one;           /* Name number one response  */
  byte       not_used3[4];           /* Not used                  */
  byte       load_session;           /* Number of sessions at load*/
  byte       load_commands;          /* Number of commands at load*/
  byte       load_names;             /* Number of names at load   */
  byte       load_stations;          /* Number of stations at load*/
  byte       not_used4[2];           /* Not used                  */
  byte       load_remote_names;      /* Number of remote names    */
  byte       not_used5[5];           /* Not used                  */
  word       ncb_dd_id;              /* NCB device driver ID      */
  byte       ncb_lana_num;           /* Adapter number            */
  byte       not_used6;              /* Not used                  */
  byte       ncb_reserve[14];        /* NCB error information     */
};
```

■ Testing and Debugging on a LAN

Testing your software is a matter of running it and verifying that it does what it's supposed to do. It helps to have a test plan; most test plans are just checklists that guide you through the testing. Debugging, on the other hand, is a lot less scientific. Most people think that finding/fixing bugs is a black art.

File Sharing

Whether you open a file on the file server for shared (*DENY_NONE*) or exclusive (*DENY_ALL*) access, the test you need to perform is to open the same file concurrently from two different workstations and see how your software behaves. If you get an "Abort, Retry, or Ignore?" message from DOS (or if your Interrupt 24 Critical Error Handler is invoked) at the second workstation, look again at the way you're opening the file. If you omit parameters in the *open()* call, or if you inadvertently used *fopen()* instead of *open()*, it may be that the second workstation is opening the file in Compatibility Mode.

Record Locking

For record locks, you need to do basically the same thing you do for file sharing—cause a controlled, concurrent collision between two workstations. It's not easy—a well-designed record lock lasts for only a brief moment in time. If you test by having two people at two workstations run your software and try to hit the enter key (to cause a record update) at exactly the same time, you'll quickly become frustrated. It's virtually impossible to cause a collision this way.

One approach you might take is to temporarily change the copy of your program on the first workstation. Insert a "wait for keypress" after acquiring the record lock(s). This lets you deliberately hold the lock for a longer period of time. While the lock is present, the person at workstation "B" can attempt an update. You can then watch to see how your program behaves.

What can go wrong inside your record locking routines? If the machine crashes at the point you issue the lock request, look carefully at your function call. If you call function 0x5C directly, look at the way the CPU registers get set.

If DOS returns an error to your lock request, look at the error code value. If it indicates the region is already locked (and you know it shouldn't be), you may be encountering the residue of a lock that was issued (without an unlock) during an earlier test. Another possibility is that the flow of your program took you through the lock request twice, without an intervening unlock. If DOS indicates some other error (perhaps invalid handle, or invalid function?), look carefully at your parameters in the call to the lock function.

The File Server as a Debugging Tool

LAN Server offers a command you can use to discover who has a file open, although the information is not presented in "real-time." You issue a NET FILE command at the file server to see which files are open. For each open file, LAN Server displays the Machine Name of the workstation that opened the file as well as the number of locks in effect for that file. NET FILE can also be used to close an open file (of course, you only want to do this if the application running at the workstation has crashed). If you want a continuous display of open files, create a .CMD file on the server that looks like this:

```
ECHO OFF
:AGAIN
NET FILE
GOTO AGAIN
```

It still isn't quite real-time, but it does save having to type the command over and over again. Use Ctrl-C to stop the display.

NetBIOS Debugging

The first time you test a program that passes messages from workstation to workstation is exciting. You tell yourself it won't work the first time, but you're hopeful nevertheless. You start the programs, and—the two workstations refuse to talk to one another. It's a bit of a letdown. After you reboot the computers, you start wondering what might have gone wrong.

In this section and the next, I offer some things you can look for that might be the culprit.

■ Adding and Deleting Names

One of the first things you need to verify is that your program has added and/ or deleted NetBIOS names correctly. If you actually have two workstations that seem to have gone out to lunch, don't reboot them quite yet. Go to a third workstation and run the NETTEST.C program (NETTEST is on the floppy disk that accompanies this book). Pick the "Adapter Status" menu option and specify that you want information about one of the test machines. If the computers are "alive" but just unable to talk to one another, the display from the Adapter Status command will tell you the contents of the local name table from one of the test machines. You'll then know whether your program at least performed a correct Add Name operation. Of course, you should check the return code from the Add Name operation and take appropriate action in your program if the call fails.

If the name isn't present in the local name table from the test machine, or if the command times out, you can start looking for the problem in the part of the program that constructs the name and adds it to the local name table. If that code looks okay, you can try backtracking from there to see if the problem occurred earlier in the execution of the program.

If the Adapter Status command times out, it may be that the Add Name operation executed properly but your program subsequently did some damage to NetBIOS or crashed the workstation entirely. If you can't find the problem in or prior to the code that does the Add Name, you might want to make what I call a "temporary assumption" —that the name was added correctly; try looking for the problem later in the program.

Are there clues you can look for to tell you whether the workstation has crashed completely? Yes. This technique may sound strange to you, but I assure you it's well-founded: Press the Caps Lock, Scroll Lock, or Num Lock key. If the green LEDs on the keyboard respond normally by toggling off and on, the computer is in a loop. The loop may well be in your program. If the LEDs don't respond, the computer has crashed. (You'll have to use the Red Switch to reboot the computer.) Of course, the loop (or the crash) may not be related to your calls to NetBIOS, but it's an informative technique.

NetBIOS Datagrams

If your program is designed to pass datagram messages "silently," without some outward sign (perhaps an on-screen message) that you can use to tell what's going on, you should put some temporary code into the program that shows message transmission or reception is occurring. It can also be advantageous to test on two workstations that are physically adjacent, so you can watch both at the same time.

Suppose you determine that Workstation "A" is sending a datagram, but Workstation "B" is simply not getting the message. The first place to look is the code that does the Send Datagram. Does it properly fill in the NCB_NUM field? Does the NCB_CALLNAME field contain the exact 16-byte name of the destination workstation? Is the NCB_LENGTH field nonzero? Are you getting a good return code from the Send Datagram call?

The next place to look is the Receive Datagram call. Is the NCB_NUM field properly filled in? Do NCB_BUFFER_PTR and NCB_LENGTH correctly express the address and length of the input buffer? Is the Receive Datagram call returning an error code? And, more generally, is the Receive Datagram call actually outstanding at the time the Send Datagram is issued?

■ Establishing Sessions

Again, to know that a session is or is not being established correctly, it's a good idea to put some temporary code in your program that gives you some sign that the Call (or Listen) command has completed. If you don't like doing this, you can use a debugger to trace through the code to see exactly how the NetBIOS calls take place. In either case, make sure you check return codes!

If you've issued the Call and Listen commands on the two workstations but it looks like the session is not being established, the first place to look is the NCB_CALLNAME field in both NCBs. For the Call command, make sure the NCB_CALLNAME field contains the name of the listening workstation. For the Listen command, make sure the first byte of NCB_CALLNAME is an asterisk ("*") if you're listening for a call from anyone, or that NCB_CALLNAME is the exact name of the caller.

If you have a complicated design that involves the creation of multiple sessions, you may find that your program exceeds the number of available sessions. In this case, look at the installation and configuration documentation for the NetBIOS software. You may be able to configure it for a higher number of available sessions.

Once a session is created successfully, make sure you save the value of NCB_LSN. You'll need it in subsequent references to the session.

■ Sending and Receiving Session Messages

Once you've gotten the session underway, it should be easy to verify that messages are sent and received correctly—your program is working! If you encounter problems, though, the likely cause is either that the NCB_LSN (Local Session Number) is not set properly, or that the NCB_BUFFER_PTR and NCB_LENGTH fields don't properly describe the input or output buffers. For the Receive operation, make sure you set NCB_LENGTH to the size of the input buffer. It's a common error to neglect setting NCB_LENGTH; if it's zero when the Receive is issued, you won't be able to receive any data.

The Send and Receive operations time out according to the NCB_STO and NCB_RTO values given at the time the Call and Listen commands are issued. If your program seems to work only intermittently, you might look at these fields to see if they're set correctly. Note that a Send operation that times out will cause the session itself to be aborted.

Don't forget that both workstations should do a Hang Up command in order to dismantle the session. And, unless you deliberately want to leave the names you've added in the local name table, make sure you do a Delete Name after the Hang Up operation is complete.

■ Summary

In this chapter, you've learned the basics of LAN programming. You understand client/server technology and, if you know how to program, you have a firm grasp of the techniques you can use to write LAN-aware computer software.

The next two parts of this book provide a command reference for LAN Server's NET command and a list of LAN Server APIs.

■ Appendix A

■ Command Reference: LAN Server NET Commands

LAN Server includes many commands you can use at a command line prompt in DOS or OS/2 sessions, full-screen or windowed. This section explains, in detail, how to use the commands. This section can be used in conjunction with Chapter 5, "Administering LAN Server."

The commands appear in alphabetical order, with command parameter values lowercased. Most of them can be used at the file server and at a workstation.

■ ACCESS

Lists, adds, changes, deletes, and applies access control profiles, and also revokes specific permissions in access control profiles. An administrator can perform all actions, and a user with P permission can perform all actions for access control profiles except for the ADD and APPLY actions.

Syntax

Use the following form of the command to list permissions for a resource or alias:

```
NET ACCESS [resource | alias] /TREE
```

Use the following form of the command to modify permissions for a resource or alias:

```
NET ACCESS [resource | alias] /subcommand
```

where the subcommand is one of the following:

[/ADD	rights
/CHANGE	rights
/GRANT	rights
/REVOKE	name
/APPLY	
/DELETE	
/TRAIL:	[YES | NO]

| /FAILURE: | [OPEN I WRITE I DELETE I ACL I ALL I NONE] |
| /SUCCESS: | [OPEN I WRITE I DELETE I ACL I ALL I NONE] |

and the other variables are

alias	Specifies the alias of the resource whose permissions you are viewing, modifying, or applying. The alias can be a file, a printer, or a serial device alias.
name	Identifies a specific logon account or group ID.
rights	Specifies the name of a user or group, as well as the permissions (N, R, W, C, X, D, A, P, Y) for the resource, in the form name:permissions. Multiple user or group names can be entered by separating sets of name:permissions with a space. You cannot combine N with other permissions, and you cannot combine Y with other permissions except P.
resource	Names the resource whose permissions you are viewing or modifying. The resource can be a disk, directory, file, spooler queue, serial device, or named pipe. Resource names that are spooler queues, serial devices, or named pipes must be preceded by \PRINT\, \COMM\, or \PIPE\, respectively.

Command Line Parameters

When you type NET ACCESS without any command line parameters, LAN Server displays a list of access control profiles and associated permissions. NET ACCESS accepts the following command line parameters:

/TREE	Reports access control profiles with associated permissions for the specified resource and all its subdirectories.
/ADD	Creates an access control profile with associated permissions for users and groups to the resource specified. You must create an access control profile before you can modify it. If access has previously been given to a resource, use the /GRANT command line parameter to add more users.
/CHANGE	Changes the permissions of users or groups for a resource.
/GRANT	Adds new user names or group names, as well as corresponding permissions, to an existing access control profile. If access has not previously been given to a resource, use the /ADD command line parameter to add users.

/REVOKE	Removes the permissions granted to users or groups to use a resource.
/APPLY	Applies the access control profile of the specified directory to all the subdirectories under it.
/DELETE	Removes the access control profile for a resource from the access control database.
/TRAIL: [YES | NO]	Turns auditing on or off for a resource. If the /TRAIL command line parameter is not specified, all successful and unsuccessful resource access attempts are audited. Do not use the /TRAIL command line parameter with the /SUCCESS or /FAILURE command line parameters.
/FAILURE	Audits failed resource access attempts. Specifies the type of information being audited by using one or more of the following values, separated by semicolons:

	OPEN	Audits failed attempts to open shared files
	WRITE	Audits failed attempts to write to shared files
	DELETE	Audits failed attempts to delete shared files
	ACL	Audits failed attempts to change permissions for a shared resource

The following /FAILURE command line parameter values cannot be used with any other value:

	ALL	Audits all failed resource attempts
	NONE	Disables failure auditing

/SUCCESS	Audits successful resource access attempts. Specifies the type of information being audited by using one or more of the following values, separated by semicolons:

	OPEN	Audits successful attempts to open shared files
	WRITE	Audits successful attempts to write to shared files
	DELETE	Audits successful attempts to delete shared files
	ACL	Audits successful attempts to change permissions for a shared resource

The following /SUCCESS command line parameter values cannot be used with any other value:

ALL   Audits all successful resource attempts

NONE   Disables success auditing

Some permissions work only with specific types of resources, as shown in the following table:

Permission	Description
Attributes (A)	Permits changing OS/2 file attributes, such as A (archive) and R (read only), as well as related file information, such as the time and date of the file's update. Some applications require the Attributes permission to copy files.
Create (C)	Permits creating subdirectories and files in a shared directory. Used alone, the Create permission lets users create a file in a directory and modify the file during its creation. After the file is created and closed, however, the same user cannot modify it again.
Delete (D)	Permits deleting subdirectories and files.
Execute (X)	Permits only running (not copying) program or command files, such as .EXE or .COM files. (Read permission includes all rights granted by the Execute permission.)
None (N)	Denies access to the resource. The None permission cannot be used with other permissions.
Permissions (P)	Permits changing resource access permissions, giving a user limited administrator authority over the resource. However, users cannot create an access control profile.
Read (R)	Permits reading and executing files in a directory, as well as copying files from a directory, but not writing to (modifying) files. Lets users view file names in a shared directory. Read permission is required for users to run .BAT files, .CMD files, and DOS applications.
Write (W)	Permits writing to (modifying) a file in a shared directory. Write used alone lets users modify files but not read, run, create, or delete them. In most cases, and always when editing files, use Write with the Read permission. In addition, the Attributes permission should almost always be used with the Write permission in an access control profile for a target subdirectory.

Permission	Description
Yes (Y)	Grants the permissions Read, Write, Create, Delete, and Attributes. The Yes permission serves as an abbreviation for this set of permissions. Yes cannot be used with other permissions except Permissions.

Examples

To view access control information and permissions:

```
NET ACCESS
```

To view permissions for the OS2\SYSTEM directory on the file server:

```
NET ACCESS C:\OS2\SYSTEM
```

To give the logon account FRED standard (RWXCDA) permissions to use the SVR-DRV-C alias:

```
NET ACCESS SVR-DRV-C /ADD FRED:Y
```

■ ACCOUNTS

The ACCOUNTS command can change the role of the Netlogon service, specify the length of time a logon account can be logged on to the network, set password expiration time, or set the number of passwords that LAN Server remembers a logon account has used before and shouldn't use again.

Syntax

```
NET ACCOUNTS
       /ROLE: [PRIMARY | MEMBER | STANDALONE | BACKUP]
       /FORCELOGOFF: [minutes | NO]
       /MAXPWAGE: [days | UNLIMITED]
       /MINPWAGE: days
       /MINPWLEN: length
       /UNIQUEPW: number
```

Command Line Parameters

If you type NET ACCOUNTS without command line parameters, the current values are displayed. Use the following command line parameters with NET ACCOUNTS:

/ROLE

Specifies the server role assigned to the machine being logged on to the domain. Select the server role from one of the following values:

PRIMARY   Specifies a server as the domain controller. Only one server per domain can be a domain controller. The domain controller contains the master user and group definition file. Updates to this file are made at the domain controller and then copied to other machines running the Netlogon service, such as member and backup servers. The domain controller also validates network logon requests. You can define other servers in the domain as backup domain controllers to also validate logons. Backup domain controllers are defined through the installation/configuration program and receive domain control database (DCDB) information from the domain controller by using the DCDB Replicator service.

MEMBER   Specifies a server as an additional server. There can be several member servers on a domain. Each member server receives a copy of the user and group definition file from the domain controller when updates are made. Member servers cannot validate network logon requests.

STANDALONE   Specifies that the machine cannot run the Netlogon service. Machines with a role of STANDALONE maintain their own copy of the user and group definitions file and do not participate in the replication of the definitions file from the domain controller. All requesters are installed as standalone machines. OS/2 LAN Servers with a role of STANDALONE are not supported. Set the role of a server machine to STANDALONE if you want to use the machine as a requester. When you want to use the machine as a server again, change the role back to PRIMARY, MEMBER, or BACKUP. If you change a server from STANDALONE back to MEMBER or BACKUP, any changes that were made to the user and group definitions file are lost.

BACKUP   Specifies that a server is a backup server. Multiple backup servers can exist in a domain. Each receives a copy of the user and group definitions file from the domain controller when updates are made. Like the domain controller, backup servers can respond to and validate network logon requests. By responding to the network logon requests, backup servers assist the domain controller in handling the user validation phase of logon, which helps to reduce the resource contention at the domain controller. You cannot use NET ACCOUNTS /ROLE:BACKUP to change a member or standalone server to a backup domain controller, because the DCDB Replicator service must also be installed. The installation/configuration program is used to install this service. Use the installation/configuration program to define backup domain controllers.

/FORCE-
LOGOFF
Causes all user sessions with the specified account to be forced off the network after the period of time specified by minutes has passed following an account expiration or a logon time that is not valid. See the /TIMES command line parameter described in NET USER Command for information on how to specify valid logon times. The NO option prevents FORCELOGOFF from working. The /FORCE-LOGOFF command line parameter disconnects all the user's sessions at the server but does not log off the user. The sessions are disconnected and automatically reconnected when the user's next logon time frame occurs. For example, if a user can log on only between 8 a.m. and 5 p.m., /FORCELOGOFF:10 disconnects the user's sessions at 5:10 p.m., but the user's sessions are reconnected at 8 a.m.

/MAXPWAGE
Sets the maximum time (in days) that a password is valid. The UNLIMITED option means there is no maximum time.

/MINPWAGE
Sets the minimum time (in days) that must pass before a user can change a password.

/MINPWLEN
Sets the minimum number of bytes for a user account password. The range is 0 to 14, and the default is 4. A 0-length password means a user can be defined without a password. User Profile Management accepts passwords of up to 8 bytes for the minimal character set and up to 14 bytes for the extended character set. The restrictions to the password length entered here control the passwords allowed in the NET PASSWORD and NET USER commands.

/UNIQUEPW	Sets the number of old passwords stored by the system for each user. The range is 0 to 8. This number specifies how many unique passwords must be used before one can be reused.

Examples

The following example identifies a server as an additional server:

```
NET ACCOUNTS /ROLE:MEMBER
```

The following example sets the number of unique passwords that a logon account must use before repeating an already-used password:

```
NET ACCOUNTS /UNIQUEPW:8
```

■ ADMIN

Runs an administrative command on a remote server (administrator only).

Syntax

```
NET ADMIN \\servername /C password "command" *
```

Typing NET ADMIN \\servername /C with no other command line parameters creates a command session on the server specified by servername.

Command Line Parameters

\\servername	Specifies the name of the server you want to use.
password	Specifies the password. Use if the specified server is not in the logon domain.
* (asterisk)	Produces a prompt for the password.
/C(OMMAND)	Runs a single non-interactive command or starts a secondary command processor on a remote server. To start a secondary command processor, press Enter immediately after typing /C. Then type as many commands as necessary on the remote server. Return to the local workstation by typing EXIT or by pressing Ctrl+Z.
"command"	Specifies the command text, including command line parameters, to run. If the command requires /Y(ES) or /N(O), enclose the command, its command line parameters, and /Y(ES) or /N(O) in double quotation marks (" ").

Examples

The following example runs an administrative command in a remote server:

```
NET ADMIN \\SERVER20 /C NET SHARE ENG=C:\ENGINEERING
```

In the preceding example, you run NET SHARE so that you can share the directory ENGINEERING on the server named SERVER20. The command actually executes in the SERVER20 computer.

■ ALIAS

Lists aliases currently defined in the domain and creates, changes, or deletes alias definitions. Only an administrator or user with server operator privilege can use this command to modify definitions.

Syntax

Use the following form of the command to list the currently defined aliases:

```
NET ALIAS
```

For information about a particular alias, use the following command:

```
NET ALIAS aliasname
```

To list all aliases defined in the current domain:

```
NET ALIAS /DO:name
```

Use the following form of the command to delete an alias definition:

```
NET ALIAS  aliasname  /DE
```

Use the following form of the command to create an alias definition:

```
NET ALIAS aliasname \\servername resource /DO:name /W: [STARTUP
| REQUESTED | ADMIN] /R:"text" [/USER:n | /UN] [/PRIN | /C /
PRIO:n]
```

Use the following form of the command to change an alias definition:

```
NET ALIAS  aliasname /W: [STARTUP | REQUESTED | ADMIN] /R:"text"
[/USER:n | /UN] /PRIO:n
```

Command Line Parameters

When you type NET ALIAS without command line parameters, a list of all currently defined aliases in the domain is displayed. You can use the following command line parameters:

aliasname	Specifies the name of the alias.
\\servername resource	Specifies the name of the server in which the resource is located, as well as the name of the resource. For a directory, resource is the absolute path. For spooler queues, resource is the queue name. For serial devices, resource is the routing for a list of devices.
/W(HEN):STARTUP- |REQUESTED|ADMIN	Specifies when the alias is shared. The following values can be used with the /WHEN option:
STARTUP	The resource is shared automatically when the server starts. This is the default.
REQUESTED	The resource is shared automatically when a user connects to it by using the NET USE command or the graphical user interface. The resource is also shared automatically if a user selects a public application that uses the resource, or if a user logs on and the resource is a logon assignment for the user. The value of /WHEN:REQUESTED cannot be used for serial devices and spooler queue aliases.
ADMIN	The resource is never shared automatically. It is shared only when an administrator uses the NET SHARE command or the graphical user interface to share it. Then the sharing continues until the administrator stops it or the server is stopped.
/R(EMARK):"text"	Specifies the description of the alias. The description must be enclosed in double quotation marks (""). The default value for /REMARK is null ("").
/USER(S):n	Sets the maximum number of users that can use the alias at the same time. The default value for /USERS is UNLIMITED.

/PRIN(T)	Defines the alias as a spooler queue. This command line parameter is valid only when creating an alias.
/C(OMM)	Defines the alias as a serial device. This command line parameter is valid only when creating an alias.
/UN(LIMITED)	Removes restrictions on the number of users that can use the alias at the same time.
/PRIO(RITY):n	Defines the priority of a serial device alias, with 1 as the highest priority and 9 as the lowest. The default value is 9. /PRIORITY is valid only for serial device aliases.
/DE(LETE)	Deletes the specified alias definition. If the resource designated by the alias is shared, users can still use it.
/DO(MAIN):name	Allows alias operations on a domain other than the logon domain. The user must be defined in the specified domain and must have administrator or server operator privilege. The default value for /DOMAIN is the logon domain.

Examples

To list aliases in the current domain, type NET ALIAS with no command line parameters.

To define a directory alias named PROSPECTS on the \\SALES server, in a domain named MKTNG:

```
NET ALIAS PROSPECTS \\SALES C:\PROSPECTS /DO:MKTNG
```

■ AUDIT

Lists or clears the contents of the network audit log of the server (administrator or user with operator privilege is required). Users with operator privilege can perform all actions except deleting.

Syntax

```
NET AUDIT [/C:n | /D]  /R
```

Command Line Parameters

When you type NET AUDIT without command line parameters, the contents of the audit log are displayed. You can use the following command line parameters:

/C(OUNT):n	Lists the first n entries in the audit log.
/R(EVERSE)	Lists the entries in reverse order so that the most recent entry is listed first and the oldest entry is listed last. If you type /R with /C:n, and n is a number, the n most recent entries in the audit log are displayed in reverse order.
/D(ELETE)	Clears the current audit log.

Examples

To display the contents of the audit log and see the most recent entries first, type:

```
NET AUDIT /R
```

■ COMM

Lists information about the queues for shared serial devices (such as modems, plotters, or fax machines). The NET COMM command also allows you to prioritize or reroute a queue, or to clear requests from a queue. Users or administrators can use NET COMM locally. Only administrators or users with comm operator privilege can use NET COMM remotely.

Syntax

```
NET COMM [\\servername \netname | devicename]
```

Use the following form of the command to delete pending requests from the queue:

```
NET COMM [\\servername \netname | devicename] /PU
```

Use the following form of the command to list and change information about serial device queues shared by a server:

```
NET COMM [devicename | netname /PU /PR:n /R:device /O]
```

Command Line Parameters

When you type NET COMM without command line parameters, information about all serial devices shared by a server is displayed. You can use the following command line parameters:

\\servername	Specifies the name that identifies the server sharing the queue.
netname	Specifies the name that identifies the network queue.
devicename	Specifies the name of the local serial device connected to the queue.
/PU(RGE)	Deletes all pending requests from the queue. Current active requests are not affected.
/PR(IORITY):n	Specifies the priority assigned to the queue. The highest priority is specified by 1, and 9 specifies the lowest.
/R(OUTE):device	Names the devices to which the serial device queue is routed. You must specify device. Multiple devices can route requests to one queue. Separate each device with a semicolon.
/O(PTIONS)	Displays the options assigned to the queue.

Examples

To display information about all shared serial devices, type

```
NET COMM
```

To see information for the queue to which the COM1 serial device is redirected:

```
NET COMM COM1
```

■ CONFIG

Lists and changes the configuration command line parameters of requesters, peer workstations, and servers.

Syntax

```
NET CONFIG service command line parameters
```

Command Line Parameters

When you type NET CONFIG without command line parameters, the services you can configure are displayed. Users type REQUESTER as the service.

The following values are valid for the service command line parameter:

REQ(UESTER)   Configures the requester command line parameters. You can use REQ, WORKSTATION, WKSTA, REDIRECTOR, REDIR, and RDR in place of REQUESTER.

SERVER   Configures the server command line parameters. You can use SRV and SVR in place of SERVER.

PEER   Configures the peer workstation command line parameters. The command line parameters for the Peer service are identical to those for the Server service except for /AUTODISCONNECT.

Use the following command line parameters to change requester configurations:

/CHARW(AIT):time   Sets the maximum time, in seconds, that your workstation is to wait for a requested serial device to become available when a program tries to use the device.

/CHART(IME):time   Sets the maximum time, in thousandths of a second, your workstation is to store data bound for a remote serial device before it sends the data to the device. Increasing this number improves network efficiency.

/CHARC(OUNT):n   Sets the number of bytes of data, bound for a remote serial device, that your workstation is to store before it sends the data to the device.

/MAXE(RRORLOG):n   Sets the maximum size of the disk error log in kilobytes.

/O(THDOMAINS):name, name   Specifies other domains that the workstation participates in. Up to four domain names can be in the list.

/PR(INTBUFTIME):time   Sets the maximum time, in seconds, for truncating a DOS print job.

Use the following command line parameters to change server and peer work-station configurations:

/AU(TODISCONNECT):nnn	Sets the number of minutes before the server automatically disconnects inactive sessions. A value of –1 means that sessions are not disconnected automatically.
/ALERTN(AMES):name,name,...	Sets the user and workstation IDs to which administrative alert messages should be sent. Do not specify group IDs. The list of names cannot exceed 128 characters, including commas.
/ALERTS(CHED):n	Sets the rate, in minutes, at which the server checks for alert conditions and sends any needed alert messages.
/E(RRORALERT):n	Sets the number of errors that can occur before the server sends an alert message.
/L(OGONALERT):n	Sets the number of logon violations that can occur before an alert is issued.
/N(ETIOALRT):n	Sets number of disk input/output (I/O) errors that generate an alert message.
/AC(CESSALERT):n	Sets the number of attempted resource access violations that can occur before the server sends an alert message.
/D(ISKALERT):n	Sets the minimum amount of free disk space, in kilobytes, that the server allows before sending an alert message.
/MAXA(UDITLOG):n	Sets the maximum size, in kilobytes, of the audit log file.

Examples

To set the character wait time to 1 second and character buffer size to 32 characters for a shared modem device, type

```
NET CONFIG /CHARTIME:1000 /CHARCOUNT:32
```

■ CONTINUE

Continues network programs and services temporarily stopped by NET PAUSE.

Syntax

```
NET CONTINUE service
```

Command Line Parameters

NETLOGON	Resumes the user logon function.
NETRUN	Resumes the NET RUN function.
REQ(UESTER)	Resumes the Requester service at your workstation so that you can use network devices again. Shared device redirection is also restored. You can use REQ, WORK-STATION, WKSTA, REDIRECTOR, REDIR, and RDR in place of REQUESTER.
SERVER	Resumes network functions on a server.
PEER	Resumes the Peer service.

Examples

To resume a previously paused NetLogon service, type

```
NET CONTINUE NETLOGON
```

■ COPY

The COPY command copies files on the network. If you copy a file from one directory on a file server to another directory on that same file server, the copy operation takes place inside that file server. Your workstation does not do the work.

Syntax

```
NET COPY source [/A | /B] destination [/A | /B] /V
```

Command Line Parameters

/A	/A denotes an ASCII copy, while /B denotes a binary copy operation.
/B	In an ASCII copy operation, a CTRL-Z character signifies the end of the file. A binary copy operation always copies the entire file regardless of CTRL-Z characters in the source file.
/V	Causes the copy operation to read what it has written and thus verify the contents of the destination file.

Examples

To copy SALES.WK1 from the PENDING directory to the SOLD directory on the remote drive letter F, type

```
NET COPY F:\PENDING\SALES.WK1 F:\SOLD\SALES.WK1
```

■ DEVICE

Lists the status of shared serial devices, or stops the current use of a device. Only an administrator or a user with comm or print operator privilege can use the /DELETE command line parameter.

Syntax

```
NET DEVICE devicename /D
```

Command Line Parameters

When you type NET DEVICE without command line parameters, LAN Server displays a list of status information about shared serial devices. You can use the following command line parameters:

devicename   Identifies the serial device.

/D(ELETE)   Stops the current use of the shared serial device.

Examples

To see the status of the COM1 device, type

```
NET DEVICE COM1
```

■ ERROR

Lists or clears the network error log.

Syntax

```
NET ERROR [/C:n | /R] /D
```

Command Line Parameters

When you type NET ERROR without command line parameters, the entire error log is displayed. You can use the following command line parameters:

/C(OUNT):n   Lists the first n entries, where n is a number, in the error log.

/R(EVERSE)   Lists the error log entries in reverse order so that the most recent entry is listed first and the oldest entry is listed last. If you type /R with /C:n, where n is a number, the n most recent entries in the error log are displayed in reverse order.

/D(ELETE)   Clears the error log.

Examples

To view the ten most recent entries in the network error log with the most recent errors first, type

```
NET ERROR /C:10 /R
```

■ FILE

Lists the names of all open files and the number of locks on each file, closes shared files left open, and releases locked records (for administrators and users with server operator privilege). The NET FILE command is used on servers and peer workstations that are sharing resources.

Syntax

```
NET FILE fileid /C
```

Command Line Parameters

When you type NET FILE without command line parameters, a list of all open files on the peer workstation or server is displayed. You can use the following command line parameters:

id   Specifies the ID number of a file.

/C(LOSE)   Closes an open file and releases locked records.

Examples

To determine which files a file server has open (on behalf of the workstations), type

```
NET FILE
```

■ FORWARD

Routes incoming messages for one messaging name to another messaging name or cancels forwarding.

Syntax

```
NET FORWARD msgname fwdname /D
```

Command Line Parameters

msgname	Specifies the messaging name originally intended to receive incoming messages. The messaging name is defined by the NET NAME command.
fwdname	Specifies the messaging name (a workstation name, user ID, or messaging name) to receive the forwarded messages. The fwd-name must be defined on the network before you can set up message forwarding to that name.
/D(ELETE)	Cancels message forwarding. This command line parameter must be used only with the msgname command line parameter.

Examples

To forward messages from logon account CHRIS to logon account JOEL:

```
NET FORWARD CHRIS JOEL
```

To cancel the message forwarding, type:

```
NET FORWARD JOEL /D
```

■ GROUP

Displays the names of groups and their members in a domain, updates the group list, and adds and deletes groups (for administrators and users with accounts operator privilege). To make changes to the domain group accounts, this command must be run at a server.

Syntax

Use the following form of the command to display a list of all groups in a domain and their members:

```
NET GROUP
```

Use the following form of the command to display a list of all users in a particular group:

```
NET GROUP groupname
```

Use the following form of the command to add a group:

```
NET GROUP groupname /A /C:"text"
```

Use the following form of the command to delete a group:

```
NET GROUP groupname /D
```

Command Line Parameters

When you type NET GROUP without command line parameters at a server, a list of the groups currently defined in the domain is displayed. When you type this command at a requester, local group information is displayed. You can use the following command line parameters:

groupname	Specifies the name of the group to be added, changed, or deleted.
username	Specifies one or more users to be added or deleted.
/A(DD)	Adds a group or adds members to a group.
/D(ELETE)	Deletes a group or deletes members of a group.
/C(OMMENT):"text"	Briefly describes the group being added. The comment is limited to 48 bytes and must be enclosed by double quotes (" ").

Examples

To add the group TECH to the domain:

```
NET GROUP TECH /A /C:"The technical support group"
```

■ HELP

Lists the NET commands for which help is available, or lists the syntax and uses of a specific NET command.

Syntax

Use the following form of the command to list the help information for a command:

```
NET HELP command /Ø
```

Use the following form of the command to list the help information for a special topic:

```
NET HELP topic
```

Use the following form of the command to list the correct syntax for a command:

```
NET command /HELP
```

Command Line Parameters

When you type NET HELP without the name of a command, a list of commands for which you can get help is displayed. You can use the following command line parameters with NET HELP:

command	Specifies the command for which you need help. You must type command without NET. For example, type NET HELP USE to see help text for the NET USE command.
/O(PTIONS)	Lists the command line parameters available with the command.
/HELP	Displays help text for the specified command.
/?	Displays the correct syntax of the command.
topic	Specifies a special topic (either SYNTAX or NAMES) for which you want help information.

Examples

Type

```
NET START REQ /HELP
```

for help text on the NET START command.

■ LOG

Starts and stops saving messages to a file or printer, or displays information about the forwarding status of the current message log.

Syntax

```
NET LOG [pathname | devicename] [/ON | /OFF]
```

Command Line Parameters

When you type NET LOG without command line parameters, LAN Server displays the current status of message logging (ON or OFF). It also displays the full name of the current message log file. You can use the following command line parameters:

pathname	Identifies the path to and the name of the log file.
devicename	Identifies the printer to which the LPT or COM device is connected.
/ON	Starts message logging.
/OFF	Stops message logging.

Examples

To log network messages to the file LAN.LOG in the HISTORY directory on the file server, type:

```
NET LOG C:\HISTORY /ON
```

■ MOVE

The MOVE command moves (rather than copies) files from one directory to another on the file server.

Syntax

    NET MOVE source destination

Command Line Parameters

The space and destination parameters identify the files and directories involved in the move operation.

Examples

To move all the files with an extension of DOC from the WP directory to the LETTERS directory, type

```
NET MOVE \WP\*.DOC \LETTERS\*.DOC
```

■ NAME

Lists names defined as messaging names, lists forwarding information, adds new names for which your workstation can receive messages, and deletes names for which you do not want to receive messages.

Syntax

NET NAME msgname [/A | /D]

Command Line Parameters

When you type NET NAME without command line parameters, the messaging names and forwarding information are displayed. You can use the following command line parameters with NET NAME:

msgname	Specifies the messaging name you want to add or delete.
/A(DD)	Adds a messaging name to the local workstation. This is the default.
/D(ELETE)	Removes a messaging name so that the workstation stops receiving messages for that name. Use this command line parameter to delete a name that has been forwarded to you and to stop receiving another user's messages.

Examples

To allow JOEL's workstation to receive messages sent to account CHRIS, JOEL would type

```
NET NAME CHRIS /A
```

■ PASSWORD

Changes passwords on a server or in a domain.

Syntax

```
NET PASSWORD [/DOMAIN:name | \\servername] username oldpassword
newpassword
```

Command Line Parameters

When you type NET PASSWORD without any command line parameters, you are prompted to type a domain, user ID, old password, and new password. You can use the following command line parameters:

/D(OMAIN):name	The name of the domain in which the password is to be changed. If you do not type a specific domain name, the default domain from the IBMLAN.INI file is used.
username	The user account whose password you are changing.
oldpassword	The current password you are changing. Type an asterisk (*) to keep the password confidential. The asterisk causes the system to prompt you to type the password. The password is not displayed.
newpassword	The new password to be used. Type an asterisk (*) to keep the password confidential. The asterisk causes the system to prompt you to type the password. The password is not displayed.
\\servername	The name of the server on which the password is to be changed.

Examples

To change your password from ABCD1 to NOVEMBER, assuming you are logon account SCOTT in the SALES domain, you would type

```
NET PASSWORD /DOMAIN:SALES SCOTT ABCD1 NOVEMBER
```

■ PAUSE

Suspends LAN Requester and LAN Server services.

Syntax

NET PAUSE service

Command Line Parameters

NETLOGON	Pauses the Netlogon service, which controls the replication of the user and group definition file (NET.ACC), and also stops accepting logon requests.

NETRUN	Pauses the Netrun service, which causes further NET RUN requests to be refused until the service is continued. Jobs already running are not affected.
REQ(UESTER)	Pauses all printer and serial device redirection. Requests for COM and LPT devices are sent to the local device instead of the shared network devices. Functions being used when the workstation pauses are not affected. You can use REQ, WORKSTATION, WKSTA, REDIRECTOR, REDIR, or RDR in place of REQUESTER.
SERVER	Pauses network functions on a server for users. The server does not accept new requests for resources from users, although administrators can still issue requests. Currently open files are not affected, and requests to these files continue to be satisfied. You can use SRV or SVR in place of SERVER.
PEER	Pauses the Peer service. The peer workstation does not accept new requests for resources from users, although administrators can still issue requests. Files currently open are not affected, and requests to these files continue to be satisfied.

Examples

To pause the server, type

```
NET PAUSE SERVER
```

■ PRINT

Controls jobs in the network spooler queues and lists the contents of network spooler queues.

Syntax

Use the following form of the command to list the contents of a spooler queue:

```
NET PRINT [\\servername\netname | devicename]
```

Use the following form of the command to manage your job in a queue:

```
NET PRINT [\\servername | devicename] jobid [/H | /DEL | /REL]
```

Use the following form of the command to manage a particular job in the queue:

```
NET PRINT jobid [/H | /DEL | /REL | /F]
```

Use this form of the command to manage all jobs in a queue:

```
NET PRINT  netname [/PU | /O]
```

Command Line Parameters

When an administrator types NET PRINT without command line parameters on a
server, a list of spooler queues for that server is displayed. You can use the following command line parameters:

\\servername	Specifies the name of the peer workstation or server shar-ing the queue.
netname	Specifies the network name of a shared queue.
devicename	Specifies the name of a local printer queue. The device-name is the name of the OS/2 printer object that handles the queue.
jobid	Specifies the number assigned to a file in the queue.
/DEL(ETE)	When used with jobid, /DEL deletes that job from the queue. If the job is currently printing, the job is canceled. Any data still in the print buffer is printed.
/H(OLD)	Holds a job in the queue to keep it from printing.
/PU(RGE)	Clears all jobs from a queue. /PU does not remove a job that is currently printing. The queue itself is not deleted. Only administrators or users with print operator privilege can use this command line parameter.
/REL(EASE)	Removes a hold on a job in the queue so the job can print.
/F(IRST)	Moves a job to the first position in the queue. Only admin-istrators or users with print operator privilege can use this command line parameter.
/O(PTIONS)	Lists the options assigned to the queue. Only administra-tors or users with print operator privilege can use this com-mand line parameter.

Examples

To view the list of print jobs in the \\SERVER1\LASERJET queue, type

```
NET PRINT \\SERVER1\LASERJET
```

To delete print job 5, one of your print jobs, from the queue:

```
NET PRINT LPT1 5 /DEL
```

■ SEND

Sends messages and files to other network users and workstations.

Syntax

```
NET SEND [name | /DOMAIN: name | * | /USERS | /BROADCAST]
[message | <filename]
```

Command Line Parameters

name	Workstation name (logon account) to send the message to.
/D(OMAIN):name	Sends a message to workstations in a specified domain.
*	Sends a message to your default domain.
/BROADCAST	Sends a message to all workstations on the network.
/USERS	Sends the message to all users currently connected to any of the server's resources. This command line parameter can only be used on a server.
<filename	A less-than symbol (<) followed by the name of a file sends the contents of the file as a message.
message	Text to be sent as a message.

Examples

To broadcast the message "Sales meeting now starting in the middle conference room." to all workstations in the SALES domain, type

```
NET SEND /DOMAIN:SALES Sales meeting now starting in the middle
conference room.
```

■ SHARE

Makes server and peer workstation resources available to network users, lists information about shared resources currently in effect, and deletes shared resources currently in effect.

This command can be used only by an administrator, or by a user with server, print, or comm operator privilege. Users with print operator privilege can perform actions on printers. Users with comm operator privilege can perform actions on serial devices.

Syntax

Use the following form of the command to list information about a shared resource:

```
NET SHARE netname
```

Use the following form of the command to change the options of a shared resource:

```
NET SHARE netname [/US:n | /UN] /R:"text"
```

Use the following form of the command to share a files resource (a directory):

```
NET SHARE netname=resource [/US:n | /UN] /R:"text"
```

Use the following form of the command to share the spooler queue of an existing printer object:

```
NET SHARE netname [/US:n | /UN] /R:"text" PRINT
```

Use the following form of the command to share a serial device pool (for a modem, plotter, fax machine, or other serial device):

```
NET SHARE netname=resource [/US:n | /UN] /R:"text" /C
```

Use the following form of the command to stop sharing a resource:

```
NET SHARE netname /D
```

To set permissions or a password for a directory, a print queue, or a serial device queue:

```
NET SHARE [netname | netname=resource] password /PERMISSIONS: A
C D R W X
```

Command Line Parameters

When you typc NET SHARE without command line parameters while logged on at a server or peer workstation, a list of all existing shares on that server or peer workstation is displayed.

netname	Specifies the network name of the shared resource. Network workstations use netname when they access the resource. For spooler queues, netname must be the name of the OS/2 printer object that handles the spooler queue.
netname=resource	Makes a resource available for network use. The resource command line parameter can be a path for shared files or a device name for shared serial devices. The resource command line parameter cannot be longer than 254 bytes.
/US(ERS):n	Sets the maximum number of users that can use a shared resource at the same time. For a peer workstation, n must be 2 or less.
/UN(LIMITED)	Removes restrictions on the number of users that can use a shared resource at the same time. This command line parameter is not valid for a peer workstation.
/R(EMARK):"text"	Specifies the comment text about the shared resource. The comment must be enclosed in double quotation marks (" "). The comment cannot be longer than 48 characters.
/C(OMM)	Defines the shared device as serial.
/PR(INT)	Shares an existing print queue.
/D(ELETE)	Cancels the sharing of the resource.
password	Specifies the password for the network resource. The password command line parameter is valid only for peer workstations configured for share-level security. The password command line parameter cannot be longer than 8 bytes.
/PERMISSIONS	Specifies the permissions for a shared directory. The /PERMISSIONS command line parameter is valid only on a peer workstation configured for share-level security. You can use any combination of the following permissions:

A   Permits changes to file attributes, such as A (archive) and R (read only), and related file information, such as the time and date the file was updated.

C   Permits creating files and directories in a shared directory. Users with this permission can change the file only when creating it.

D   Permits deleting subdirectories and files.

R   Permits reading, copying, and executing files, as well as changing from one subdirectory to another.

W   mPermits writing to a file.

X   Permits running (but not copying) program or command files such as .EXE or .COM files. R permission implies (includes) X permission.

Examples

To see the list of resources a server is sharing, type the following at that file server:

```
NET SHARE
```

To begin sharing the file server's \DEPT145\SALES directory with a netname of SALES, type the following at the file server

```
NET SHARE SALES = C:\DEPT145\SALES /UN
```

■ START

Starts network services or lists the services already started.

Syntax

```
NET START service command line parameters
```

Command Line Parameters

When you type NET START without command line parameters, a list of network services already started is displayed.

Workstations can use the following command line parameters:
REQUESTER
MESSENGER
REPLICATOR
PEER

Servers can use the following command line parameters:
REQUESTER
SERVER
ALERTER
GENALERT
LSSERVER
MESSENGER
NETLOGON
NETRUN
REMOTEBOOT
TIMESOURCE
UPS
DCDBREPL
REPLICATOR

REQUESTER Connects your workstation to the network server as a requester, allowing you to access shared network resources. You can use REQ, WORKSTATION, WKSTA, REDIRECTOR, REDIR, and RDR in place of REQUESTER.

SERVER Starts your workstation as a server. This command line parameter is for servers only. You can use SRV or SVR in place of SERVER.

PEER Starts the Peer service, which allows requesters to share resources.

ALERTER Starts the local Alerter service.

LSSERVER Starts the LSserver service. This service supports remote requests from requesters for such tasks as spooling, querying users, logging on, and logging off. The LSserver service starts automatically with the Server service.

NETLOGON Copies the master user and group definition file (NET.ACC) located on the domain controller to network servers. At the domain controller, this service controls logon requests. This service is available only on servers.

NETRUN Starts the local Netrun service. This service can only be started by servers.

REMOTE-BOOT Starts the Remote IPL service on servers with the Server service already started. This service allows the server to load files for a particular operating system onto a workstation at the user's request. You can use RIPL or RPL in place of REMOTEBOOT.

TIMESOURCE	Designates the domain controller as a source of a reliable time and date with which other workstations in the same domain or other domains can synchronize.
UPS	Starts the Uninterruptible Power Supply (UPS) service, which is used with a battery to protect a server from data loss during a power failure.
DCDBREPL	Starts the DCDB Replicator service, which controls the replication of the domain control database (DCDB) information on domain controllers to backup servers. This command line parameter works only on the server.
REPLICATOR	Maintains identical sets of files and directories on different machines. Servers can replicate data to other servers, peer workstations, or requesters.

Examples

To start the LAN Server requester at your workstation, so you can access a file server, type

```
NET START REQUESTER
```

To see the list of services running on a file server, type the following at that file server

```
NET START
```

■ STATISTICS

Displays and optionally clears a list of usage statistics for a workstation.

Syntax

Use the following form of the command on a requester:

```
NET STATISTICS REQ /C
```

Use the following form of the command on a server:

```
NET STATISTICS SERVER /C
```

Use the following form of the command on a peer workstation:

```
NET STATISTICS PEER /C
```

Command Line Parameters

When you type NET STATISTICS without command line parameters, the services for which usage statistics can be obtained (server, requester, or peer) are listed.

REQ(UESTER)	Provides usage statistics for the Requester service
SERVER	Provides usage statistics for the Server service
PEER	Provides usage statistics for the Peer service
/C(LEAR)	Clears the list of statistics

Examples

To see a file server's usage statistics, type the following at an OS/2 command prompt at that file server:

```
NET STATISTICS SERVER
```

■ STATUS

Lists information about current network shares and server definition settings.

Syntax

    NET STATUS

Command Line Parameters

None.

Examples

To see status information for a file server, type the following at that file server:

```
NET STATUS
```

■ STOP

Stops the network service your workstation was using and frees the memory the service used.

Syntax

```
NET STOP service /Y
```

Command Line Parameters

The service command line parameter can be one of the following:

REQ(UESTER)	Stops the Requester service on your workstation.
SERVER	Stops the Server service running on a file server. (The computer is no longer a file server after you use this command.)
PEER	Stops the Peer service.
ALERTER	Stops the Alerter service, which sends administrative alerts on the network.
LSSERVER	Stops the LSserver service that supports remote requests from requesters.
GENALERT	Stops the Generic Alerter service, which generates generic alerts and sends them either to the log file or to a LAN management software product.
MESSENGER	Stops the Messenger service.
NETLOGON	Stops the Netlogon service, which controls the replication of the user and group definition file (NET.ACC). At the domain controller, stopping this service prohibits any further logon requests from being processed by this domain controller.
NETRUN	Stops the Netrun service.
REMOTEBOOT	Stops the Remote IPL service.
REPLICATOR	Stops the Replicator service (which replicates files).
DCDBREPL	Stops the Domain Control Database (DCDB) Replicator service, which copies the DCDB on the domain controller to designated backup servers.
TIMESOURCE	Stops the Timesource service.
UPS	Stops the Uninterruptible Power Supply (UPS) service.

When you use NET STOP, you can optionally include the following command line parameter:

/Y	Carries out the NET STOP command without first prompting you to provide information or confirm actions.

Examples

To stop the file server, perhaps before performing a shutdown of OS/2 at that computer:

```
NET STOP SERVER
```

■ TIME

Displays the current clock setting on a remote server and sets the local clock to the time on a remote server or a remote domain. It also sets the clock of the specified domain controller and synchronizes the clocks of all active additional servers with that of the specified domain.

Syntax

Use the following form of the command to display the current time at the primary domain or the specified domain:

```
NET TIME /DOMAIN:name
```

Use the following form of the command to display the current time at any server on the network:

```
NET TIME \\servername
```

Use the following form of the command to synchronize your workstation computer's time with a remote server's or domain's clock:

```
NET TIME [/DOMAIN:name | \\servername] [/SET /YES | /SET /NO]
```

Use the following form of the command to set the clock of the specified domain and synchronize the clocks of all active additional servers with that of the specified domain:

```
NET TIME /DATE:datestring /TIME:timestring /DOMAIN:name
```

Command Line Parameters

When you type NET TIME without command line parameters, the time and date of the domain controller are displayed. You can use the following command line parameters with NET TIME:

\\servername	Identifies the name of the server whose time you want to view or synchronize with.
/D(OMAIN):name	Identifies the domain.

/SET	Synchronizes the time on this workstation with the server or domain time.
/Y(ES)	Sets the workstation time without displaying a prompt.
/N(O)	Does not set the workstation time.
/DATE:datestring	Sets the date at the specified domain controller and synchronizes the clocks of all active additional servers with that of the specified domain.
/TIME:timestring	Sets the time at the specified domain controller and synchronizes the clocks of all active additional servers with that of the specified domain.

Examples

In the following example, LAN Server displays your workstation's time as well as that of the primary domain controller. LAN Server then asks if you want to set your workstation's clock to the time value of the primary domain controller.

```
NET TIME /SET
```

To set the date and time at the logon domain and synchronize the clocks of all the active additional servers with the clock of the logon domain, type the following command

```
NET TIME /DATE:06-23-95 /TIME:02:15
```

■ USE

Lists the network resources in use, or connects or disconnects your workstation to or from shared resources on the network.

Syntax

Use the following form of the command to list all the network resources in use:

```
NET USE
```

Use the following form of the command to display information about a particular network resource in use:

```
NET USE [devicename| \\servername\netname]
```

Use the following form of the command to connect to a resource using its Universal Naming Convention (UNC) name:

```
NET USE \\servername\netname /C password
```

Use the following form of the command to connect to a resource using an alias:

```
NET USE devicename aliasname /DOMAIN:domainname /C password
```

Use the following form of the command to disconnect from a resource:

```
NET USE [devicename | \\servername\netname] /D
```

Command Line Parameters

When you type NET USE without command line parameters, the list of network resources currently in use is displayed. You can use the following command line parameters:

devicename	Specifies the drive, printer port, or serial port currently connected to a shared resource. You can use the following device names:
	Drive letter D through Z
	Printer port (LPT1 through LPT9)
	Serial device port (COM1 through COM9)
\\servername\netname	Specifies the UNC name containing the server name or peer workstation name and net name of the shared resource.
aliasname	Specifies the alias of the shared resource.
/DOMAIN:domainname	Specifies the domain in which the alias of the shared resource is defined. If a domain is not specified, the logon domain is used.
/D(ELETE)	Ends the NET USE connections.
/C(OMM)	Requests use of the device for direct input/output.
password	Allows connection to resources that require a password.

Examples

To view a list of shared resources you are currently using, enter

```
NET USE
```

To connect to the shared resource known by the alias name SVR-DRIVE-D and use that resource as drive G, type

```
NET USE G: SVR-DRIVE-D
```

■ USER

Lists, adds, removes, and modifies user accounts in the domain.

To make changes to the domain user accounts, this command must be run at a server, or from a peer workstation or requester using the NET ADMIN command and specifying the domain controller as the remote server.

Only an administrator or user with accounts operator privilege (as defined in the local accounts database) can use this command. Users with accounts operator privilege cannot add and manage administrators or other users with accounts operator privilege.

NOTE. *Requester and peer workstations maintain a separate user accounts database locally that is different from the domain's user accounts database.*

Syntax

Use the following form of the command to list user accounts:

```
NET USER
```

Use the following form of the command to add or modify a user account:

```
NET USER username [password | *] /ACTIVE [YES | NO] /
PRIVILEGE:priv /COUNTRYCODE:nnn /PASSWORDCHG: [YES | NO] /
PASSWORDREQ: [YES | NO] /PASSWORDEXP: [YES | NO] /COMMENT:"text"
/USERCOMMENT:"text" /EXPIRES: [date| NEVER] /FULLNAME:"name" /
HOMEDIR:pathname /SCRIPT:pathname /MAXSTORAGE: [nn | UNLIMITED] /
OPERATOR:list /TIMES: times /WORKSTATIONS: {* | ALL | name] /
LOGONSERVER: [\\servername | \\* ]
```

Use the following form of the command to add assignments for a user:

```
NET USER username /ASSIGN [device:alias | PUBLIC:appid |
PRIVATE:appid]
```

Use the following form of the command to delete a user's assignments:

```
NET USER username /UNASSIGN [device:alias | PUBLIC:appid |
PRIVATE:appid | PUBLIC:ALL | PRIVATE:ALL | LOGASN:ALL]
```

Use the following form of the command to remove a user account from the domain:

```
NET USER username /DELETE
```

Command Line Parameters

When you type NET USER without command line parameters at a server, a list of all user accounts in the domain is displayed. When you use this command at a requester or peer workstation, information is displayed about the local user accounts database. You can use the following command line parameters:

username	Specifies the name of the account to be added, deleted, or modified.
password	Specifies the password to be assigned to the user-name in the command. A password must satisfy any minimum-length requirements set by NET ACCOUNTS and must not exceed 14 characters.
*	Displays a prompt for the password.
/ACTIVE:YES|NO	Specifies whether this is an active account. An account must be active for the user to log on.
/ADD	Adds a user to the domain.
/PRIVILEGE:priv	Specifies the user's privilege level. The priv variable can be either USER, ADMIN, or GUEST.
/COMMENT:"text"	Provides a descriptive comment about the user's account (maximum of 48 characters). Enclose the text in double quotation marks ("").
/COUNTRYCODE:nnn	Sets the user's country code. The default value is 0 and indicates that the user is treated as having the same country code value as the local workstation.
/EXPIRES: date|NEVER	Causes the account to expire if date is set. NEVER sets no time limit on the account. An expiration date is in the form mm/dd/yy or dd/mm/yy, depending on the country code.
/FULLNAME:"name"	The user's full name (rather than a username). Enclose the name in double quotation marks ("")
/HOMEDIR:pathname	The path name of the user's home directory.

/SCRIPT:pathname	Specifies a command file to be run when the user logs on. The file specified by pathname can have the extension .CMD, .EXE, .BAT, or .PRO.
/MAXSTORAGE:nn|-UNLIMITED	Sets the maximum amount of storage, in kilobytes, for a user's home directory. UNLIMITED is the default.
/OPERATOR:list	Enables a user to act as an administrator for the listed entries only. Separate entries in the list with commas. The privileges are:
	ACCOUNTS Adds, deletes, and modifies user accounts, and updates logon requirements for the user accounts database.
	COMM Controls shared communication-device queues from the command line.
	PRINT Controls shared printer queues from the command line or Print Manager.
	SERVER Controls shared resources on a server, reads and closes the error log, and closes sessions and files that are open.
/PASSWORD-CHG:YES|NO	Specifies whether users can change their own passwords.
/PASSWORD-REQ:YES|NO	Specifies whether a password is required for this user account. The default is YES.
/PASSWORD-EXP:YES|NO	Specifies that the user's record is marked for a required password change the next time the user logs on. NO, the default, does not mark the password as expired.
/USERCOMMENT:text	Provides a descriptive comment about the user's account. The text must be enclosed in double quotation marks (" ").
/DELETE	Deletes the specified user account from the domain.
/TIMES:times|ALL |""	Specifies the logon hours, using the following notations:
	Specify day to day and time to time, limited to 1-hour increments.

Type the day of the week as the complete name (for example, Monday) or one of these abbreviations: SU, M, T, W, TH, F, S.

For time based on the 12-hour clock, use am, pm, or a.m., p.m., in uppercase or lowercase; the hour can be a single digit (5PM) or full time (9:00 AM). The 24-hour clock notation must use full time (12:00-24:00).

Separate multiple day and time entries with semicolons (;).

Separate day entries from time entries with commas (,).

ALL means that a user can always log on. A null string ("") means that a user can never log on. ALL is the default.

/WORKSTATIONS: *|""|name1;name2;...

Lists the workstations from which a user can log on. Separate entries with a semicolon (;) or with a comma. If you type an asterisk (*) or a null string (""), the user can log on from any workstation. You can specify up to eight workstation names with this command line parameter.

/LOGONSERVER: \\servername|*|""

Specifies the name of the preferred server that will validate logon requests for this user. The server name should be preceded by a double backslash (\\) and should be the name of a domain controller or backup server in the domain.

/ASSIGN

Specifies that the list of assignment pairs that follow the /ASSIGN command line parameter are to be added as assignments for the specified user. At least one assignment pair must follow the /ASSIGN command line parameter.

/UNASSIGN

Specifies that the list of assignment pairs that follow the /UNASSIGN command line parameter is to be removed as assignments for the specified user.

device:alias	When used with the /ASSIGN or /UNASSIGN command line parameter, specifies an item to be added to or removed from the specified user's logon assignments. The alias must be an existing alias, and the device specifies the device that is used to connect the alias at logon time.
PUBLIC:appid	When used with the /ASSIGN or /UNASSIGN command line parameters, specifies that the indicated application is to be added to or removed from the specified user's application assignments.
PRIVATE:appid	When used with the /ASSIGN and /UNASSIGN command line parameters, specifies that the indicated application is to be added or removed from the user's application assignments.
PUBLIC:ALL	When specified with the /UNASSIGN command line parameter, indicates that all of a user's public application assignments are to be deleted.
PRIVATE:ALL	When specified with the /UNASSIGN command line parameter, indicates that all of a user's private application assignments are to be deleted.
LOGASN:ALL	When specified with the /UNASSIGN command line parameter, indicates that all of the user's logon assignments are to be deleted.

Examples

To see a list of all user accounts in the domain, type

```
NET USER
```

To add the logon account SUSAN with a password of ABCD1, make the account active, assign the account USER privileges, require the account to use passwords, and indicate that SUSAN manages the forms unit, type the following

```
NET USER SUSAN ABCD1 /ACTIVE:YES /ADD /PRIVILEGE:USER /
PASSWORDREQ:YES /USERCOMMENT:"Susan manages the forms unit"
```

■ VIEW

Lists the names of the active servers on the domain and information about the resources of a specific server or peer workstation.

Syntax

NET VIEW \\servername

Command Line Parameters

When you type NET VIEW without command line parameters, a list of all servers on the domain is displayed. Use the following command line parameter with NET VIEW:

\\servername   Specifies the name that identifies a server or a peer workstation on the network.

Examples

To see a list of servers on the network, type

```
NET VIEW
```

To see a list of resources shared by the SERVER1 file server, type

```
NET VIEW \\SERVER1
```

■ WHO

Lists the users who are logged on to the current or to a remote domain, displays logon information about a user, and lists users with sessions to a specific server.

Syntax

Use the following form of the command to list the users currently logged on to the domain or who have sessions to a server in the domain:

```
NET WHO
```

Use the following form of the command to view information about the named domain:

```
NET WHO /DOMAIN:name
```

Use the following form of the command to view information about the specified user:

```
NET WHO username
```

Use the following form of the command to list users with sessions to a specified server:

```
NET WHO \\servername
```

Command Line Parameters

When you type NET WHO without command line parameters, a list of all the currently logged-on users is displayed. You can use the following command line parameters with NET WHO:

/D(OMAIN):name	Identifies the domain for which you want information.
username	Specifies the name of the user about whom you want information.
\servername	Specifies the name of the server for which you are requesting information.

Examples

To list all logged on accounts, type

```
NET WHO
```

■ Appendix B: Programming Reference

■ LAN Server API

LAN Server comes with online programming documentation in the file A3A4AM02.INF. Chapter 4, "Installing LAN Server," explains how to install the programming documentation and the online documentation files. To read the documentation, you can use the OS/2 VIEW utility or you can double-click the book icon labeled Programming Guide and Reference, located in the LAN Server Documentation folder.

The online Programming Guide and Reference does a good job of explaining each of the individual functions a programmer can take advantage of. However, finding the right function to use in a particular programming situation can be difficult with online documentation. For this reason, this book lists the individual LAN Server API functions and identifies basically what the functions accomplish. Chapter 9, "LAN Server Programming," discusses the LAN Server programming environment. You should use Chapter 9 along with this part of the book to help navigate your way through the online documentation.

The following list shows the frequently used categories of functions available to a programmer on a LAN Server LAN:

Access Permissions

Alerts

Aliases

Applications

Auditing

Configuring

Connections

Domains

DOS LAN Requester

Error Logging

Files

Groups

Mailslots

Messages

Named Pipes

NetBIOS

Network Statistics

Printing

Requester

Serial Devices

Server

Sessions

Workstations and Logon Accounts

Using the Import Libraries

As a practical matter, knowing which libraries to reference when linking a program is an important consideration. The following lists give the names of the LAN Server API import libraries, their locations, and the functions the libraries contain.

NETAPI.LIB, located in \IBMLAN\NETSRC\OS2\LIB, contains these functions:

NetAccessAdd

NetAccessApply

NetAccessCheck

NetAccessDel

NetAccessEnum

NetAccessGetInfo

NetAccessGetUserPerms

NetAccessSetInfo

NetAlertRaise

NetAlertStart

NetAlertStop

NetAliasAdd

NetAliasDel

NetAliasEnum

NetAliasGetInfo

NetAliasSetInfo

NetAppAdd

NetAppDel

NetAppEnum

NetAppGetInfo

NetAppSetInfo

NetAuditClear

NetAuditRead
NetAuditWrite
NetBiosClose
NetBiosEnum
NetBiosGetInfo
NetBiosOpen
NetBiosSubmit
NetCharDevControl
NetCharDevEnum
NetCharDevGetInfo
NetCharDevQEnum
NetCharDevQGetInfo
NetCharDevQPurge
NetCharDevQPurgeSelf
NetCharDevQSetInfo
NetConfigGet2
NetConfigGetAll2
NetConnectionEnum
NetCreateRIPLMachine
NetDASDAdd
NetDASDCheck
NetDASDCtl
NetDASDDel
NetDASDEnum
NetDASDGetInfo
NetDASDSetInfo
NetDeleteRIPLMachine
NetErrorLogClear
NetErrorLogRead
NetErrorLogWrite
NetFileClose2
NetFileEnum2
NetFileGetInfo2
NetGetDCName
NetGetRIPLMachine

NetGroupAdd

NetGroupAddUser

NetGroupDel

NetGroupDelUser

NetGroupEnum

NetGroupGetInfo

NetGroupGetUsers

NetGroupSetInfo

NetGroupSetUsers

NetHandleGetInfo

NetHandleSetInfo

NetLogonEnum

NetMessageBufferSend

NetMessageFileSend

NetMessageLogFileGet

NetMessageLogFileSet

NetMessageNameAdd

NetMessageNameDel

NetMessageNameEnum

NetMessageNameFwd

NetMessageNameGetInfo

NetMessageNameUnFwd

NetRemoteCopy

NetRemoteExec

NetRemoteMove

NetRemoteTOD

NetServerAdminCommand

NetServerDiskEnum

NetServerEnum2

NetServerGetInfo

NetServerSetInfo

NetServiceControl

NetServiceEnum

NetServiceGetInfo

NetServiceInstall

NetServiceStatus

NetSessionDcl

NetSessionEnum

NetSessionGetInfo

NetSetRIPLMachine

NetShareAdd

NetShareCheck

NetShareDel

NetShareEnum

NetShareGetInfo

NetShareSetInfo

NetStatisticsGet2

NetUseAdd

NetUseDel

NetUseEnum

NetUseGetInfo

NetUserAdd

NetUserDCDBInit

NetUserDel

NetUserEnum

NetUserGetAppSel

NetUserGetGroups

NetUserGetInfo

NetUserGetLogonAsn

NetUserModalsGet

NetUserModalsSet

NetUserPasswordSet

NetUserSetAppSel

NetUserSetGroups

NetUserSetInfo

NetUserSetLogonAsn

NetUserValidate2

NetWkstaGetInfo

NetWkstaSetInfo

NetWkstaSetUID2

NETAPI32.LIB, located in \IBMLAN\NETSRC\OS2\LIB, contains these functions:

Net32AccessAdd
Net32AccessApply
Net32AccessCheck
Net32AccessDel
Net32AccessEnum
Net32AccessGetInfo
Net32AccessGetUserPerms
Net32AccessSetInfo
Net32AlertRaise
Net32AlertStart
Net32AlertStop
Net32AliasAdd
Net32AliasDel
Net32AliasEnum
Net32AliasGetInfo
Net32AliasSetInfo
Net32AppAdd
Net32AppDel
Net32AppEnum
Net32AppGetInfo
Net32AppSetInfo
Net32AuditClear
Net32AuditRead
Net32AuditWrite
Net32CharDevControl
Net32CharDevEnum
Net32CharDevGetInfo
Net32CharDevQEnum
Net32CharDevQGetInfo
Net32CharDevQPurge
Net32CharDevQPurgeSelf
Net32CharDevQSetInfo
Net32ConfigGet2

Net32ConfigGetAll2

Net32ConnectionEnum

Net32CreateRIPLMachine

Net32DASDAdd

Net32DASDCheck

Net32DASDCtl

Net32DASDDel

Net32DASDEnum

Net32DASDGetInfo

Net32DASDSetInfo

Net32DelRIPLMachine

Net32EnumRIPLMachine

Net32ErrorLogClear

Net32ErrorLogRead

Net32ErrorLogWrite

Net32FileClose2

Net32FileEnum2

Net32FileGetInfo2

Net32GetDCName

Net32GetRIPLMachineInfo

Net32GroupAdd

Net32GroupAddUser

Net32GroupDel

Net32GroupDelUser

Net32GroupEnum

Net32GroupGetInfo

Net32GroupGetUsers

Net32GroupSetInfo

Net32GroupSetUsers

Net32LogonEnum

Net32MessageBufferSend

Net32MessageFileSend

Net32MessageLogFileGet

Net32MessageLogFileSet

Net32MessageNameAdd

Net32MessageNameDel

Net32MessageNameEnum

Net32MessageNameFwd

Net32MessageNameGetInfo

Net32MessageNameUnFwd

Net32RemoteCopy

Net32RemoteExec

Net32RemoteMove

Net32RemoteTOD

Net32ServerAdminCommand

Net32ServerDiskEnum

Net32ServerEnum2

Net32ServerGetInfo

Net32ServerSetInfo

Net32ServiceControl

Net32ServiceEnum

Net32ServiceGetInfo

Net32ServiceInstall

Net32ServiceStatus

Net32SessionDel

Net32SessionEnum

Net32SessionGetInfo

Net32SetRIPLMachineInfo

Net32ShareAdd

Net32ShareCheck

Net32ShareDel

Net32ShareEnum

Net32ShareGetInfo

Net32ShareSetInfo

Net32StatisticsGet2

Net32UseAdd

Net32UseDel

Net32UseEnum

Net32UseGetInfo

Net32UserAdd

Net32UserDCDBInit

Net32UserDel

Net32UserEnum

Net32UserGetAppSel

Net32UserGetGroups

Net32UserGetInfo

Net32UserGetLogonAsn

Net32UserModalsGet

Net32UserModalsSet

Net32UserPasswordSet

Net32UserSetAppSel

Net32UserSetGroups

Net32UserSetInfo

Net32UserSetLogonAsn

Net32UserValidate2

Net32WkstaGetInfo

Net32WkstaSetInfo

NetBios32Close

NetBios32Enum

NetBios32GetInfo

NetBios32Open

NetBios32Submit

HPFS386.LIB, located in \IBMLAN\NETSRC\OS2\LIB, contains these functions:

HPFS386GetInfo

HPFS386GetInfo16

OS2286.LIB (for 16-bit programs) and OS2386.LIB (for 32-bit programs), located in one of your OS/2 compiler product's directories, contains these functions:

DosBufReset or 32-bit DosResetBuffer

DosCallNmPipe or 32-bit DosCallNPipe

DosClose
DosConnectNmPipe or 32-bit DosConnectNPipe
DosDisConnectNmPipe or 32-bit DosDisConnectNPipe
DosMakeNmPipe or 32-bit DosCreateNPipe
DosOpen
DosPeekNmPipe or 32-bit DosPeekNPipe
DosPrintDestAdd or 32-bit SplCreateDevice
DosPrintDestControl or 32-bit SplControlDevice
DosPrintDestDel or 32-bit SplDeleteDevice
DosPrintDestEnum or 32-bit SplEnumDevice
DosPrintDestGetInfo or 32-bit SplQueryDevice
DosPrintDestSetInfo or 32-bit SplSetDevice
DosPrintJobContinue or 32-bit SplReleaseJob
DosPrintJobDel or 32-bit SplDeleteJob
DosPrintJobEnum or 32-bit SplEnumJob
DosPrintJobGetId
DosPrintJobGetInfo or 32-bit SplQueryJob
DosPrintJobPause or 32-bit SplHoldJob
DosPrintJobSetInfo or 32-bit SplSetJob
DosPrintQAdd or 32-bit SplCreateQueue
DosPrintQContinue or 32-bit SplReleaseQueue
DosPrintQDel or 32-bit SplDeleteQueue
DosPrintQEnum or 32-bit SplEnumQueue
DosPrintQGetInfo or 32-bit SplQueryQueue
DosPrintQPause or 32-bit SplHoldQueue
DosPrintQPurge or 32-bit SplPurgeQueue
DosPrintQSetInfo or 32-bit SplSetQueue
DosQFHandState or 32-bit DosQueryFHState
DosQHandState or 32-bit DosQueryHType
DosQNmPHandState or 32-bit DosQueryNPHState
DosQNmPipeInfo or 32-bit DosQueryNPipeInfo
DosQNmPipeSemState or 32-bit DosQueryNPipeSemState
DosRead
DosReadAsync
DosSetFHandState or 32-bit DosSetFHState

DosSetNmPHandState or 32-bit DosSetNPHState

DosSetNmPipeSem or 32-bit DosSetNPipeSem

DosTransactNmPipe or 32-bit DosTransactNPipe

DosWaitNmPipe or 32-bit DosWaitNPipe

DosWrite

DosWriteAsync

SplQmAbort

SplQmClose

SplQmEndDoc

SplQmOpen

SplQmStartDoc

SplQmWrite

MAILSLOT.LIB, located in \IBMLAN\NETSRC\OS2\LIB, contains these functions:

Dos32DeleteMailslot

Dos32MailslotInfo

Dos32MakeMailslot

Dos32PeekMailslot

Dos32ReadMailslot

Dos32WriteMailslot

DosDeleteMailslot

DosMailslotInfo

DosMakeMailslot

DosPeekMailslot

DosReadMailslot

DosWriteMailslot

UPM.LIB, located in \IBMLAN\NETSRC\OS2\LIB, contains these functions:

U32ELOCL

U32ELOCU

U32EULGF

U32EULGN

U32EUSRL

UPMELOCL

UPMELOCU

UPMEULGF

UPMEULGN

UPMEUSRL

NOTE. *If your software will run on LAN Server version 2.0 or 3.0, you should link your application to NETOEM.LIB as well as NETAPI.LIB (or NETAPI32.LIB). Place a reference to NETOEM.LIB before the references to other libraries, as shown in the following example:*

```
link386 myprogram,,,netoem.LIB+netapi.LIB+os2.LIB;
```

LAN Server installs NETOEM.LIB in the same directory, \IBMLAN\NETSRC\ OS2\LIB, as the other LAN Server import library files.

Four DLLs correspond to the LAN Server import libraries. The LAN Server installation process copied the four DLLs, identified in the following list, to the MUGLIB\DLL directory:

Library	Contains
MAILSLOT.DLL	Mailslot API library
NETAPI.DLL	Base network API library
NETAPI32.DLL	32-bit base network API library
NETOEM.DLL	Stub library for legacy applications

Access Rights by Function

The following section is a table listing each LAN Server API function and the access rights that must be in effect at run time for a function to succeed. The Requirements column of the following table indicates the access rights a function requires. The following list explains the meaning of the letters used in the Requirements column:

Code	Definition
W	Requires Requester service
M	Requires Messenger service
S	Requires Server service
R	Can be run remotely
A	Requires administrative privileges (remote only)
P	Requires partial administrative privileges
L	Has a local-only library available

The operator rights that must be in effect for an API function to succeed are listed in the Operator Rights column of the table. An operator can have one or more of the following rights, or privileges, in a LAN Server environment:

Accounts	Administers logon accounts
Print	Maintains printer queues and devices
Comm	Maintains communication queues and devices
Server	Maintains normal server operations and shared resources

API Name	Requirements	Operator Rights
DosBufReset or 32-bit DosResetBuffer	W L	Any
DosCallNmPipe or 32-bit DosCallNPipe	W L	Any
DosClose	W L	Any
DosConnectNmPipe or 32-bit DosConnectNPipe	W L	Any
DosDeleteMailslot or Dos32DeleteMailslot	W L	Any
DosDisConnectNmPipe or 32-bit DosDisConnectNPipe	W L	Any
DosDupHandle	W L	Any
DosMailslotInfo or Dos32MailslotInfo	W L	Any
DosMakeMailslot or Dos32MakeMailslot	W L	Any
DosMakeNmPipe or 32-bit DosCreateNPipe	W L	Any
DosOpen	W L	Any
DosPeekMailslot or Dos32PeekMailslot	W L	Any
DosPeekNmPipe or 32-bit DosPeekNPipe	W L	Any
DosPrintDestAdd or 32-bit SplCreateDevice	W A	Print
DosPrintDestControl or 32-bit SplControlDevice	W A	Print
DosPrintDestDel or 32-bit SplDeleteDevice	W A	Print
DosPrintDestEnum or 32-bit SplEnumDevice	W	Any
DosPrintDestGetInfo or 32-bit SplQueryDevice	W	Any
DosPrintDestSetInfo or 32-bit SplSetDevice	W A	Print
DosPrintJobContinue or 32-bit SplReleaseJob	W P	Print
DosPrintJobDel or 32-bit SplDeleteJob	W P	Print
DosPrintJobEnum or 32-bit SplEnumJob	W	Any
DosPrintJobGetId	W	Any
DosPrintJobGetInfo or 32-bit SplQueryJob	W	Any

API Name	Requirements	Operator Rights
DosPrintJobPause or 32-bit SplHoldJob	W P	Print
DosPrintJobSetInfo or 32-bit SplSetJob	W P	Print
DosPrintQAdd or 32-bit SplCreateQueue	W A	Print
DosPrintQContinue or 32-bit SplReleaseQueue	W A	Print
DosPrintQDel or 32-bit SplDeleteQueue	W A	Print
DosPrintQEnum or 32-bit SplEnumQueue	W	Any
DosPrintQGetInfo or 32-bit SplQueryQueue	W	Any
DosPrintQPause or 32-bit SplHoldQueue	W A	Print
DosPrintQPurge or 32-bit SplPurgeQueue	W A	Print
DosPrintQSetInfo or 32-bit SplSetQueue	W A	Print
DosQFHandState or 32-bit DosQueryFHState	W L	Any
DosQHandType or 32-bit DosQueryHType	W L	Any
DosQNmPHandState or 32-bit DosQueryNPHState	W L	Any
DosQNmPipeInfo or 32-bit DosQueryNPipeInfo	W L	Any
DosQNmPipeSemState or 32-bit DosQueryNPipeSemState	W L	Any
DosRead	W L	Any
DosReadAsync	W L	Any
DosReadMailslot or Dos32ReadMailslot	W L	Any
DosSetFHandState or 32-bit DosSetFHState	W L	Any
DosSetNmPHandState or 32-bit DosSetNPHState	W L	Any
DosSetNmPipeSem or 32-bit DosSetNPipeSem	W L	Any
DosTransactNmPipe or 32-bit DosTransactNPipe	W L	Any
DosWaitNmPipe or 32-bit DosWaitNPipe	W L	Any
DosWrite	W L	Any
DosWriteAsync	W L	Any
DosWriteMailslot or Dos32WriteMailslot	W L	Any
HPFS386GetInfo16 or HPFS386GetInfo	R S	Any
NetAccessAdd or Net32AccessAdd	W R A	Any
NetAccessApply or Net32AccessApply	W R A	Any
NetAccessCheck or Net32AccessCheck	W	Any
NetAccessDel or Net32AccessDel	W R A	Any
NetAccessEnum or Net32AccessEnum	W R A	Any

API Name	Requirements	Operator Rights
NetAccessGetInfo or Net32AccessGetInfo	W R A	Any
NetAccessGetUserPerms or Net32AccessGetUserPerms	W R A	Any
NetAccessSetInfo or Net32AccessSetInfo	W S R A	Any
NetAlertRaise or Net32AlertRaise	W	Any
NetAlertStart or Net32AlertStart	W	Any
NetAlertStop or Net32AlertStop	W	Any
NetAliasAdd or Net32AliasAdd	W R A	Server
NetAliasDel or Net32AliasDel	W R A	Server
NetAliasEnum or Net32AliasEnum	W R P	Server
NetAliasGetInfo or Net32AliasGetInfo	W R P	Server
NetAliasSetInfo or Net32AliasSetInfo	W R P	Server
NetAppAdd or Net32AppAdd	W R P	Server
NetAppDel or Net32AppDel	W R P	Server
NetAppEnum or Net32AppEnum	W R P	Server
NetAppGetInfo or Net32AppGetInfo	W R P	Server
NetAppSetInfo or Net32AppSetInfo	W R P	Server
NetAuditClear or Net32AuditClear	W R A	Any
NetAuditRead or Net32AuditRead	W R A	Accounts, Server, Print, Comm
NetAuditWrite or Net32AuditWrite	W S	Any
NetBiosClose or NetBios32Close	W	Any
NetBiosEnum or NetBios32Enum	W R	Any
NetBiosGetInfo or NetBios32GetInfo	W R	Any
NetBiosOpen or NetBios32Open	W	Any
NetBiosSubmit or NetBios32Submit	W	Any
NetCharDevControl or Net32CharDevControl	W S R A	Comm
NetCharDevEnum or Net32CharDevEnum	W S R	Any
NetCharDevGetInfo or Net32CharDevGetInfo	W S R	Any
NetCharDevQEnum Net32CharDevQEnum	W S R	Any
NetCharDevQGetInfo or Net32CharDevQGetInfo	W S R	Any
NetCharDevQPurge or Net32CharDevQPurge	W S R A	Comm

API Name	Requirements	Operator Rights
NetCharDevQPurgeSelf or Net32CharDevQPurgeSelf	W S R	Comm
NetCharDevQSetInfo or Net32CharDevQSetInfo	W S R A	Comm
NetConfigGet2 or Net32ConfigGet2	W R A	Accounts, Server, Print, Comm
NetConfigGetAll2 or Net32ConfigGetAll2	W R A	Accounts, Server, Print, Comm
NetConnectionEnum or Net32ConnectionEnum	W S R A	Server, Print, Comm
NetDASDAdd or Net32DASDAdd	W R A P	Any
NetDASDCheck or Net32DASDCheck	W R A	Any
NetDASDCtl or Net32DASDCtl	W R A	Any
NetDASDDel or Net32DASDDel	W R A P	Any
NetDASDEnum or Net32DASDEnum	W R A	Any
NetDASDGetInfo or Net32DASDGetInfo	W R A	Any
NetDASDSetInfo or Net32DASDSetInfo	W R A P	Any
NetErrorLogClear or Net32ErrorLogClear	R A	Any
NetErrorLogRead or Net32ErrorLogRead	R A	Any
NetErrorLogWrite or Net32ErrorLogWrite	W	Any
NetFileClose2 or Net32FileClose2	W S R A	Server
NetFileEnum2 or Net32FileEnum2	W S R A	Server
NetFileGetInfo2 or Net32FileGetInfo2	W S R A	Server
NetGetDCName or Net32GetDCName	W R	Any
NetGroupAdd or Net32GroupAdd	W R A	Accounts
NetGroupAddUser or Net32GroupAddUser	W R A	Accounts
NetGroupDel or Net32GroupDel	W R A	Accounts
NetGroupDelUser or Net32GroupDelUser	W R A	Accounts
NetGroupEnum or Net32GroupEnum	W R A	Accounts
NetGroupGetInfo or Net32GroupGetInfo	W R A	Accounts
NetGroupGetUsers or Net32GroupGetUsers	W R A	Accounts

API Name	Requirements	Operator Rights
NetGroupSetInfo or Net32GroupSetInfo	W R A	Accounts
NetGroupSetUsers or Net32GroupSetUsers	W R A	Accounts
NetHandleGetInfo	W R S	Any
NetHandleSetInfo	W R S	Any
NetLogonEnum or Net32LogonEnum	W R	Any
NetMessageBufferSend or Net32MessageBufferSend	W R A	Accounts, Server, Print, Comm
NetMessageFileSend or Net32MessageFileSend	W R A	Accounts, Server, Print, Comm
NetMessageLogFileGet or Net32MessageLogFileGet	W M R A	Any
NetMessageLogFileSet or Net32MessageLogFileSet	W M R A	Any
NetMessageNameAdd or Net32MessageNameAdd	W M R A	Any
NetMessageNameDel or Net32MessageNameDel	W M R A	Any
NetMessageNameEnum or Net32MessageNameEnum	W M R A	Any
NetMessageNameFwd or Net32MessageNameFwd	W M R A	Any
NetMessageNameGetInfo or Net32MessageNameGetInfo	W M R A	Any
NetMessageNameUnFwd or Net32MessageNameUnFwd	W M R A	Any
NetRemoteCopy or Net32RemoteCopy	W R	Any
NetRemoteExec or Net32RemoteExec	W R	Any
NetRemoteMove or Net32RemoteMove	W R	Any
NetRemoteTOD or Net32RemoteTOD	W R	Any
NetServerAdminCommand or Net32ServerAdminCommand	W S R A	Any
NetServerDiskEnum or Net32ServerDiskEnum	W R A	Server
NetServerEnum2 or Net32ServerEnum2	W R	Any

API Name	Requirements	Operator Rights
NetServerGetInfo or Net32ServerGetInfo	W S R A	Accounts, Server, Print, Comm
NetServerSetInfo or Net32ServerSetInfo	W S R A	Server
NetServiceControl or Net32ServiceControl	W R A	Server
NetServiceEnum or Net32ServiceEnum	W R	Any
NetServiceGetInfo or Net32ServiceGetInfo	W R	Any
NetServiceInstall or Net32ServiceInstall	W R A	Server
NetServiceStatus or Net32ServiceStatus	W	Any
NetSessionDel or Net32SessionDel	W S R A	Server
NetSessionEnum or Net32SessionEnum	W S R A	Server
NetSessionGetInfo or Net32SessionGetInfo	W S R A	Server
NetShareAdd or Net32ShareAdd	W S R A	Server
NetShareCheck or Net32ShareCheck	W S R	Any
NetShareDel or Net32ShareDel	W S R A	Server
NetShareEnum or Net32ShareEnum	W S R	Server, Print, Comm
NetShareGetInfo or Net32ShareGetInfo	W S R	Server, Print, Comm
NetShareSetInfo or Net32ShareSetInfo	W S R A	Server
NetStatisticsGet2 or Net32StatisticsGet2	W R A	Server
NetUseAdd or Net32UseAdd	W R A	Any
NetUseDel or Net32UseDel	W R A	Any
NetUseEnum or Net32UseEnum	W R A	Any
NetUseGetInfo or Net32UseGetInfo	W R A	Any
NetUserAdd or Net32UserAdd	W R A	Accounts
NetUserDCDBInit or Net32UserDCDBInit	W R P	Accounts
NetUserDel or Net32UserDel	W R A	Accounts
NetUserEnum or Net32UserEnum	W R A	Accounts
NetUserGetAppSel or Net32UserGetAppSel	W R P	Accounts
NetUserGetGroups or Net32UserGetGroups	W R A	Accounts

API Name	Requirements	Operator Rights
NetUserGetInfo or Net32UserGetInfo	W R A	Accounts
NetUserGetLogonAsn or Net32UserGetLogonAsn	W R P	Accounts
NetUserModalsGet or Net32UserModalsGet	W R A	Accounts
NetUserModalsSet or Net32UserModalsSet	W R A	Accounts
NetUserPasswordSet or Net32UserPasswordSet	W S R A	Any
NetUserSetAppSel or Net32UserSetAppSel	W R P	Accounts
NetUserSetGroups or Net32UserSetGroups	W R A	Accounts
NetUserSetInfo or Net32UserSetInfo	W R A	Accounts
NetUserSetLogonAsn or Net32UserSetLogonAsn	W R P	Accounts
NetUserValidate2 or Net32UserValidate2	W	Any
NetWkstaGetInfo or Net32WkstaGetInfo	W R A	Accounts, Server, Print, Comm
NetWkstaSetInfo or Net32WkstaSetInfo	W R A	Any
NetWkstaSetUID2	W	Any
SplQmAbort	R	Any
SplQmClose	R	Any
SplQmEndDoc	R	Any
SplQmOpen	R	Any
SplQmStartDoc	R	Any
SplQmWrite	R	Any
UPMELOCL or U32ELOCL	L	Any
UPMELOCU or U32ELOCU	L	Any
UPMEULGF or U32EULGF	L	Any
UPMEULGN or U32EULGN	L	Any
UPMEUSRL or U32EUSRL	L	Any

DOS and Windows Functions

DOS and Windows 3.x programs can also use LAN Server API functions. The functions that simply communicate information across the LAN (in the NetBIOS, Named Pipes, and Mailslots categories) don't necessarily reference a LAN Server file server. The remainder of the functions, which perform administrative, auditing, or other LAN Server tasks, must reference a LAN Server file server.

NOTE. *LAN Server programs running on DOS or DOS-plus-Windows don't benefit from OS/2's insulation of application address spaces. DOS and Windows do not support pointer checking, semaphores, or shared memory segments. DOS and Windows programs cannot access files with long file names on a file server that's sharing an HPFS drive.*

DOS LAN Services supports the following four services:

Service	Purpose
Messenger	Lets DLS workstations send and receive messages across the LAN
Netpopup	Displays messages as pop-up notifications on the screen
Requester	Allows DOS computers to use shared resources
Peer	Permits DOS workstations to share printers and drives

LAN Server comes with two dynamic link libraries, NETAPI.DLL and PMSPL.DLL, for use with Windows 3.x. To call LAN Server APIs, a Windows application must link to the NETAPI.LIB and PMSPL.LIB (for DosPrint API support) libraries. You link a non-Windows DOS application to the DOSNET.LIB library. The DOSNET library file provides network functions for applications on DLS workstations to access LAN Server. The following example shows the link libraries you use to resolve LAN Server API function calls in your software:

For non-Windows DOS applications:

```
LINK MYDOSAPP.OBJ, MYDOSAPP.EXE, MYDOSAPP.MAP, DOSNET.LIB
```

For Windows 3.x applications:

```
LINK MYWINAPP.OBJ, MYWINAPP.EXE, MYWINAPP.MAP, NETAPI.LIB PMSPL.LIB
```

Functions by Category

The following sections identify the LAN Server API functions by category and show which header files you'll need to include in your programs.

Access Permission APIs examine or change user or group access permissions for server resources. These functions use the ACCESS.H and NETCONS.H header files.

NetAccessAdd

NetAccessApply

NetAccessCheck

NetAccessDel

NetAccessEnum

NetAccessGetInfo

NetAccessGetUserPerms

NetAccessSetInfo

Alert APIs provide a system for notifying network service programs and applications of network events. These functions use the ALERT.H and NETCONS.H header files.

NetAlertRaise

NetAlertStart

NetAlertStop

Alias APIs examine or change aliases. In OS/2 LAN Server, an alias is a name for a shared resource. An alias can have a file, print, or serial type. These functions require the NETCONS.H and DCDB.H header files.

NetAliasAdd

NetAliasDel

NetAliasEnum

NetAliasGetInfo

NetAliasSetInfo

Application APIs manage information about network applications. These functions use the NETCONS.H and DCDB.H header files.

NetAppAdd

NetAppDel

NetAppEnum

NetAppGetInfo

NetAppSetInfo

Auditing APIs control the audit log file, which contains an audit trail of operations that occur on a server. These functions use the AUDIT.H and NETCONS.H header files.

NetAuditClear

NetAuditRead

NetAuditWrite

Configuration APIs retrieve network configuration information from the IBM-LAN.INI file. The NetConfigGet2 API retrieves a single parameter value for a given network component; NetConfigGetAll2 returns all the parameters for the given component. These APIs use the CONFIG.H and NETCONS.H header files.

NetConfigGet2

NetConfigGetAll2

The NetConnectionEnum API lists all connections made to a server by a requester client, or all connections made to a shared resource of a server. This API uses the SHARES.H and NETCONS.H header files.

NetConnectionEnum

The DOS LAN services (DLS) category provides several function calls for compatibility with existing DOS programs that run in the LAN Server version 2.0, LAN Server version 3.0, or PC LAN Program environment.

Installation Check

Network Print Stream Control

Get User ID and Logon Status

DLS Installation Check

Network Version Check

NetWkstaSetUID2

Error-logging APIs control the error log file. These functions use the ERR-LOG.H and NETCONS.H header files.

NetErrorLogClear

NetErrorLogRead

NetErrorLogWrite

File APIs provide a system for monitoring which file, device, and pipe resources are opened on a server and for closing one of these resources when necessary. These functions use the SHARES.H and NETCONS.H header files.

NetFileClose2

NetFileEnum2

NetFileGetInfo2

The group APIs control logon account and group IDs. They use the ACCESS.H and NETCONS.H header files.

NetGroupAdd

NetGroupAddUser

NetGroupDel

NetGroupDelUser

NetGroupEnum

NetGroupGetInfo

NetGroupGetUsers

NetGroupSetInfo

NetGroupSetUsers

Handle APIs operate on the handles of remote serial devices and remote named pipes. These functions use the CHARDEV.H and NETCONS.H header files.

NetHandleGetInfo

NetHandleSetInfo

The APIs in the 386HPFS category control functions that are specific to the 386HPFS file system, which includes limiting disk space by logon account. These functions use the DASD.H file.

HPFS386GetInfo

NetDASDAdd

NetDASDCheck

NetDASDCtl

NetDASDDel

NetDASDEnum

NetDASDGetInfo

NetDASDSetInfo

Programs can use the Mailslot API functions to communicate through the LAN cable. These functions use the MAILSLOT.H and NETCONS.H header files.

DosDeleteMailslot

DosMailslotInfo

DosMakeMailslot

DosPeekMailslot

DosReadMailslot

DosWriteMailslot

The Message API functions can send, log, and forward messages. The functions use the MESSAGE.H and NETCONS.H header files.

NetMessageBufferSend

NetMessageFileSend

NetMessageLogFileGet

NetMessageLogFileSet

NetMessageNameAdd

NetMessageNameDel

NetMessageNameEnum

NetMessageNameFwd

NetMessageNameGetInfo

NetMessageNameUnFwd

Print destination APIs control the printers that receive spooled print jobs on a server. A print destination is any spooled device, such as a line or laser printer, that physically is connected to a server. These APIs use the NETCONS.H, NETERR.H, and DOSPRINT.H header files.

DosPrintDestAdd

DosPrintDestControl

DosPrintDestDel

DosPrintDestEnum

DosPrintDestGetInfo

DosPrintDestSetInfo

Print job APIs control the print jobs in a printer queue on a server. A print job is a file submitted for printing. The print job APIs use the NETCONS.H, NETERR.H, and DOSPRINT.H header files, and support 16-bit applications.

DosPrintJobContinue

DosPrintJobDel

DosPrintJobEnum

DosPrintJobGetId

DosPrintJobGetInfo

DosPrintJobPause

DosPrintJobSetInfo

Printer queue APIs control the printer queues on a server. A printer queue is an ordered list of submitted print jobs on a server. The printer queue APIs use the NETCONS.H, NETERR.H, and DOSPRINT.H header files.

DosPrintQAdd

DosPrintQContinue

DosPrintQDel

DosPrintQEnum

DosPrintQGetInfo

DosPrintQPause

DosPrintQPurge

DosPrintQSetInfo

Remote utility APIs enable applications to copy and move remote files, remotely run a program, and access the time-of-day information on a remote server. They use the REMUTIL.H and NETCONS.H header files.

NetRemoteCopy

NetRemoteExec

NetRemoteMove

NetRemoteTOD

Requester APIs control the operation of requesters. The Requester functions enable applications to control the configuration of a requester. The functions in this category use the ACCESS.H, NETCONS.H, and WKSTA.H header files.

NetWkstaGetInfo

NetWkstaSetInfo

Server APIs let a program perform remote administrative tasks on a local or remote server. These APIs use the ACCESS.H, SERVER.H, and NETCONS.H header files.

NetGetDCName

NetServerAdminCommand

NetServerDiskEnum

NetServerEnum2

NetServerGetInfo

NetServerSetInfo

Sessions APIs control network sessions established between requesters and servers. The functions in this category use the SHARES.H and NETCONS.H header files.

NetSessionDel

NetSessionEnum

NetSessionGetInfo

Share APIs control shared resources. These functions use the SHARES.H, ACCESS.H, and NETCONS.H header files.

NetShareAdd
NetShareCheck
NetShareDel
NetShareEnum
NetShareGetInfo
NetShareSetInfo

Use APIs examine or control connections between requesters and servers. Include the USE.H and NETCONS.H header files in your program to access these functions.

NetUseAdd
NetUseDel
NetUseEnum
NetUseGetInfo

User APIs control logon accounts. These functions use the ACCESS.H and NETCONS.H header files.

NetLogonEnum
NetUserAdd
NetUserDCDBInit
NetUserDel
NetUserEnum
NetUserGetAppSel
NetUserGetGroups
NetUserGetInfo
NetUserGetLogonAsn
NetUserModalsGet
NetUserModalsSet
NetUserPasswordSet
NetUserSetAppSel
NetUserSetGroups
NetUserSetInfo
NetUserSetLogonAsn
NetUserValidate2

■ Index

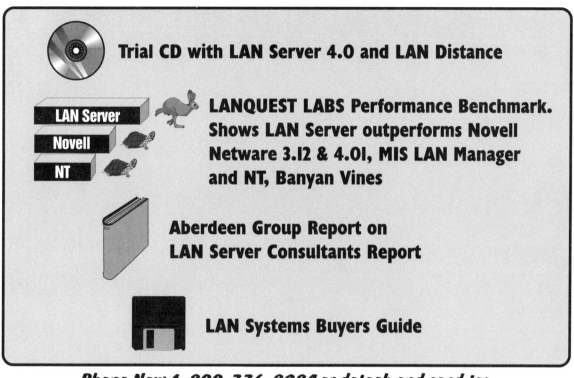

FREE Migration Utility

for LAN Server 4.0 from

*Novell or
LAN Manager*

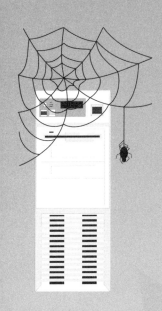

INDELIBLE
BLUE
Inc.

LAN Server 4.0

**Migration from Novell Netware or Microsoft LAN
Manager can be as simple as "Dragging & Dropping"**

Ride the Fast Lane on the Information Highway

with Ziff-Davis Press.

Driving lessons for online newcomers.
The latest waves for expert net surfers.

In these just-released books from Ziff-Davis Press, noted authors share their passion for the online world. Join them on a thrilling ride down the information highway from the comfort of your home or office.

THE INTERNET VIA MOSAIC AND WORLD-WIDE WEB

$24.95 ISBN: 1-56276-259-1

PC Magazine UK Labs Manager Steve Browne focuses on Mosaic, the most popular Web browser. Browne concisely explains how to gain access to the Web and how to take advantage of the Web's hyper-linked environment through Mosaic. Included are valuable discussions on the ways business can take advantage of the Web.

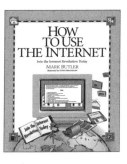

HOW TO USE THE INTERNET

$17.95 ISBN: 1-56276-222-2

Colorfully illustrated how-to guide; the easiest way for beginning Internet users to have fun and get productive fast.

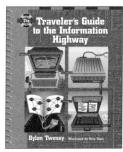

THE TRAVELER'S GUIDE TO THE INFORMATION HIGHWAY

$24.95 ISBN: 1-56276-206-0

The ultimate atlas to online resources including CompuServe, America Online, the Internet, and more.

THE INTERNET BY E-MAIL

$19.95 ISBN: 1-56276-240-0

Fun and informative Internet services available at no extra charge from the e-mail system you already know.

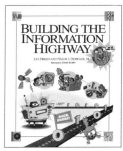

BUILDING THE INFORMATION HIGHWAY

$24.95 ISBN: 1-56276-126-9

Our present and future information structure, delightfully illustrated and clearly explained for anyone who's curious.

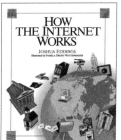

HOW THE INTERNET WORKS

$24.95 ISBN: 1-56276-192-7

Best-selling, full-color presentation of the technological marvel that links people and communities throughout the world.

© 1995 Ziff-Davis Press

Ziff-Davis Press Survey of Readers

Please help us in our effort to produce the best books on personal computing.
For your assistance, we would be pleased to send you a FREE catalog
featuring the complete line of Ziff-Davis Press books.

1. How did you first learn about this book?

Recommended by a friend . . . . ☐ -1 (5)

Recommended by store personnel . . . . ☐ -2

Saw in Ziff-Davis Press catalog . . . . ☐ -3

Received advertisement in the mail . . . . ☐ -4

Saw the book on bookshelf at store . . . . ☐ -5

Read book review in: _____ ☐ -6

Saw an advertisement in: _____ ☐ -7

Other (Please specify): _____ ☐ -8

2. Which THREE of the following factors most influenced your decision to purchase this book? (Please check up to THREE.)

Front or back cover information on book . . . ☐ -1 (6)

Logo of magazine affiliated with book . . . . . . ☐ -2

Special approach to the content . . . . ☐ -3

Completeness of content . . . . ☐ -4

Author's reputation. ☐ -5

Publisher's reputation . . . . ☐ -6

Book cover design or layout . . . . ☐ -7

Index or table of contents of book . . . . ☐ -8

Price of book . . . . ☐ -9

Special effects, graphics, illustrations . . . . ☐ -0

Other (Please specify): _____ ☐ -x

3. How many computer books have you purchased in the last six months? _____ (7-10)

4. On a scale of 1 to 5, where 5 is excellent, 4 is above average, 3 is average, 2 is below average, and 1 is poor, please rate each of the following aspects of this book below. (Please circle your answer.)

Depth/completeness of coverage	5 4 3 2 1	(11)
Organization of material	5 4 3 2 1	(12)
Ease of finding topic	5 4 3 2 1	(13)
Special features/time saving tips	5 4 3 2 1	(14)
Appropriate level of writing	5 4 3 2 1	(15)
Usefulness of table of contents	5 4 3 2 1	(16)
Usefulness of index	5 4 3 2 1	(17)
Usefulness of accompanying disk	5 4 3 2 1	(18)
Usefulness of illustrations/graphics	5 4 3 2 1	(19)
Cover design and attractiveness	5 4 3 2 1	(20)
Overall design and layout of book	5 4 3 2 1	(21)
Overall satisfaction with book	5 4 3 2 1	(22)

5. Which of the following computer publications do you read regularly; that is, 3 out of 4 issues?

Byte . . . . ☐ -1 (23)

Computer Shopper . . . . ☐ -2

Home Office Computing . . . . ☐ -3

Dr. Dobb's Journal . . . . ☐ -4

LAN Magazine . . . . ☐ -5

MacWEEK . . . . ☐ -6

MacUser . . . . ☐ -7

PC Computing . . . . ☐ -8

PC Magazine . . . . ☐ -9

PC WEEK . . . . ☐ -0

Windows Sources . . . . ☐ -x

Other (Please specify): _____ ☐ -y

Please turn page.

6. What is your level of experience with personal computers? With the subject of this book?

	With PCs	With subject of book
Beginner	☐ -1 (24)	☐ -1 (25)
Intermediate	☐ -2	☐ -2
Advanced	☐ -3	☐ -3

7. Which of the following best describes your job title?

Officer (CEO/President/VP/owner) ☐ -1 (26)
Director/head ☐ -2
Manager/supervisor ☐ -3
Administration/staff ☐ -4
Teacher/educator/trainer ☐ -5
Lawyer/doctor/medical professional ☐ -6
Engineer/technician ☐ -7
Consultant ☐ -8
Not employed/student/retired ☐ -9
Other (Please specify): _____ ☐ -0

8. What is your age?

Under 20 ☐ -1 (27)
21-29 ☐ -2
30-39 ☐ -3
40-49 ☐ -4
50-59 ☐ -5
60 or over ☐ -6

9. Are you:

Male ☐ -1 (28)
Female ☐ -2

Thank you for your assistance with this important information! Please write your address below to receive our free catalog.

Name: _____

Address: _____

City/State/Zip: _____

Fold here to mail.

2702-07-18

_____

_____

_____

BUSINESS REPLY MAIL

FIRST CLASS MAIL   PERMIT NO. 1612   OAKLAND, CA

POSTAGE WILL BE PAID BY ADDRESSEE

Ziff-Davis Press
ZD PRESS
5903 Christie Avenue
Emeryville, CA 94608-1925
Attn: Marketing